In Search Of…
Literary L.A.

In Search Of…
Literary L.A.

By Lionel Rolfe

California CLASSICS BOOKS

LOS ANGELES, CALIFORNIA

ISBN 1-879395-00-2

■

Portions of this book have appeared in different form in the Los
Angeles *Times*, the late and lamented Los Angeles *Herald-Examiner*,
the Los Angeles *Reader* and *Angeles* magazine. Portions were also
excerpted in two anthologies, *On Bohemia: The Code of the Self-Exiled*
(Transaction Publishers, Rutgers University) and *Unknown California*
(Macmillan Publishing Company).

■

Typography by Ken Boor
Cover color by Bill Winters

*This book is dedicated to
John Ahouse and Nigey Lennon,
who have been central
in its creation.*

NOTES ON THE ILLUSTRATIONS

The cover photograph of Charles Bukowski is © 1982 by Michael Montfort and the color work was done by Bill Winters. The photo on page six is © Phil Stern, as are his photos on pages 10, 71, 79, 126. A *Standard Solution* on page 19 is © Lair Mitchell as is his *Jungian Origami* on page 22. The photographs for the chapter "Grand Old Man of L.A. Letters" were all supplied to me by Jake Zeitlin, who also gave me for this book the autographed photo of Louis Adamic on page 164. My deep appreciation to the Special Collections Department of the University of Southern California for the photographs of Thomas and Katia Mann on page 109, Aldous Huxley on page 121 and Upton Sinclair on page 144. USC was given the extensive *Herald-Examiner* photo collection when that paper ceased publication. Occidental College's special collections also supplied the photo of Jeffers on page 131. The photo of John Fante on page 162 was supplied by Michael Montfort. The snapshot of Raymond Chandler on page 165, in which he looks more like his hero-protagonist Philip Marlowe, is © Alfred Knopf. Knopf was Chandler's publisher. The other photos in the book were taken by the author.

TABLE OF CONTENTS

Hidden Links

The California Bohemian Movement, under whose shadow my life has been lived, is basically a journalistic one that, like its progenitors in England, saw its activities growing out of certain coffeehouses. It can claim ancestry in the early writings of Samuel Clemens during the Comstock Lode period, and it touched most of the really great American writing. One must include Mark Twain, Bret Harte, Ina Coolbrith, George Sterling, Jack London, Ambrose Bierce, Upton Sinclair, John Steinbeck, Theodore Dreiser, Henry Miller, and Jack Kerouac, in any list of California Bohemians. These were the American writers who owed their literary personas to California Bohemianism.

These were not hack journalists; rather, journalism gave their writing a certain stamp that the New England Ivy League academics never had. My mentor was Scott Newhall, the last great living California Bohemian newspaper editor. For nearly two decades, during its most creative and imaginative years, he edited the San Francisco *Chronicle*. The Bohemian Club, from which sprang the California Bohemian movement, started meeting in the kitchen of one of the *Chronicle*'s editors in the 1860s, and then moved to Montgomery Street in the City — and finally to its present location up on the Russian River, considerably north of its original San Francisco location.

This book tells the stories of some of these intriguing figures — and describes what they, as California iconoclasts, gave to the nation and the world in terms of the written word. It does not purport to be an exhaustive history, merely a personal record by one who readily acknowledges how deep its influence on him has been.

☐

When I was a kid growing up on the west side of Los Angeles in the '40s and '50s, uncouth Russian Jews like myself only rarely ventured to the Pacific Palisades to visit the high and mighty. One day, after a particularly stern warning to be on my best behavior, my mom took me to call on former United States Senator James Phelan, then in his 90s. Phelan had been a patron of the Bohemian arts since the late 1800s into the 1920s. My mother, pianist Yaltah Menuhin, also concertized with violist Michael Mann, the son of Thomas Mann, the great writer. The Manns lived a few miles west of us, in the Palisades. Lion and Marta Feuchtwanger, who were in fact Jewish German refugees, lived at Villa Aurora, in the Palisades, after 1942 — several decades earlier, it had been built as a showpiece California villa by Harry Chandler, publisher of the Los Angeles *Times*.

In my childhood memories, the Palisades was a beautiful wooded place, with great mansions nestled in beautiful canyons loaded with green trees, all sloping gently to the Pacific. Mann was of an old German aristocratic background and Phelan was certainly as WASP as the great poet, Robinson Jeffers, whom he had patronized. Ronald Reagan, perhaps the most famous Palisadian, certainly wasn't Jewish.

I reflected on the fact that although I sometimes visited the homes of the elite in the Palisades, I grew up elsewhere. I didn't live in the Palisades — few Jews seemed to. I went to public schools in West Los Angeles and attended what is now called Brentwood Academy for some years. I lived next door to the Palisades, and those occasions when I went there were usually memorable.

Randy Young, known as the historian of the Palisades, has authored two volumes, *Rustic Canyon: The Story of the Uplifters* and *Pacific Palisades, From Mountains to the Sea*. He says that the Methodists founded what is now the village of Pacific Palisades in 1921, but about a year later others were developing other parts of the Palisades. A group known as the Uplifters had purchased a large ranch next to the Methodist portion. These were the opposite of Methodists — they were descended from the Bohemian Club in San Francisco. The most prominent of Los Angeles pioneer Jewish family names were Hellman and Newmark, and they were members of the Uplifters. Marco Hellman himself, who founded Hellman's Bank (which later became Union Bank), in 1923 built a beautiful log cabin in Rustic Canyon that is still a landmark on Haldeman Road (named after the grandfather of Bob Haldeman of Watergate notoriety). During the 1940s the place served as the home of then-Governor Earl Warren. Camp Josepho, the Boy Scout camp in the Palisades since the '30s, was donated by a prominent Jewish businessman and philanthropist, who was also a member of the Uplifters.

The Uplifters, who didn't mind drunken reveling, and the performance of other hedonistic bacchanalia on occasion, frankly horrified the Methodist fundamentalists, who had great plans for turning the area into a Chautauqua — a Christian cultural and educational fairground. That the Uplifters had Jews as members only further horrified the Methodists. "The Uplifters were," says Young, "the antithesis of the Methodists."

A couple of years after the '60s came to an end, I found myself in Northern California, a writer-in-residence at a place called Villa Montalvo Center for the Arts. It was a genuine Italian villa in Saratoga, inland a little way from Carmel — a villa with great exotic gardens and rare birds, surrounded by hundreds of acres of prime and hilly California chaparral, nestled in the green Los Gatos hills. Villa Montalvo was Senator Phelan's old place.

I had gotten the residency for six months to write my novel. My intention was to sum up the meaning of my career as a wandering small-town newspaperman in the California Bohemian mode during the '60s. I called the novel *Last Train North* — and in it I was trying to create a definitive statement of the '60s — and, more than that, an enduring testimony to the last hurrah of the California Bohemian movement.

I was partially writing about Newhall, just the other side of the Los Angeles basin north on Highway 5, in the '60s. I saw Newhall as one of those special Bohemian places and times, where special people came together and created something, such as occurred at Carmel after the 1906 San Francisco earthquake, and also occurred during the '50s in San Francisco. Scott Newhall, who then owned the Newhall *Signal*, was obviously a prototype for one of the main characters — the last great California Bohemian editor. And, in fact, Newhall was just that — he was the last major editor of the San Francisco *Chronicle*, a position he held for over two decades. He edited the paper with a definite consciousness of its original Bohemian tradition.

So I went to Villa Montalvo, now run by private donations and Santa Clara County, hoping to deal with the subject. While there I did get a feeling of Phelan, who in his younger days had been known for having a penchant both for fine women and fine arts. When I spent time there in the early 1970s, legends from the villa's halcyon days were everywhere to sense, especially if you got to know the villa and grounds day after day, night after night, as I did. For walking around the grounds was the main thing to do when you weren't writing, making music, or whatever during the 1920s. Bohemian bacchanals, orgies and poetry readings had been the order of the day. The young hermit Robinson Jeffers is said to have come here regularly to recite his epic poetry.

Villa Montalvo was my Magic Mountain. It wasn't so far away from Carmel, although it was far away from the original Bohemian encampment on the Russian River, which had been a sort of Socialist and writer's utopia in the previous century. But in the 20th century, the grounds were getting too difficult for the real Bohemians to maintain, so monied people from academia and commerce took it over.

That, too, was the history of the California Bohemian movement. Montalvo itself was very monied and Bohemian at the same time. It was ironical that the Bohemian Club, founded in the kitchen of an editor of the *Chronicle*, became today's Bohemian Club, which has few Socialists or writers in it today.

I always ended my day's work on *Last Train North* during those initial Montalvo days impatiently awaiting the first gloom of evening. No light from the surrounding cities seemed to touch Montalvo, and the night was very dark. The first thing I would do was take a walk, beginning from the flower garden at the bottom of the long, sloping lawn. I would walk up the lawn, watching the old villa draw closer, sensing the shadowy old place as she must have been.

When the light was on the main floor of the villa, the two huge windows were lit up so that from the outside, looking up, the lighted windows looked like great cat's eyes.

Buildings and places tell stories — don't believe that it isn't so. There's a mansion in *Last Train North*, and there was a Newhall Mansion House in "real life." I'm obsessed with mansions, with places that harbor dark Bohemian secrets.

This brings us back to Newhall in the '60s when I worked there. Newhall was an old art student of the '20s, a passable ragtime pianist, and an innovative metal sculpturist. His hobby for the last several years has been restoring mid-'50s Chryslers on a grand scale — we're talking several warehouses full of them.

I soaked up the California Bohemian tradition at Newhall's feet. I was fascinated by this last of the great Bohemian newspapermen — working for him gave meaning to my years as a wandering small town newspaperman during the '60s. Everything seemed connected at that point — Montalvo, the Newhall Mansion House, the coffeehouse culture I had come of age in, all the other newspapermen and editors I met there, many brilliant ranconteurs, and then that passing breed — the hippies, with whom I was not entirely comfortable.

At Newhall's Mansion House, we had thrown regular Bohemian soirees, where we ate lavish meals at dinner tables whose size can only be compared to what might be found in a dank European castle or on the Russian River, in the Bohemian groves. We ate lavish meals: then we talked or played chess or admired the house and gardens, or swam in the great tile pool outside, and perhaps relaxed in the jacuzzi and watched the dusk creep in across the narrow Santa Clarita Valley, dusk that spread her gloomy purple brilliance first on the orchards and then on the great house itself. We felt as if we were the elite o' the '60s — in summers especially, the rounded, tall, narrow doors of the Newhall Mansion House parlor were thrown wide open and the hot summer air was full of restless spirits flowing in and out. We were alive with the spirit of the rebellions of the '60s.

And yes, we were frank hedonists. Perhaps I overdid the sex and drug descriptions of our great parties in *Last Train North*, but they had that zeitgeist of a high jinx and rite in the Bohemian Groves. Robert Corrigan, the first president of California Institute of the Arts, on whose board Newhall sat, before Cal Arts even had a campus, frequented our parties often — and he would talk about Cal Arts, as if it really were going to be a place to rival the Bauhaus of the '20s. Cal Arts was originally supposed to have been built in Placerita Canyon, near the Oak of the Golden Dream, where gold was first discovered in California. But the geology turned out to be unsafe, so a site sitting to the side of Highway 5 was offered for the Disney school in the Valencia development by the Newhall Land and Farming Company, on whose board Scott Newhall also sat.

As the '80s were coming to a close, it did not look as if Cal Arts was going to become the equivalent of a Bauhaus. The '60s might have been the nation's equivalent of China's Cultural Revolution, but then one wonders how indelible a mark the Cultural Revolution made in China?

The notion of the Bohemian writer faced hard times in the somber '70s because of the harsh, ugly reality of reaction and hard times. The underground press ebbed as quickly as it had thrust itself upon the scene. By the Reagan '80s, Babbitts and Strangeloves were the order of the day, and the notion that the arts were more noble than commerce and militarism, was not a popular one.

This project of mine, writing about writers and a city, dates back to my childhood love of the Bohemian grandfather Mark Twain in San Francisco. Most of the writers I ever loved after that could be counted among the ranks of the California Bohemians. Since a big part of the tradition of the Bohemian writers was journalistic, I went to work on newspapers when I was nineteen years old.

But it wasn't until one lazy afternoon, not long before I ended up at Montalvo, that I listened to Scott Newhall expounding at great length on his views of newspapers and literature. Newhall said that real newspapermen were called to the profession the way others were called to the priesthood. He said that newspapermen should understand that journalism, despite what the cynics say, really should be practiced as a kind of daily literature, with the same commitment to truth — truth, he explained, which is not the same as so-called 'objectivity'.

I got the same feeling of what he was talking about more than a decade later, when I walked up the wide flight of stairs to the second story cityroom of the old *Herald-Examiner*, and was confronted by Dick Adler, the editor of the Sunday magazine section. Adler was a burly, balding, bearded man — which, incidentally, is not a bad description of me, either. Adler told me that he couldn't pay well, so I ought to have fun and write stories I cared about. I began writing about writers and Los Angeles and this book is the result.

☐

All through the '50s and '60s, I rode the old Southern Pacific Daylight up and down the coast of California — I started doing so as a kid and I kept on doing so and even do so now, every once in a while. On one particular trip, I remember that all the way up the coast, everyone I talked with was thinking about death, which was a strange topic considering the beautiful green-yellow-brown landscape just outside the window. As the Daylight wove its way along the top of the ocean cliffs just north of Santa Barbara, the widow of beatnik poet Stu Perkoff talked of death. She talked of the last few weeks of her husband's life, how as he was wasting away from cancer, her husband had become "beautiful, philosophical and very religious." Stu Perkoff was the most famous poet of the scene in Venice in the '50s, which Lawrence Lipton of the Free Press had written about in his book *The Holy Barbarians*. He was sort of the Los Angeles Ginsberg.

Photographer Phil Stern shot this photograph of the author making his way up the stairs to the newroom of the old Herald-Examiner, *where the "search for literary L.A." began. The sentence on the wall, "YOU ARE GETTING CLOSER TO GOD," was the photographer's joke. The old cityroom was not heaven.*

Just how much things were changing didn't hit home to me until 1984, when Papa Bach Bookstore in West Los Angeles closed its doors forever. John Harris, the poet-proprietor, partly blamed himself in closing the store, which had been much more than a store when it opened in 1964 as the city's, if not the country's, first all-paperback bookstore on Santa Monica Blvd., just a couple of blocks west of the San Diego Freeway. It should be explained that in the early '60s, quality paperbacks — not the cheap, pulp paperbacks found in drugstores and supermarkets, but books with content, ideas, enduring cultural values — were still something new in publishing. Until then, if a manuscript was worth printing, it was as a hardcover, unless it was banal, cheap, and formulaic enough to become a pulp paperback that fell apart after the first sweaty reading.

Even back in the '50s and '60s, with the exception of the Modern Library's wonderful classic series, hardcovers were expensive and people were resistant to the idea of paying a lot for them. On the other hand, quality paperbacks were the basis of mass left-wing publishing projects of the political '30s; in fact, most of the country's important new writers published by Grove Press, New Directions, and City Lights in the '50s and '60s reached thousands of people because they were first published in paperback. Paperbacks were more democratic and hence a bit subversive; and this aura rubbed off on Papa Bach when it dedicated its shelves to them in 1964.

Papa Bach's proprietor John Harris was L.A.'s Ferlinghetti.

Papa Bach quickly became the center of the city's burgeoning counter-culture movement and remained so during the twenty-odd years it remained a fixture on Los Angeles's cultural scene. Papa Bach was a meeting place and a cultural institution of its own. Papa Bach was where people went to announce their meetings, to give away their seditious literature, as well as a book store where a serious scholar on many different subjects had as good a chance as any of finding just what he or she really needed. This was because of Harris's catholic and eclectic intellect as much as anything else. I was proud that the book signings for my first two books — *The Menuhins: A Family Odyssey* and *Literary L.A.* — were at Papa Bach. When Papa Bach finally closed, Koki Iwamoto, the owner of Chatterton's Bookshop in the

Los Feliz district, called it a crime. Chatterton's today is the last survivor among the old-time general-interest literary bookstores.

Harris was the victim of the normal factors facing proprietors of real book-shops: greedy landlords, chain bookstores, and parking problems, and worst of all, the ominous signs that the television generation now coming of age really is illiterate. They can't read and they can't think. Otherwise, it is unlikely that we would have been saddled with two decades of Reaganism. But there was more than that. The closest thing Los Angeles ever had to a publisher-author of the likes of San Francisco's Lawrence Ferlinghetti, prop-rietor of City Lights bookstore and publishing company in North Beach, was Harris, but he was truly burned out, he said.

Not only could you buy the Communist Party's *People's World* or the demo-cratic socialist *In These Times*, there was a large browsing area in the rear of the store for small-press (mostly poetry) books you'd never find at Crown or B. Dalton. Papa Bach's walls reflected the tenor of the place — the Nixon mask which peered out of the front window throughout most of the bookstore's two decades, the cats prowling around the store or snoozing on top of the magazine racks. Papa Bach was the counterculture bookstore in Los Angeles before there even was a counterculture. It was the place where lefties came to argue politics, or literary people came to debate the merits of their respective heroes and heroines.

After graduating from USC, Harris spent the '50s as an industrial-relations honcho for aerospace firms. During the '60s he served as an executive in the War on Poverty's job-training programs; while working near San Francisco, he discovered the beat movement, whose philosophy, if not every aspect of its lifestyle, grabbed him. Born in China, the son of Seventh-Day Adventist missionaries, Harris disavowed his father's religion but obviously was motivated by a quest for the spiritual.

His view of the deity is obviously in the mode of his mentor, Robinson Jeffers, who grew up in Los Angeles and attended Occidental and USC in the teens, moved to the Big Sur coast in Northern California in the early '20s, then died as the famous poet of Big Sur in the '50s. Oddly enough, Harris was generally a man of the left politically, but he accepted without a shrug as his own spiritual and artistic mentor Jeffers, who was politically a conservative Republican.

Papa Bach published its own *Bachy* magazine, which made the bookstore as important to the Los Angeles poetry scene as Sylvia Beach's Shakespeare and Co. was in Paris in the '20s. Harris admits that he was trying to do what City Lights, the bookstore and the imprint, did for the beat generation. "I don't think there would have been a beat generation of poets without Ferlinghetti and his bookstore to publish them. I mean, some of the people from that era might have emerged anyway, but there wouldn't have been the beat movement."

Harris was ambivalent about Ferlinghetti, but he never denied that Papa Bach was always Los Angeles's last true beatnik institution, very much in the Ferlinghetti tradition. Excitement entered his voice when he talked about the effect the beats had on him — the beats whom he knew in San Francisco in the early '60s. "I discovered the beats and modern poetry and I stopped writing pretty and started writing true," he said. "There was always a fascination both with the lifestyle and the literature. You can't separate the two in the beats, but there was something adventuresome and risky, something vital about the beats. There was an honest quality to the writing."

Among other things, Harris also kept in print a fine but little recognized Los Angeles poet named William Pillin, not so famous as Charles Bukowski or Allen Ginsberg, but a man perhaps as well as endowed as a writer as these two men. Pillin died in 1985 at the age of 75. He had been born in the Ukraine, during a time of terrible pogroms. Pillin made it to Chicago in 1923, and English became his adopted language. He wrote often about Los Angeles, its streets and neighborhoods. His poetic imagery had a lot of substance. Consider this one, from "Akriel's Consolation":

> This morning I wrote a poem
> on the sadness of this street
> loud new youths, rude new neighbors,
> rot in the walls, ruts in the pavement.
> Said my angel, Akriel,
> invisible, soft-tongued
> "Stop your griping, Bill Pillin!
> All things grow old and rotten.
> You may even grow fond
> of rotted planks and decaying plaster
> and include them in one
> of your mist-ridden poems."

He was not religious but his Jewishness was part of his world. Now consider this snatch of his poetry:

> "I have not felt God's presence
> in my house or on my street
> for some time; and frankly I
> have no need for a God
> in the sky...
> I want a deity dwelling in the kitchen or the bedroom..."

The California Bohemian movement began in the last century in San Francisco, but it found its best definition by default in the next century in Los Angeles. The peculiar alchemy of writer and city is the subject of the following pages.

One of the last book signings at Papa Bach.

Cafe Au L.A.

My old friend from the coffeehouse days, Walden Muns, appears to have a good, solid head on his shoulders, but, on occasion, he has been morbidly attracted to the most pretentious and decadent stuff. For a while, he took to showing up on my doorstep carrying on about

Walden Muns, a.k.a. Monty Muns

punks, new-wavers, and similar half-human jetsam. As if they and their coffeehouse activities were somehow worthy of a comparable scene where Muns and I first met 30 years ago. Since Muns's initial enthusiasm for Al's Bar, establishments that *look* like real coffeehouses have sprung up all over town. I guess they are coffeehouses, although I don't get that sense from the conversations I've overheard. Maybe I am just a coffeehouse troglodyte.

In fairness to Muns — in fairness to punks — I decided to investigate some of the punk dives Muns was always mentioning — places like Al's Bar, in downtown Los Angeles, besides several other clubs in Hollywood. Al's Bar has become nothing but a nightclub, with hardly a coffeehouse pretense left at all. But the coffeehouse phenomenon, from the vantage point of the early '90s, seems to have Los Angeles firmly in its grip — there are dozens of them, with new ones opening every day. And now I'm beginning to understand why Muns was excited. They look like the real thing — like coffeehouses. And some of the patrons even resemble their counterparts in the great establishments of old. The only problem is that they all seem to be writing screenplays instead of essays and novels and articles; worse, in the "good" real-estate times, all they talked about was real estate, and in the bad real-estate times, they're still talking about real estate. Or so, at least, has been my impression.

I know it's an unfair impression. Gee, I almost fell into reveries in several nightspots, for peeling paint and tired old couches summoned up great memories. But when the sullen, moronic punk "music" of Al's started up, still to be duplicated in others of today's generation of "coffeehouses", the reveries short circuited — and this would-be patron took to his heels in disgust.

In the coffeehouses of old, we all loved intelligent music — classical, jazz or folk. Moreover, the coffeehouse generation from which Muns and I sprang was a literate one. We also loved books and writers and conversation; we were voracious readers ourselves; we were — or wanted to be — writers. Listening briefly to what passed for conversation at Al's, I knew that I couldn't go home again.

Muns must be desperate for a revival of the coffeehouse scene if he's willing to carry on so favorably about those punk places just because they physically resemble yesteryear's establishments. Like a lot of us, he yearns for the days when young minds hadn't been scrambled by television, before people — young and old alike — forgot how to talk and think.

But at least Muns was doing something about it. A former journalist and coffeehouse entrepreneur himself, Muns lives on the western slope of the Sierra and, when not working on his poetry, is writing a detailed narrative of the coffeehouse tradition in Los Angeles in the early '50s and '60s.

Bohemian meeting places date back two or three centuries to the coffeehouses of Paris and London, to the early days in the professions of journalism, insurance and international finance. The scene began in London in the early 1700s when men of enterprise abandoned taverns and hastened to strange, dark places called coffeehouses, where "pretty wenches" served a sooty drink from Turkey called *kaufy*. Most Londoners found the drink unpatriotic, seditious and downright smelly to boot. The most famous coffeehouse was Lloyd's, which became a great name in insurance. Later on, in Paris, the greatest Bohemian coffeehouses came into being in the 1830s and 1840s; Balzac was one of their ardent patrons. In the 1870s San Francisco's "Monkey Block" (which today is Montgomery Street in the financial district) was where the action was.

Muns and I reminisced about the old L.A. coffeehouse days and came to the conclusion that they had been grossly underrated. Monty — for that is what the name Walden Muns's friends all knew him by — is ten years older than I, so he remembers the '50s beatnik coffeehouse days in the shabby environs of Venice far better than I do. I did hang around some of those legendary places, like the Venice West and the Gas House, but I was merely a naive teenager who was attracted by the dense, sticky atmosphere of lust, sin and gratification which I had hoped would serve as a jumping-off place for my first genuine real-life sexual encounter. As for such obligatory coffeehouse art forms as reading abstract poetry, mouthing existential platitudes, and painting on Masonite boards, I didn't understand them. But the lewd, pulsating rhythm of the jazz was different and exciting. I marveled at the way the women doted on the singsong words of the male jazz poets, for their sonorous drones rarely made sense to me. In fact, by the time I began hanging out at the old Xanadu on Melrose Avenue (next to the Ukrainian Cultural Center), a whole new scene was flourishing. There, Muns served coffee and sandwiches and wit. I was only nineteen and still a virgin of the mind as well as the spirit and body, and the scene drew me like a magnet.

By the beginning of the '60s perhaps 50 coffeehouses were operating in the Los Angeles area, all in a modified beatnik mode. They had wonderful names like the Unicorn, I TAFANI, The New Balladeer, The Blue Grotto, Mother Neptune's, Vieteloni, Pogo's Swamp, the Couch, The Insomniac, the Bridge, The Epicurean, Deja-Vu, Wampeter, Cafe Frankenstein, The Coffeehouse, The Garret — to name a few.

The Xanadu was my shrine. And of all the coffeehouses of that period I believe it was the most influential. Chess and conversation appeared to be the chief activities there; at the Epicurean, ping-pong held sway. When "ping-pong diplomacy" first opened up negotiations between China and the United States, a couple of the regular ping-pong players from the Epicurean led the first American team to China. Another Xanadu regular, musician and writer Bonnie White, daughter of the well-known jazz vocalist Kitty

White, ran a coffeehouse called The Bridge in the late '60s, long after the Xanadu had closed. It was at the Bridge that poet Charles Bukowski gave his first poetry reading. Other California poets who read at The Bridge included Harold Norse and Jack Hirschman.

Still, I always felt the most comfortable around the Xanadu, and not just because it was next to Los Angeles City College, where I was attending classes. I had been part of coffeehouse clienteles that had shifted their allegiance to the Xanadu, having moved from such places as Pogo's Swamp, just across the street, and the Viteloni, up on Hyperion Avenue northeast of the campus. The "Vit" had had its share of famous folks coming in — Cisco Houston, who had been right up there with Woody Guthrie and Pete Seeger, showed up pretty regularly. In retrospect, I think I was initially drawn to the Xanadu by its book-lined walls. The Xanadu had once been the London Book Shop, and the combination of sofas and assorted other soft chairs gave the place the seedy air of a private club that had known better days. When you sat and conversed or played chess, you could always pull a book from the wall to bolster an argument. Pogo's Swamp, across the street, was owned by Levi Kingston, then a young black draft resister, now a community activist. It was literally a dark hole in the wall.

To my mind, the Xanadu deserves the most historical recognition of all the coffeehouses, even though it was one of the most ardent in appearance. For it was only out of the Xanadu that the Los Angeles *Free Press* was really born. Not only did the "Freep" first publish such writers as Charles Bukowski, who later became important, but by the end of the '60s, it had spawned the whole underground press movement across the country. It was not just coincidence that so many of the Xanadu regulars were working journalists. Even Muns had once worked for the Deal newspapers, weekly shoppers that still exist under different ownership, and other newspapers and magazines along the way. Gene Vier would putt-putt up in his battered old black Volkswagen; sometimes he'd bring in his fellow *Times* rim rats — copyeditors — and great political conversations would ensue. Then there was Ridgely Cummings, columnist and City Hall reporter, who inadvertently played a kingpin role for Sam Yorty, helping him to get elected mayor. Ridgely became a close, dear friend of mine; he looked like what he had been — a Liberty Ship captain during World War II. After some years roaming the seas, he became a tramp — a wandering newspaperman.

Ridgely became "Gridley Kuminski" in the *Free Press*, writing about City Hall politics with a lot more savvy than other reporters did in either the *Times* or the *Herald*. He used a pseudonym in the Freep because the newspapers that paid his salary didn't want to see his byline in the disreputable Freep. Ridgely made good money but supported a dozen children from several marriages.

All these people, including the *Free Press*'s founder, Art Kunkin, were regulars at the Xanadu. And one of the favorite topics of conversation was about the need for "a good newspaper in Los Angeles." When Kunkin hired me as a staff writer for the *Free Press* in 1970, we talked about the old days, for Kunkin was proud of the publishing empire he thought he was building then.

The difference between Kunkin and everyone else at the Xanadu in the early '60s was that Kunkin actually went out and started the paper, whereas the rest of us talked about it. Kunkin then adopted as his editorial guru Larry Lipton, who wrote a rather turgid and shrill column right from the first issue called "Radio Free America." Lipton had written *The Holy Barbarians*, a bestseller about beatnik life in its Venice heyday. After Kunkin hired me, I had to go take counterculture lessons from Lipton, because he and Kunkin had detected a certain lack of fervor in my prose. I needed that weekly paycheck, so I went. Mostly, Lipton had the bad taste not to talk about me, however, but about himself. I apparently showed the proper humility. The job continued a few more months.

The Xanadu closed in 1963, and many of the old crowd went to the Fifth Estate, at 8226 W. Sunset Boulevard, in whose basement Art Kunkin began the *Free Press* in 1964. The owner of the Fifth Estate, Al Mitchell, offered Kunkin space for the newspaper because he saw the publication as the beginning of the long-proposed Fifth Estate coffeehouse newsletter. But Kunkin actually issued his first number for Pacifica radio station KPFK's Renaissance Pleasure Faire.

The *Free Press* went along, not doing anything sensational, until the Sunset Strip demonstrations in 1966, which Mitchell organized because the cops were constantly harassing the Fifth Estate. The demonstration against police violence occurred in front of Pandora's Box, a music club at Crescent Heights and Sunset, next door to the site of the old Garden of Allah Hotel and less than a block away from the Xanadu. The demonstration became a riot — and suddenly the generational conflict of the '60s had exploded. "There were so many kids around," Kunkin explained, "They'd bring their knapsacks to the offices, take a bundle of papers, and go make some money. As many as one out of every four cars on the strip would stop and pay a dime for the *Free Press*." Soon, the old newspaper was no longer an intellectual coffeehouse publication — it developed a reputation as a hippie weekly, with a paid circulation of nearly 100,000 people. Soon underground papers were springing up in cities and towns across the country. The underground press, which had had its beginnings in those fervent conversations back at the Xanadu, became a reality.

Before the *Free Press* was born, the folks at the Xanadu all had a strong media focus. One of the earliest pieces in the Freep was by Les Claypool Jr., whose radio show did an unsung amount toward linking folk music to that stormy decade. Claypool had a nightly show on KRHM. Claypool's show was where the folkies of the burgeoning coffeehouse scene tuned in to listen and congregate. Claypool kept up a socially conscious Mort Sahl stream-of-consciousness rap, including countless folk songs, of which he had a magnificent collection, but he also improvised guerrilla radio theater, whose targets always included then-governor Ronald Reagan and the Vietnam War.

Claypool's show was actually quite influential. For example, he introduced Woody Guthrie's two best disciples to the L.A. airwaves, including the more talented disciple, Phil Ochs. Claypool was also chiefly responsible for introducing a young strummer named Bob Dylan, then just a nobody with a social conscience.

When Claypool wasn't on the air, he was on at the Xanadu. He and Muns were close friends; in fact, much of the guerrilla theater done on the show was sketched and spoken by Claypool and Muns. When the Xanadu finally closed, some of the old regulars spent as much time up at Claypool's house, at the top of Echo Park Avenue, as they did at the Fifth Estate. Claypool lived with his wife, Anne, in one of the same group of redwood cabins at the top of the street where bookman Jake Zeitlin had lived in the '20s, a tale we will get to in a later chapter.

The redwood bungalows still remain in a glen of trees and ivy. Muns lived across the way from Claypool. True Bohemian bacchanals took place in that "Bohemian Grove," hedonistic affairs, full of sexual outrageousness. At the crest of Echo Park Avenue, the old style of Bohemianism, such as had been practiced on the beaches of Carmel and on the Russian River nearly a century ago, was combined with '60s civil-rights activism, antiwar beliefs, and sexual revolution.

The Xanadu was the central city coffeehouse when the great civil-rights struggle was just beginning, both in Los Angeles and in the Deep South. The Xanadu was "where it was at" in terms of whites and black getting it together. Such great black blues singers as Lightnin' Hopkins, Sonny Terry, and Brownie McGhee hung around the Xanadu and its related scenes, because of the presence of Carroll Perry. Perry was more than a Xanadu regular: he was one of its pillars. One of the best Scrabble players around, Perry had even written a couple of books on the subject. Perry, a black writer, had counted among his friends in New York the great jazz musician Charlie "Bird" Parker. And that was no jive.

Perry had originally hung out at Pogo's Swamp. When owner Levi Kingston began closing down, Perry spent more and more time across the street at the Xanadu. Muns describes him: "Perry used to call himself the world's greatest Marxist dishwasher. He was Ed Perl's kitchen man, a jack-of-all-trades at the old Ash Grove. He had also once been a columnist for the *Daily Worker*, in New York. A charismatic guy, black, who said he was born in Jamaica, although I always figured he was born in Oakland in '31." Slipping into mock-heroic tones, Muns declares, "a true Communist, he strode the world like a Colossus. He's become the patron of San Pablo. I've heard he's been running a place in Berkeley, on San Pablo, called the Cabal, for years now. Don't know if it's still there."

Brownie McGhee, Muns continues, "was just one of the old black guys playing, who always came in and played in the corner of the Xanadu. Except that he happened to be the world's foremost blues guitar player. Been so judged, been to Europe. Yeah, and loved Scotch. Loved that J & B Scotch. They'd sit in the corner away from the window, keeping the beat; truly jazzed up. McGhee was a jived-up person. Always keeping the beat. He didn't use drugs. None of them did. Just drank Scotch. Those were the pure old days, those were the days that were pure. They had a natural high." Although Hopkins, McGhee and Terry used to get together often at the Xanadu, Muns says the Xanadu was really only a staging point for where they did some of their best playing at Echo Park parties they found out about through the Xanadu.

Or were specially invited to. Muns mentions the case of party giver Jane Borak, who ran the jewelery concession at the Ash Grove. You could tell who she was by the fact that she sported long African earrings. She had somehow obtained a house from a hard-up veteran of the Spanish Civil War who was being foreclosed on for back taxes. Borak's Saturday night parties were famous from about '59 to '64, he says. "Sometimes parties would break up the next morning, sometimes they'd still be going through the next day. People like Judy Collins and Pete Seeger came up and played. And if you gave them (Hopkins, McGhee and Terry) a bottle of J & B, they would come and play straight through until the next morning."

Muns says that he always enjoyed Borak's parties more than Claypool's, which I remember best. "He always thought he was running the satyricon," Muns sneers, "but in reality he was a puritan. He had his own little court system up at his house in the wilderness, and he thought he was the Henry David Thoreau of Echo Park, but it was hard to accept him as that when he fell down in his own barf. If you got to know him well, your skin was always being singed by his ego. It poured out like an erupting volcano." Muns and Claypool, in case you couldn't tell, had something of a falling out.

Spin-off parties from the Xanadu also took place in the student housing east of Vermont Avenue. The Chambers Brothers, who achieved some moderate musical success in the '60s and '70s and some even into the '80s, often played for these. They practically lived at the Xanadu. The effect of the Xanadu therefore was not confined to its narrow walls — often one would merely go to the coffeehouse to learn where the parties were, for they all drew from that wellspring.

Black and white talent mixed not only in music but in the literary arts. According to Muns, a young black playwright, then known as LeRoi Jones, hung around his place. I met my one-time roommate, an aspiring black playwright named Ed Bullins, at the Xanadu. He and I used to tell each other we'd never make it as writers, an exchange I had forgotten about until one day when I read a full-page profile on Bullins in *Newsweek*, where he was being acclaimed as a major playwright on the American scene. A young man named Ron Everett, the student body president at City College, was another roommate. After Everett left City College, he changed his "slave name" to Ron Karenga and became both famous and notorious in the then-emerging black-power movement.

☐

Even though Art Kunkin was around for much of the Xanadu scene, he is less inclined than I am to see the paper as an outgrowth of the coffeehouse movement. He sees it more as something he did on his own, observing that a lot of the old coffeehouse writers disdained his power at first. Kunkin, who has turned from the Marxism he followed from the late '40s to the '60s, to alchemy and metaphysics in the '80s and '90s, says, "The reason history touched me to found the Los Angeles *Free Press* and what it spawned in the '60s was that I was supertuned to the mental direction of the nation, to the emotional desires of the nation. I knew it wasn't Art Kunkin doing it, but before the forces emerged, I was responsive to them. I was looking for those little molecular developments that make up social change, and I was doing this with a sense of history."

In a long conversation about those days, Kunkin held out an old issue of the *Free Press* and pointed at the cover of a dark, mysterious, half-portrait of "staffer" Norman Hartweg. Where had Hartweg come from? A playwright who rented a room at the Fifth Estate, he had won some acclaim as the author of "The Pit," Kunkin told me. He won even more notoriety later on as a real-life character in Tom Wolfe's *The Electric Kool-Aid Acid Test*, the saga of Ken Kesey's Merry Pranksters on their trip across the country in a bus painted in Day-Glo, Kunkin added.

But the tale that really best summed up the Zeitgeist of the Xanadu was the Defeat of Chess Player Ted Jester by Master Walden Muns, Kunkin insisted emphatically. "You can't write about the coffeehouse scene without telling that," Kunkin insists.

I was around when the event occurred, but I wanted to recreate it accurately.

A Standard Solution *by Lair Mitchell.*

So I went and talked with Lair Mitchell (who is not to be confused with Fifth Estate proprietor Al Mitchell). Lair Mitchell was managing the Xanadu then, along with Muns and Norman Bollerup. (Another early contributor to the Freep, Mitchell, who died in 1989, was an artist and writer of considerable originality in Hollywood.)

"We were always on the lookout for people with wit and grace who could contribute to the conversation," Mitchell told me. "Then this gawky young man came in, and he could talk about nothing but himself and what a brilliant chess player he was. His name was Ted Jester — you ask, what's in a name? Out of a certain desperation we all came up with a plan at once. Jester was asked if he had ever played chess with Master Muns. Jester allowed as to how he hadn't even heard of Master Muns. Muns, it developed, had retired from the Game after causing a friend to die of a heart attack because of losing one game too many to Muns. Jester agreed — enthusiastically — to a match. Muns of course hadn't played a lick of chess in his lifetime, but he was soon taught enough to move the pieces, or at least he could if he had someone else's notations to follow.

Came the great night. Klieg lights were burning and "reporters" were dashing about with note pads and cameras. Letters and telegrams of congratulations from chess enthusiasts from as far away as the Soviet Union, welcoming the return of Master Muns, adorned the walls of the Xanadu. When Jester walked in, he was roundly ignored. Right behind him came Master Muns in a trench coat and scarf. He was led to an imposing throne next to the oversize chess set in the corner. A bevy of beautiful women danced attendance on him. Then between sips of coffee and wine, he slowly and majestically moved his pieces. The reason Muns took his time moving the pieces was that he had to read each move off a piece of cardboard held on a waiter's tray behind Jester. The notations were worked out by three top-rate and ranked chess players, who were following the game in the Xanadu kitchen. At one point Muns misread a cue and lost an important piece, but inevitably he won the game.

Afterwards, however, people began feeling sorry for Jester, sunk in confusion and humiliation. The "elder statesmen" of the Xanadu took him to coffee at the 24-hour Norms that used to be at Sunset Boulevard and Vermont Avenue for years and years. They decided to tell him what had really happened — so that he would just laugh it off. By the time they got back to the coffeehouse, Jester was saying that he had figured out the whole thing was a fake when he walked in the door. The next morning he was quoted as saying he had known it was a fake the morning of the match. A week later, he said he had known from the beginning that Master Muns was a phony. On the basis of his misadventure, however, Jester was accepted by the Xanadu's Illuminati, and the whole story is remembered as one of the great Bohemian high jinx of the Xanadu period. Today, Jester lives in a cave in Santa Barbara, and other times on the beach in Morro Bay. He has changed his name to Cyril Jasmine III. He tells people that during the ensuing years he has been writing a novel.

Lair Mitchell also described a number of other outrageous characters of the old Xanadu. "A couple of them that I just have to mention," he said, "were Owsley Stanley III and George Hunter. Stanley became especially famous as a manufacturer and distributor of LSD in San Francisco. And both Stanley and Hunter were prime movers, along with Ken Kesey, in the development of The Grateful Dead, the first psychedelic rock band."

Muns, also wanting to add some famous names to the story, mentions that Mort Sahl came in occasionally, and Christopher Isherwood stopped by a few times, saying he especially liked the "European" atmosphere — perhaps he meant the books on the wall. (As previously mentioned, the Xanadu had originally been a bookstore and the landlord, who liked the idea of a coffee-house in a bookstore, made that part of the deal.) Hoyt Axton hung around a lot, a gruff but obviously talented guitar player, who was trying to impress an attractive girl named Victoria Valentino, who later went on to become not only Axton's girlfriend but also a *Playboy* centerfold in 1963. Muns says that Axton made connections at the Xanadu that allowed him to go on to fame and fortune. There were also other local literati around, such as poet Curtis Zahn and writer Bard Dahl.

The most colorful, however, from Muns's point of view, may have been J.D. Jones, who roamed the Xanadu dressed in a safari jacket and Bermuda shorts, whatever the weather, and made his living not only by writing poetry, which of course didn't pay, but also by selling pen-and-ink drawings of vaginas that he smuggled in under his coat. "A true con man, a great boulevardier," laughed Muns.

Nigey and Muns and I sat around discussing these good times over a bottle of wine (the coffee would come later). We talked of how, despite the best efforts of Carroll Perry, that street-wise philosopher, and his sidekick "Mad Dog Wilburn," the Xanadu was finally done in by a contingent of Satan's Slaves, an outlaw motorcycle gang that drove everyone else away after a while. Muns was spending more time in San Francisco than Los Angeles then, because, he said the old Beat thing was coming back up north. "There's a renaissance of jazz and poetry in North Beach again," he optimistically insisted. (Muns hasn't talked about the old Beat thing coming back in North Beach in a while now, and has instead bought some land in Ireland, where he's planning to retire to the old sod.)

We talked about San Francisco, but Muns admitted that he still missed the old Xanadu. We pondered just what the chemistry was that occurred in that rather unprepossessing storefront, which, incidentally, as of this writing, is a western boutique called Y Que. Perhaps, Muns suggests, the Xanadu was to Los Angeles what San Francisco's North Beach had been to the entire

A Jungian Origami *by Lair Mitchell*

beatnik movement, "back when," Muns said rhetorically, "I'd hike a thousand miles to meet a friend."

Is there anything going on in Los Angeles today? I asked Monty, hoping he'll know of something I've missed. He shook his head. How about Beyond Baroque, down in the old Venice City Hall? "It would be hard to duplicate down here what they even take for granted in San Francisco today. What is a coffeehouse movement? Well, for one thing it's people who work all night, using their imaginations. That is what it amounts to." Then Monty was quite convinced that the coffeehouse scene will never thrive again in Los Angeles. If nothing else, the cost of rents is prohibitive.

"Yeah," I say. "Do you know something strange? You know *Los Angeles Magazine*, that big, glossy, boring city magazine? A good friend of mine, Lincoln Haynes and a group of his friends, founded it as a nice Bohemian literary monthly. Then they lost control of it. They went on to collaborate on a famous project of the Johnson years — a book called *The Begatting of a President* that Orson Welles later did on a record. Then they did one on

Reagan, but it didn't seem to hit."

Muns said he had heard of Haynes and read the old magazine, but he said it was of a slightly earlier generation of coffeehouse people than we were — more '50s. "But I liked it. They had articles by people who were brought up in the Los Angeles River before it had concrete levees; when the kids would go and catch frogs in it. A fine little magazine. It drew some artists and writers together and it was important. Didn't last long, though."

And so there we sat talking, Nigey, Muns and I — all of us sounding like a bunch of old Bohemian reprobates talking about this city's hidden literary tradition, about the better days.

Damn, they were better.

Why Norman Is Still On The Bus

I've always wondered what Benjamin Bufano's St. Francis of Assisi might have thought of that strange night back in 1966 when Ken Kesey's Merry Pranksters reveled for several hours in front of the Longshoremen's Hall in San Francisco, shortly before departing for Los Angeles in their Day-Glo-painted bus. The great sculptor's rendition of the gentle, animal-loving Catholic saint looked enigmatic to me through the dope-hazed stroboscopic madness of that crazy evening that lingered in my mind as a time-frozen snapshot of the era. I remember the outlandish costumes of Kesey and the Pranksters, the ugly and pervasive noise of the acid rock sounds of the Grateful Dead, as well as the startling sight of a phalanx of women dancing topless, and the cops who hovered as if they were about to pounce, but then didn't. Just as Kesey had intended, they had become part of the bizarre proceedings. The Merry Pranksters was an apt name.

Kesey had just finished telling the court, suddenly sounding as chaste as an old Baptist maiden lady, that his new Acid Tests, of which this was one, would be LSD-free. The LSD experience without the LSD, he announced — which everyone knew was a big joke. The joke was for the benefit of the courts, where Kesey was facing various marijuana charges. Another big prank. Too big a prank. For after the San Francisco Acid Test, Kesey had to escape to Mexico. The idea was that the Pranksters would drive the bus south, holding Acid Tests all the way down the coast into Mexico, where eventually they would rendezvous with the fugitive from justice. LSD was not yet clearly illegal — it would be in a few months, but not quite yet. No doubt one of the reasons it did become illegal were the various Acid Tests conducted by the Pranksters as they headed south, especially the four in Los Angeles, and in particular the Acid Test in L.A.'s Watts, where LSD-spiked Kool-Aid — so called Electric Kool-Aid — left a number of innocents so freaked out they had to be hospitalized. Kesey's Pranksters without Kesey were as outrageous as McMurphy, the main character in Kesey's 1962 novel, *One Flew Over the Cuckoo's Nest*.

A couple of years later Tom Wolfe (again, the journalist, not the real novelist) published *The Electric Kool-Aid Acid Test*, his best-seller based on Kesey's adventures with his Merry Pranksters aboard their 1939 Day-Glo-painted former church bus. I was one of thousands who rushed out to buy the book. Then the following year, which was 1969, I was brought full circle back to that original night under St. Francis's nose. A fellow from Filmways

24

invited me in to discuss doing something about Kesey's thousands of hours of movie footage, which because of misfocusing and overexposure and other amateur problems had boiled down to half an hour of usable footage. Wolfe's book had already been published, so everyone was aware of the existence of "The Movie," shot by Kesey's Pranksters during their initial trip across the country. The studio wanted someone who would work with Kesey, a writer who could devise a script that could be shot around the usable footage. We talked a long time — yes, I was anxious to work on the film. Certainly I had heard of Kesey. The Filmways executive warned me that Kesey was difficult to work with — in fact, several other writers already had failed. But the Filmways executive thought I might be successful with Kesey, just as he no doubt had thought that the others would.

I think he meant what he said, however, for he viewed me as a more bona fide hippie than his other writers, with their fancy digs in Malibu and the Hollywood Hills. And, of course, I had done LSD, and I had followed the doings of those priests of LSD, such as Timothy Leary and Ken Kesey. I had read and been deeply impressed by Kesey's novels. The executive said he would hire me when Kesey got back, for no one was quite sure where he was at that moment, except that he was on the road in the Day-Glo bus. He had gone with a whole truckload of the studio's equipment to do what, no one was precisely sure. As happens so often in such flaky deals, the executive finally called me back and said that the studio was dropping out of the whole project — they had come to the conclusion that Kesey was simply impossible.

I spent much of that psychedelic decade traveling between Los Angeles and San Francisco, as did many of my generation. Gas was cheap, and the big old American cars we drove were, if nothing else, reliable and comfortable. The psychedelic tide carried us, the remnants of the late beatnik coffeehouse scene in the early '60s, to and fro between Los Angeles and San Francisco. When the waves were out, we always found ourselves in Los Angeles, waiting for the next tide that would carry us to the Jerusalem that San Francisco was for us. In those days, we Angelenos saw ourselves as the pikers when the psychedelic revolution overtook us: everything was happening up north, it seemed. With hindsight, it now seems as if that may not have been quite the truth. For down here, we were reading Aldous Huxley's *Doors of Perception*, in part, no doubt, because we were all impressed by the fact that the great British author who adopted the Southland as his native home for more than the last two decades of his life, went out on his deathbed in his Hollywood Hills home under the influence of LSD — notes of which were dutifully kept by his widow, Laura Huxley. Kesey and Leary may have been the gurus of the psychedelic movement, but it is doubtful if they would have found so many followers had it not been for the influence of Huxley's slim but potent little volume.

☐

One day Jeanne Morgan, the first wife of Art Kunkin, left a note for me at Chatterton's Bookstore on Vermont Avenue. She was going to meet Norman Hartweg at a coffee shop across from the bookstore to talk about old times. Would I like to join them? Hartweg had been one of Kesey's Merry Pranksters. In fact, much of Wolfe's book, since Wolfe himself never actually was on the bus, was based on material taped by Hartweg: Hartweg had been a major character in *The Electric Kool-Aid Acid Test* as well, and his was, in a sense, the ultimate story of what happened to much of the writing talent of my generation in Los Angeles. He was the great writer who might have been; but he was living in obscurity in a tiny, dingy little apartment in North Hollywood. Hartweg survived Kesey's various acid tests as well as the notorious stoned driving of Neal Cassady. The irony of Hartweg's life is that he was a paraplegic, confined to a wheelchair as the result of a broken back suffered in an auto accident that occurred right after he left Kesey's bus in Los Angeles in 1967.

When Kesey approached him in 1964, however, Hartweg was riding high. He was a columnist at the *Free Press*, which had just started at the Fifth Estate coffeehouse, on Sunset Blvd. Hartweg also lived at the Fifth Estate, in a cheap basement apartment that had no windows. He had recently won an award for his play "The Pit," which the prestigious *Tulane Drama Review* not only published, but gave him an award for. The play was being performed all over the country — eventually, it would be produced on public television in Boston. Hartweg was deeply involved in a small Hollywood playhouse called Theatre Event in what was then The Bridge coffeehouse (later the Deja Vu). He had also directed the West Coast premier of Genet's "The Maze." Through the rumor mill, he had also heard that the *New Republic* was considering him for a position as drama critic. But he threw all this up, which included giving away his personal library, to go off and become one of Kesey's Merry Pranksters.

Hartweg wouldn't have been interested in Kesey's proposal that he abandon all of this in Los Angeles and come up to his place in the redwoods (just south of San Francisco) had it not been for the mention of the legendary Neal Cassady's name. For Cassady was none other than the Dean Moriarty of Kerouac's *On the Road*, which Hartweg considered to be one of his biggest influences.

Hartweg couldn't resist the chance to be around Cassady. Their introduction, however, was not entirely auspicious. Cassady's first love, as one of the Merry Pranksters, was cars and driving. He was a whiz with old cars — and the bus was one of the oldest. He was a whiz at fixing it, and a whiz at driving. In Tom Wolfe's book there are some memorable descriptions of the Pranksters' first cross-country trip, some truly terrifying moments with Cassady, his mind blowing on too many mics of LSD, maneuvering the old vehicle down the slopes of the great mountains without the benefit of brakes.

Hartweg had a similar hair-raising experience when he first met Cassady. They had gone for a drive in the country around Kesey's home and again Cassady was at the wheel. And while he was driving, especially down one long winding curve coming out of the hills, Cassady kept up an incessant patter about the bus and old cars and anything else that crossed his mind, looking not at the road but directly at the terrified Hartweg. Hartweg saw the truck coming up the grade, but he was also sure that Cassady had not. At the last moment, as the bus approached the truck, Cassady looked back to the road, fishtailed the old bus out of the truck's path along the edge of the road, and without comment looked back again at Hartweg, his patter resuming where it had left off a second before.

Back at La Honda, where Kesey lived, the famed author suddenly appeared before his guest, as if he knew that Hartweg needed an explanation, saying, "Cassady doesn't have to think anymore." By which, Hartweg presumed, he was supposed to believe that Cassady had moved on to ever-higher and more-noble plains of pure thought, helped, of course, by the large doses of acid he had taken.

There was a lot of history behind Hartweg's journey to meet the prototype Dean Moriarty. In the early '50s, Hartweg had written a play called "Joe Brown," which was performed and won a prize in Oklahoma. "The play recorded my distress at just discovering racial prejudice," Hartweg told me at a second meeting in another coffeeshop. He laughed at himself as he told me about it. "I thought this was really good stuff. I was going to write plays against war and mob violence and see if I couldn't straighten some of these things out." He also read On the Road, which had a tremendous effect on him, introducing him not only to the fantastic character of Moriarty but the fact that marijuana was used elsewhere besides the ghettoes.

Soon after this, he ended up in the army and found himself stationed in Denver, which was extraordinary luck. He thought he could go searching for Moriarty's famous lost drunken father on Larimer Street, as described in On the Road.

But Larimer had changed. It had gone uptown; the old slum part of town was undergoing urban renewal. As if to make up for the fact, however, the fates smiled kindly on Hartweg. He was assigned to work in the library of an army hospital, and mostly what he did was read. "There were five or six souls of my ilk on the post," he says. "We made up the 'Beat contingent.' We went out and got the obligatory bongo drums, berets, and Miles Davis records and had a good time. We managed to survive the army that way. We all wanted to be writers, but we also had trouble finishing anything." One of his buddies, a fellow named Kent Chapman, was from California and knew Venice well. In fact, Chapman had been portrayed as a Venice Beat in Larry Lipton's *The Holy Barbarians*, and that impressed Hartweg no end.

Chapman introduced Hartweg to names he had never heard of — writers such as Malcolm Lowry and Christopher Isherwood, and the Vedanta Society. The latter was what originally got Hartweg interested in going to the West Coast after the army, "for I heard there was this whole Eastern trip submerged on the West Coast."

The first thing that Hartweg did on being mustered out in 1960 was to head for Los Angeles, where he looked up his old friend Chapman. The two of them rented an apartment in Hollywood for $40 a month. The fascination with the "Eastern thing" persisted, and no doubt through the influence of Huxley and other writers, whom Hartweg read avidly, drugs were mixed into the brew of Eastern mysticism developing on the West Coast. At first, Hartweg says, "Marijuana provided a pleasant way to draw and write that also made you think that what you were doing was terrific. You felt warm and relaxed and euphoric." So when Hartweg first decided to take Kesey upon his offer, to meet Moriarty, he thought that he would find the Pranksters "into the Tibetan thing." What he found, instead, was not the "Tibetan," (meaning a lot of flies buzzing around a meditating wise man) but Kesey's own rather odd kind of Americana — among the Day-Glo mania at La Honda were the Hell's Angels, all the movie-making gear, the sound equipment, and all the other paraphernalia of Kesey's northern loonybin environment. The only real "Eastern thing" around La Honda was Kesey's rampant anti-intellectualism, as revealed in his statement to Hartweg about the nobleness of Cassady's dope dementia.

The period 1964 to 1967 was an "extraordinary time in human history," Hartweg proclaims. "Leaders sprang up all over the place from the grass roots. They came in all types, colors, and descriptions. They gave names to things for people. That's still what I'm most interested in now, and the physics of that phenomenon — what it was that happened around them. It doesn't exist now. Maybe some of the same people are around, but they're doing different things, or maybe even the same things. But the leaders and the clusters are gone."

Hartweg looked me squarely in the eye. "That's what the lamentation over coffeehouses and the '60s was all about when we met the first time with Jeanne Morgan. About how it's all gone, and how we wish it were back again," he said. I nodded my agreement that indeed this might be true. I wasn't convinced by all that Hartweg said, but I also felt that his must have

have been the most archetypical '60s writer's story ever to come out of the Los Angeles coffeehouse scene. Which meant, naturally, that despite talent and intelligence, even brilliance, he ultimately produced very little. Hartweg explained the process precisely. He said that the whole generation of young painters, writers, and musicians stopped being painters, writers, and musicians as a result of the psychedelic revolution. In his case, this voyage began with his leaving Los Angeles to join Kesey and the Pranksters. Basically, Hartweg insisted, his generation left their arts and went off into two different directions. One group went into radical politics, and the other went into psychedelics. "There just wasn't much writing or painting going on if you were going to be doing the other things."

□

There is some sense of this parting of the generational ways in Wolfe's description of the meeting between Kesey and Kerouac in *The Electric Kool-Aid Acid Test*. Here was the most important writer of the '50s in the same room with Kesey, who looked as if he were going to be the best writer of the '60s. And although it was as if Kesey had picked up the banner that Kerouac had wearily put down, in Wolfe's description, there was no rapport between the two men. Neither had much to say to the other.

To this day, Hartweg shares Kesey's militant anti-intellectualism, which was, of course, a hallmark of the psychedelic generation. Hartweg will hardly even admit to himself that he was, and in fact remains, a hero worshipper of Kesey. Hartweg argues that it would be pointless to say what he felt, or feels today, about Kesey, the man who snatched him out of his developing career and former life, even though he admits what he thinks indirectly. "Kesey was an enormously powerful personality," he says, "and he was also huge. He's not that tall, but he had neck muscles like oilfield wire lines; he was a collegiate heavyweight wrestler aiming at going to the Olympics, which he never did. Now, if you take an unsure person and run him across a huge man like that with a powerful personality who is dead sure of what he believes, you will find circles of insecure people around him, trying to figure out if they agree with him or not, sort of like the way little fish latch onto the side of a whale." Later, Hartweg insists that in actual fact Kesey did not seek out followers, that "he did not expect worship at all, that he simply one day looked around and realized he had acquired a lot of people who centered their identity on his, most of whom were underfoot, who were making it harder and harder for him to move." On the other hand, I pointed out, it was his money that supported all these people, to which Hartweg replied with what I thought was an unconvincing response, namely, that if "someone wasn't really contributing by doing his or her thing, they would eventually be kicked out."

Hartweg eventually left the Merry Pranksters on his own. After the well-publicized Acid Tests in Los Angeles, some of the Pranksters continued south with Kesey on his Mexican sojourn, and others just "scattered."

It was in the process of scattering that the accident occurred that, more than any of his previous experiences with the Los Angeles coffeehouse scene or Kesey's Pranksters, changed the rest of Hartweg's life. Yet even the crash seemed to me a logical culmination for an archetypical Los Angeles coffeehouse experience. The sheer velocity of that generation could only end in a crash. Hartweg and his old friend Evan Engber, and famed Prankster Marge the Barge, piled into an ancient, uninsured automobile and headed out to New York. Hartweg drove the first leg of the journey, to Las Vegas. It was three in the morning when they arrived in town. They all had a quick sandwich, and then Hartweg curled up in the right front seat and went to sleep. He doesn't even remember who was actually driving after that. "Halfway out in the desert, we banged into something. I don't know exactly what happened, except that I was thrown out and my back was broken. The other two sustained only slight injuries and bruises."

For a year after that, Hartweg lay in a hospital bed in his native Ann Arbor, Michigan. The convalescence gave him a lot of time to think. One of the things he thought about the most was his goal of wanting to be a writer. He came to the conclusion that it wasn't so much that he wanted to be a writer as he was in love with the idea of others thinking that he was one. Except for a few brief book reviews and articles, he's hardly written a thing since then. Instead, he spent the next ten years trying to regain his sanity after the turmoil of the '60s.

He went back to the University of Michigan, where he had already earned a master's degree, figuring he would check things out "with the people who do philosophy for a living." He entered the doctoral degree program and also got a job teaching at the university — "They gave me easy stuff to teach, like symbolic logic." After three years he only had to write a dissertation to earn his doctorate. But he found he had nothing to write about. "The philosophy professors knew nothing, either — only how to articulate the dilemmas." He now believes that the best answer to the old philosophical questions is the proverbial Zen reply, which is to hit anyone who asks such questions with a big stick, and then run away giggling. "I decided that anybody who giggles is probably all right," he said, giggling.

Hartweg also pretty much abstains from marijuana, alcohol, and other drugs these days, with the exception of coffee and cigarettes. He's adamantly opposed to cocaine and speed and thinks that LSD is really only appropriate for those whose situation is so hopeless that "They might as well try blasting powder. But then it's still very risky. You might blow up. People are in loony bins to this day from it." He described some of the scenes from the '60s in San Francisco's Haight-Ashbury so vividly that you almost wonder that he's not totally against drugs. "You'd find these dismal crash pads with people in terribly desiccated states, dark hollows around their eyes, still saying 'wow' and 'groovy.' They came out from Des Moines to San Francisco to wear flowers in their hair, but they found only sharks who said they could score a kilo. Suddenly, instead of consciousness-raising, it had become drug dealing, and it was scummy."

Yet despite his disavowal of drugs, the psychedelic way of looking at things is still there — one might even suggest that it is these very attitudes that effectively prevented him from finding his way back to the typewriter. He explains that he just doesn't take words, or, for that matter, his own beliefs and thoughts, very seriously. He paraphrases that old '60s shaman, Marshall McLuhan, who said, "Words have just become reality probes." "You try them out to see what works," says Hartweg. "You throw them away when they don't work. Words just aren't engraved in stone anymore. Don't look for the meaning of words, look for their use."

For a while, Hartweg and I debated the meaning of great writing. He still retains the notion that says there is nothing but everyone's subjective truth, and hence no one statement is really more valid than another because there really is no such thing as truth. I argued that Mark Twain's works, for instance, have survived because their author had the breadth of vision that made his works immortal. But neither of us was convincing the other. To Hartweg, my statement was no more true and no more false than his or anyone else's statement. After fifteen minutes of that, my head started to hurt.

Hartweg even refused to see any significance in his coming home again to Los Angeles in 1977, after his decade of soul-searching in Michigan. He admits that he had a "whole mess of California stuff still hanging over my head undone." He admitted that he "wanted to see what had become of the underground newspapers, the coffeehouses." And you certainly could sense his disappointment as he discovered "every spit, every scrap" gone. "It was like an organism that had grown," he said, "lived its life, and then decomposed back into the initial elements from which it had sprung. The places were still there — Venice, the Pacific Ocean, a whole mess of the individuals." But the group consciousness was gone.

Hartweg had originally come to Los Angeles in 1960, to check out the scene for a few weeks before going to New York to settle down. But he stayed. "You can spend 25 years in L.A. never buying a six-pack of Coke because at any moment you may be leaving for New York." Before he came back to L.A. for the last time, he had checked out New York once again. But he found the mobs and its nastiness and tension "inhuman. It was like finding good things in postwar Berlin. If you have to be there, fine, make the most of it." By then, however, it wasn't for him. Thus he returned West.

There was one brief moment after his arrival back in town when it looked as if some of the old gang would materialize. Art Kunkin and Paul Krassner hired him to be the editor of a new *Realist* that Larry Flynt, owner of the *Hustler* empire, was planning to resurrect. But then Flynt got shot, either by the Mafia or the CIA, and Kunkin, Krassner, and Hartweg were on the streets again.

He still wanted to settle in. He drove up and down the old streets with names like Alvarado Street and Hollywood Boulevard, so he could renew "the tapes" and destroy the old mystique of L.A. that he had built up in his mind since he left it the last time in '67. He sat down with maps to figure out where the city's backbone, where its nervous system was. He even went out to look at the powerlines and foundries. He read books on the unstable geology underneath. And he sat high on the top of the Hollywood Hills so he could contemplate the city as it really was, not as his own personal self, or the mystique, had made it seem.

He seemed please to report that the same "muscle layers" were there — the big retail stores, the jammed freeways, the phone company, the service clubs. But he noted that the culture signified nothing. The art and writing of the '70s, which had gone on in his absence, affected no one. "In the mid-'50s and '60s art mattered," he said. "It had an effect. There was a great arch of the artistic, political, and Bohemian, all linked in one great swirl. It made a difference. But nowadays, the fleas aren't jumping. They're not biting the dog. The exciting issues that enflame the human spirit are gone. Things still happen — important things like the sun coming up, the tide coming in, the flowers growing. But the fleas just ain't jumping."

Like many other people in town, Hartweg had a tough time surviving in the Reagan depression of 1982. Just finding work was tough — he was running a one-man office for a man who sold drilling equipment to Texas oil fields. He was glad to have the job, which, from the trade journals spread all over his apartment, you could tell he took seriously. He was getting his rent paid. He conceded, with what seemed some wistfulness, that he could see some possible signs of a cultural awakening in Los Angeles. Hartweg firmly believed that art needs some oppression to give it impetus, and that's just beginning to happen now. For him, and for many of his generation, there was a spurt, an eruption — then the futility of the dreary '70s and '80s, when little was written, less was painted, and ultimately nothing was said.

Tales Of An
Extraordinary Madman

In 1972, when I first saw fellow Los Angeles *Free Press* writer Charles Bukowski's book in the window of a bookstore in West Hampstead in London, I felt a lot of jealousy. It was called *Notes of a Dirty Old Man*, the same title as his column in the paper. It was a City Lights book, with Bukowski's amazing pocked alcoholic face adorning its cover. I viewed Bukowski as only doing a limited shtick — he rarely came into the office himself, but I knew all about him through the grapevine, or so I thought. I hadn't realized how popular Bukowski was getting until I was confronted by a book display in London. Years later, after realizing that this guy had paid more dues than me and maybe was even more of a writer I set about reconstructing his life, and I was surprised to find out how much I knew and how much I hadn't known.

Charles Bukowski down and out in Hollywood.

He was more than just a good offbeat columnist. Everyone knows about Bukowski, who for many years was able to walk the decaying, slummy streets of Los Angeles — as a mailman, a hobo, an alcoholic on Skid Row — while his writing was just beginning to sell by the thousands in Europe, especially in Germany. His work was selling only a few hundred in his own country. He's an ethnic Polish-German who has become more famous even in his hometown of Los Angeles in years of late. Even though the movie "Barfly" didn't do well at the box office, it helped draw more attention Bukowski's way. Mickey Rourke did a fine job playing Bukowski, and Faye Dunaway was his girl. The director was Barbet Schroeder, one of the alienated German variety.

There was an earlier movie, "Tales of Ordinary Madness," in which Ben Gazzara also did a good job of playing a slicked up Bukowski. Let me tell you about the time I reconstructed Bukowski.

□

It was one of those rare moments when it really was impossible to figure out whether art imitates life, or life imitates art. The occasion was an informal, lightly-attended afternoon movie premiere of "Tales of Ordinary Madness" at a theatre in West Los Angeles. "Tales of Ordinary Madness," distributed by Fred Baker, was an Italian film about a mad and drunken Los Angeles poet, based on various autobiographical short stories by Bukowski.

As the movie began, Ben Gazzara appeared on the silver screen taking a swig from a brown-bagged wine bottle. I turned around to see what the real Charles Bukowski thought of all this — he was sitting three or four rows back. He, too, was swigging away from a "freeway bag" full of wine in sync with the character on the screen.

Bukowski had lived in Los Angeles since 1920. His parents brought him to L.A. from his native Andernach, Germany, when he was two years old. For most of the years after that, he was an unknown: a day laborer, a postman, and, for more than a decade, an out- and out- Skid Row bum. He ended up with his stomach hemorrhaging at L.A. County General Hospital, where the doctors warned him that unless he stopped drinking, he would die. Characteristically, the minute that Bukowski was discharged, he found a bar. He has never apologized for his drinking since. He revels in it. "Two things kept me from suicide — writing and the bottle," he said.

He began writing seriously in the '50s. "To have the nerve to attempt an art form as exacting and unrenumerative as poetry at the age of 32 is a form of madness," Bukowski recently explained. "But crazy as I was, I felt I had something to say, as I had lived with degradation, and on the edge of death... what had I to lose?"

Bukowski's poetry began appearing regularly in little literary magazines, but it wasn't until the '60s that he really came to public prominence with his raunchy, outrageous, and often hilarious prose column, "Notes of a Dirty Old Man," in the "underground" Los Angeles *Free Press*. "Notes" described the misadventures of Bukowski's alter-ego, a fellow named Henry Chianski.

One woman after another hopped in and out of Chianski's bed. All this occurred on Bukowski's turf, the underbelly of L.A., mostly downtown and Hollywood and various states in between.

The columns were first published as a book by Lawrence Ferlinghetti's City Lights in 1969. But most of Bukowski's later books were published from the West Los Angeles garage of publisher John Martin, who issued Bukowski's first novel, *Post Office*, in 1971. Anyone who's ever hated a job could appreciate this *Catch 22* of the workaday world. *Post Office* was the first Bukowski volume in which his unique, gut-wrenchingly lyrical style really began to emerge. Soon afterward, Martin moved Black Sparrow Press a hundred miles up the coast to Santa Barbara. He has since gone further north, to Santa Rosa. But he's still publishing Bukowski — close to 30 volumes by now of poetry and fiction, some of which have now sold hundreds of thousands of copies.

Bukowski's reputation grew quickly in the '70s especially in Europe: Germany, Spain, Italy, Norway, Finland and France — although not generally as much in England, Sweden or the West Coast of the U.S.A.

Bukowski himself says he once spent three months in New York in the '40s and came to the conclusion that "Maybe it's a nice place now, only I'm not going to try it." Bukowski is still more famous in Europe than on the turf he writes about. "I can go into the supermarket and buy a dozen eggs." In fact Bukowski lives down in San Pedro rather than in Hollywood because "you're not going to find a bevy of poets sipping espresso" in L.A.'s primarily blue-collar port town. He figures that the reason he is acclaimed in Europe is that "it's an older culture. The people…they know more."

Bukowski has definitely evolved as a writer to where comparisons between him and his cultural heroes Henry Miller and Louis-Ferdinand Celine are not just being whispered anymore. (Miller once called Bukowski the "poet satyr of today's underground.") Not everyone is enamored of Bukowski, of course. Some folks find him a terrible downer.

John Harris, when he was still the proprietor of Papa Bach Bookstore, used to insist that Bukowski was a terrible downer — "He doesn't celebrate anything but his own stool," said Harris. Walden Muns, whom we have met in previous chapters and who is still working on a book about the '50s and '60s Hollywood milieu that Bukowski was a part of, says "He's good, I suppose, if you like reading about toilets and whorehouses."

On the other hand, the San Francisco *Chronicle* said that "Bukowski is pure Los Angeles — in the insane, exciting, frenetic, electrical sense of that whole incredible scene." And the Los Angeles *Times* declared that "Bukowski is the most important short story writer since Hemingway." The German newspaper *Die Welt*: "Bukowski is what you'll have to call the

the American anti-guru. He's so authentic he can make you cringe." And another German magazine proclaimed: "American nightmares. Very brutal, very honest, very apocalyptical — and very funny." Bukowksi has become a literary phenomenon and like Hemingway was in his last years, the author himself has become bigger than life — and his legend is looming larger than his works.

One sensed this that afternoon at the Royal as Bukowski moved slowly out of the theater lobby after the premiere of "Tales of Ordinary Madness." Upon this, his first viewing of the movie, he seemed genuinely touched by it. As Bukowski moved out of the lobby, he stopped for a few moments to warmly greet Baker, who seemed relieved that Bukowski had liked the film. Baker was not a close friend of Bukowski's, but a few nights previously he had gotten a rare invitation to visit Bukowski in San Pedro. Bukowski, Baker said, had treated him well enough — at first. But as the evening wore on, Bukowski continued his two-fisted drinking until he was becoming surly and even a little threatening. Baker said that it was only when he got up to leave that Bukowski quickly seemed to regain some of his gruff, warm charm. When I told Baker that I was going to try to interview Bukowski, he warned me that Bukowski is a different kind of guy from the rest of us.

Even so, over the next several days, I approached Bukowski, by mail, phone, and through intermediaries — I talked to many people who had known him well at different points of his career. In a letter to Bukowski, I even apologized to him for having slighted him in my original Literary L.A.. But nothing seemed to work — Bukowski, of late, has taken to turning down most interviews. His standard line is that everything is there in his books. ("Make up quotes," he told one would-be interviewer, "it's all right by me.") Still, I kept trying, hoping there might be someone Bukowski trusted who could convince him to make an exception for me. Instead, I found some of his acquaintances angry at me for even trying to interview Bukowski. "The recent waves of attention are not good for him, because when he gets into uncomfortable situations, he drinks even more than usual and these situations are genuinely uncomfortable for him," I was told by one possessive admirer, who reminded me that Bukowski routinely turned down thousands of dollars for public appearances — he used to make his living doing poetry readings, but his last one was years and years ago, when he then said he would never do one again.

Finally, I was reduced to trying to put Bukowski's story together from all my interviews with friends and former lovers and such. I was saved from this fate, however, by one of the world's greatest eccentrics, and a good friend of mine from coffeehouse days. Gene Vier is an old newspaper and magazine staffer whom you would know if you ever saw Detective Columbo on television.

Actor Peter Falk used Vier as a model for Columbo's physical appearance and mannerisms. Vier is one of those rare people who either knows everyone in the world, or knows someone who knows someone. He didn't know Bukowski directly, but a couple of his good friends, Laura and Frank Cavestani, just happened to be drinking partners of Bukowski's. If I showed up at the official premiere of "Tales of Ordinary Madness," being held at the Encore Theatre in Hollywood, Vier assured me that I would get my chance to at least go out drinking with Bukowski — if not to interview him.

Gene Vier

The night of the official premiere was cold and rainy, and none of what unfolded seemed to hold much promise at first. When Bukowski and his girlfriend, Linda Beighle, walked into the theater, the author was immediately mobbed by hordes of autograph seekers. Bukowski planted himself at a counter to sign books on which the movie was based, and before he began, he loudly protested and with mock gruffness referred to all his fans with the colloquial term for excrement, and then openly raised a bottle, uncovered by the traditional brown bag, to his lips.

Nigey and I joined Vier, the Cavestanis, Bukowski, and Linda in the rear corner of the theatre, near the door. We were told that Bukowski might want to slip out early. I was also warned not to bring any tools of my trade, such as a tape recorder or a pen and paper. In fact, I was warned to refrain from asking interview-type questions, that is, about literature or modern poets or politics or such. (I already knew that the evidence about his politics was mixed — he is enamored of fascist writers like Celine and Ezra Pound, but one close friend of his told me that he also likes Sartre and Marx, on occasion.) Just come prepared to observe what was going to probably be a night of vintage Bukowski, I was told, since Bukowski had already been drinking heavily even for himself that night.

Perhaps because of all the alcohol he had consumed, or perhaps because there was a large audience of fans, Bukowski wasn't being nearly as charitable about the movie the second time he saw it. I didn't find that it had worn well, either. Gazzara looked too much like a matinee idol to portray the pock-marked, alcohol-ravaged character that has become Bukowski's trademark over the years. Vier suggested that the problem was that the film insisted on making Bukowski into kind of a saint of the dispossessed.

In actuality, Bukowski just didn't want to be nominated for sainthood. So he played movie critic that night by shouting out his objections as the movie progressed. For example, during a scene in which a beautiful prostitute lay down on his bed, while the Gazarra-Chianski character just kept typing at his desk, Bukowski yelled out, "If that were me I would have stopped typing long ago!" As a scene in a flophouse rolled by, Bukowski cried out that "I've never seen a flophouse as empty and clean as that one." As a stream of such comments kept emanating from our corner of the theater, someone in the audience yelled at Bukowski to shut up. Bukowski replied, "Hey, I'm the guy they made the movie about. I can say anything I want to. You shut up." Toward the end of the film, a woman strolled up the aisle past Bukowski and told him that she loved him but was bored by the movie. He responded by saying he would give her his phone number.

It was raining as if it were the end of the world when our entourage finally left the theater. We headed toward a bar several blocks away from the theater. This was familiar Hollywood territory to Bukowski. As we walked past the old Monogram Studios on Melrose Avenue (now remodeled in modernistic high-tech style with another name), just west of Van Ness, Vier was leading the way, but Bukowski caught up with him and put his arms around Vier as if they were long-lost friends. We couldn't hear what Bukowski was saying, but he was obviously well on his way to a state of total inebriation. We finally reached the bar, but it was on the other side of Melrose. As we were lining up, waiting for a break in the rain and traffic, Bukowski suddenly made a dash for the middle of the street. He was choo-chooing drunkenly, going in circles like a locomotive on a fast track to nowhere, looking back at us yelling, "Hey, I thought you guys would follow me wherever I go." A car was bearing down on Bukowski through the darkened, rain-slicked street, and Frank and Linda both ran out and dragged Bukowski back. Eventually we made it safely into the bar — a rather typical blue-collar bar with a loud jukebox, torn red vinyl booths and a pool table in the back. We headed for the rear, where it was uncrowded.

Nigey and I sat directly across from Bukowski, who began pounding on the table and demanding booze. Red wine appeared out of nowhere and more drinking began. A Judy Garland song from a 1931 movie crooned its tinny heart out on the jukebox. This occasioned a monologue from Bukowski about how he was a creature of the '40s, "no make that the '30s, maybe even the '20s." From there, his monologue made its way to some half-hearted comments about all the women troubles he was having. (Bukowski's books are always full of women troubles.) None of this seemed to bug Linda, who was sitting by his side, seemingly oblivious to this patter which she had no doubt heard many times before. "When I'm lying in bed and reach out, I like to feel nothing," he grumbled. Then he told the story of Sir John Gielgud, the famous British actor who Bukowski said was married to a madwoman for 19 years. Whenever Gielgud mentioned a good review from the previous night's performance, the mad wife — at least according to Bukowski's pickled version — "would start to shriek at him to pick up his socks." Bukowski ended his little yarn with a knowing look at Linda, but then he relieved the tension with a rather self-deprecating sounding laugh. "Being married to the mad-woman made him feel alive," Bukowski had to explain. He leaned over and kissed Linda, who didn't look in the least mad but rather nobly patient.

Tired of us by now, Bukowski looked over to the pool table where a couple of working stiffs were playing. "The dead pool table of nowhere," he said, pulling himself out of his chair and meandering over to their direction. From where we were, we could hear Bukowski trying to explain to the pool players that he was "a celebrity now, because a movie had been made about my life." They might have been impressed had they understood English. But neither seemed to know what to make of Bukowski, even though Bukowski made it plain to us when he came back that he considered himself more one of them than one of us. Bukowski sat down again across from Nigey and I and said, "I hate intellectuals." Thus we had our first direct encounter.

"I'm the toughest guy in town," he said, looking right at me — the first time he would utter the phrase that would become his refrain in each of the three bars around Hollywood that we journeyed to that night. I made some sort of barroom reply, and Bukowski quickly backed down. We talked a while and Bukowski seemed to warm up a bit. "You have an honest face, a good face, but behind it is a lot of bull shit, in the way you have dealt with people," he said to me. This undoubtedly was so of most of us in this life, I replied. "See what I mean," Bukowski rejoined, triumphantly. "All of mankind means nothing. Mankind is all cowardice. Has no courage. So let's drink."

Vier, meanwhile, had been sitting on the other side of Bukowski. With an unexpected vehemence, Vier burst out that Bukowski was full of it. "Hank," he said, "you can't tell us that even in your own negative way, you don't celebrate life. It's there in your poetry." Bukowski looked at Vier, and for the longest time I thought he was going to be speechless. Finally, Bukowski said, "You're a funny man." A little later, he looked into Vier's face and said, "You are a tormented man. Hey, man, I'm sorry I can't make you happy." His tone of voice sounded sincere, although also quite drunken. He kept repeating to Vier over and over again, "Hey man, I wish I could make you happy. I wish I could make you happy."

Not much more time elapsed before everyone agreed it was time to move onto the next place. We would go further down Melrose, to Lucy's El Adobe, the Mexican restaurant made famous by the fact that the former California governor Jerry Brown was a regular there. Bukowski became more raucous as we moved on (still friendly but sounding more and more street wise) and obviously felt it was time to say something. Vier again interjected, "Hey, Bukowski, for you, life is a horserace. You're competitive. I think it's a dance. Remember style; don't you hear those words of yours at the beginning of the movie, about everything being style? You're handling stardom very badly, Hank."

Bukowski seemed chagrined at that. It was a while before he responded. But in a few minutes, Bukowski was out and ahead, loudly demanding more booze. The management said no, which, of course, made Bukowski even angrier and more incessant in his demands. I jumped in with a compromise. I ordered three beers, and handed them to Bukowski. He quieted down for a while, happy with his liquor. Soon he was entertaining us with vulgar references and jokes about his and Linda's sex practices. Then he suddenly eyed a group of big, muscular punks in the next booth. He cried out loudly, so that they could hear too, "Hey, look at the fags. Looks at the fags." His voice rested awhile on the word fags. After a few minutes of this, he managed to succeed in getting what he wanted — he had outgrossed the punks; they left, muttering angrily among themselves and glaring at him out of the corners of their eyes. Bukowski really didn't give a shit, if they came over and started a fight or not, but something told the youths to keep their distance.

By the time we finally got back to the parking lot behind Lucy's, the trick had become getting Bukowski to stay seated in the rear of Frank's Volkswagen. He didn't seem angry at anyone in particular, just intent on getting out of the car when he had just finished getting into it. No one could keep him there. He was oblivious to the sheets of black rain as he insisted on climbing out of the car. Finally, however, he got the idea that he should stay in the car. He became very apologetic — if you spend much time around Bukowski, you hear a lot of apologies — and sat down meekly in the back of Cavastani's car.

Cavastani drove Bukowski and Linda back to their car, and now there was a three-car procession through the rain to Dan Tana's, next to the Troubadour, on the literal edge of Beverly Hills. It wasn't long before the maitre d' was inviting Bukowski to leave the premises again, as Bukowski obstreperously demanded booze. Bukowski looked at the waiter's smooth face and said, "You have an empty face." The maitre d' came over, and a compromise was arrived at — Frank would have responsibility for Bukowski, who was getting a little more subdued again.

Bukowski was generous. He brought us all a fine bottle of expensive red wine and got serious enough to first apologize for preaching, and next observe "You guys are looking for a hero. I don't want to be your hero."

I thought of telling him that he was being a little presumptuous, but I didn't. Bukowski wanted to talk about death. "I'm 63 years old. I'm closer to death than any of you here."

Then he looked at Nigey and I. "These people are going to be killed," he announced in a sonorous kind of voice. I wasn't sure if his tone of voice was supposed to be threatening — it wasn't particularly. It was only the content that was. How do you know? I asked. "With bullets," he replied. How do you know that? I asked. "I don't," he laughed. "I'm only a poet. I only know how to write poems. Other than that one thing, I'm an ignorant man." Then he pulled back, and returned to the evening's refrain. "Hey man, do you know, I'm the toughest guy in town. And also the kindest."

By now, the conversation was lagging. Bukowski and Linda were bickering. He'd throw oral barbs her way, and then make up by kissing her, or mussing her hair. Then he fell completely silent. He slid away from Linda, and chugged his way rather precariously to the bar.

"Oh, oh, I hope Papa will be okay," Linda said with obvious concern. But "Papa" made it up to the bar, and he plunked himself down next to Cavastani, who was studying a racing form. We talked a while more with Linda and Laura, and then made our way up to the bar to say goodbye to Bukowski. He put down his racing form, and put his hand on Nigey's arm and bid her farewell with an impromptu poem. Then he did the same with me. I bent over to hear what my poem was, but I heard only a phrase or two, and mostly mumbling. Outside the bar, I asked Nigey if she had heard what her poem had been. She, too, had had the same problem — whether it had been poetic and sonorous she would never know, for it had been unintelligible. She did note, however, that the drunker he got, the more poetic he became. Probably, Nigey said, he was just summing up everything he had said all evening. I told her I wished I could have heard those summings-up. We also said goodbye to Linda, who seemed genuinely sad to see us go.

Several days later, we walked into Sholom Stodolsky's Baroque Bookstore on Las Palmas, in Hollywood — now long gone. We told Stodolsky about our night of drinking with Bukowski, and about how he had begun damning us as "intellectuals." Stodolsky, who knows Bukowski pretty well, said that was just "Bukowski playing Bukowski." But then he told us that on the night of the premiere, police had stopped Bukowski and Linda on the way home from leaving Dan Tana's. They hadn't been taken to jail. The cops just took away Bukowski's keys and let him sober up because they knew who he was. I heard another version of the same incident a few days later. The second story was that when the cops found Bukowski, his BMW was on the sidewalk, and his face was scratched up — he and Linda had been fighting. The cops took his keys away, but sly old Bukowski simply took out another set he had hidden in his pocket, and he and Linda drove home. Both stories had an authentic ring, even if neither was one hundred percent accurate.

A while later, Vier and I were again comparing notes about Bukowski. Vier said that what makes Bukowski fascinating to Europeans is that being down-and-out in Los Angeles is much more degrading and alienating than being down-and-out in Europe. Vier opined, in fact, that Bukowski's down and out L.A. experiences were better literature than had been George Orwell's down and out times in London and Paris in the '30s. Being down and out in a demi-paradise, where so many have so much, Vier argued, is to belong to nothing. In Europe, even the down and out belong to a class, and have their place in the society. "Bukowski's style," said Vier, "is pure Skid Row. It's a style that was developed on the streets. When you're down that far, style is all you have. There is no such thing as getting status through money — it's all style." Vier had actually discussed his idea with Bukowski, who himself had noted that many of his characters were people who "had one out — death." Even though Bukowski had pontificated to me that "the middle class has no courage," he had told Vier that he didn't reject "middle-class luxury, I only reject the price people play to get it."

And truly, Bukowski has mastered the art of good living. He writes poems about how much he likes to drive his $30,000 BMW. Libraries and collectors seek out his special editions. Even his paintings are now collectors' items. Walden Muns, who is as good a friend of Vier's as he is of mine, owns a Bukowski original that was given to him a few years back by Larry Miller, a friend of Bukowski's. Miller knew Bukowski primarily because Miller's sister Pam was one of Bukowski's girlfriends. The oil painting is a large childlike profile of what looks like an abstract cow, a rather strange apparition that Muns keeps in his closet at his home. He figures that it can only appreciate in value.

Like a lot of observers of the L.A. literary scene, Muns has closely followed the growing Bukowski legend. Recently, Muns saw Bukowski come into a fancy South Bay restaurant (close to his San Pedro home) "wearing Picasso-like pants, checkerboard abstracts of a multicolored-thick material like clowns wear, with green suspenders." Muns avoided going up to talk to Bukowski, but he remembered the first time he had seen Bukowski, when Bukowski was living in much different circumstances. Then, Bukowski was still living in a sleazy court near Western Avenue and Hollywood Boulevard, hanging out with Pam Miller. "It was a small, drab apartment," Muns recalled, "dark inside, the shades all pulled, no curtains, old furniture, newspapers. And first editions of his own books arranged on a crude counter."

Pam, an attractive redhead, had taken Muns to visit Bukowski on that occasion. Today, she is married to a lawyer, and a sales representative for a large title company. She had been Bukowski's girlfriend in the mid-70s, between Linda Beighle and a sculptor-poet named Linda King. Bukowski wrote a book of poems about Pam called "Scarlet." Pam was also a character named "Tammie" in Bukowski's popular novel *Women*. Muns remembered that much of the visit was taken up with Pam and Bukowski talking about things that only they understood. Muns never became a big Bukowski fan. But still Muns concedes that Bukowski might ultimately end up being compared to Hemingway. "In his own crazy way, Bukowski is more of an existentialist, closer to the marrow of existentialism than Hemingway ever was."

Gerald Locklin, who writes poetry in the Bukowski manner (and even looks sort of like his hero) has won high praise from Bukowski. Locklin is a poet and English instructor at Cal State University at Long Beach — despite this, Bukowski says that Locklin is one of the few modern poets he can stand. Locklin rarely visits or calls Bukowski — the last time Locklin saw Bukowski in person was years ago. But because of the voluminous correspondence that's carried on between Bukowski and Locklin, the two are considered close. Locklin explained his mentor this way: "Miller said Orwell gave the proletariat a voice. I think Bukowski does this even more than Miller. He is a man who has lived at the lowest socio-economic level, yet he can write realistically about it. Most social realism is written from the outside, by fairly well educated people who may be temporarily sharing the lives of the lower classes, but Bukowski writes as one." Still Locklin agreed that despite this, Bukowski is not terribly political. Locklin quotes Bukowski as saying that "politics are just like women: get into them seriously and you're going to come out looking like an earthworm stepped on by a longshoreman's boot." In Bukowski's view, said Locklin, politics is mostly "irrelevant, naive, wrong and ineffective."

Now that I knew more about Bukowski's politics, I wanted to know more about him as a man and lover. After all, he was the one who called his column "Notes of a Dirty Old Man." So I asked Muns to put me in contact with Larry and Pam Miller. Is Bukowski really a violent womanizer who loves them and leaves them, as he does in his books? The answer, according to both Larry and Pam, was absolutely not. Both of them found Bukowski to be a soft pussycat, jealous and possessive of his women, "and needing women far more than they need him." He's also a romantic, Pam claimed. When Bukowski was courting Pam, and they were living apart, Bukowski would leave poetry in her door whenever she hadn't called him for a day or two.

"There was nothing at all violent about him — at least, he never exhibited anything violent in front of me," Pam told me. Sometimes, she admitted later, they would have boozy fights and throw things at each other. They did that on several occasions, when they were eating at Musso and Frank's in Hollywood because usually he would falsely accuse her of having affairs with the postman, the milkman, and everyone else. When Pam knew Bukowski, he was just beginning to achieve financial independence — sometimes he would leave his uncashed checks around the house for weeks, while they would gather wine and beer stains.

Pam says that Bukowski was kind to her personally, but very unkind in print. "He took a lot of poetic license. He always pictures himself as a Romeo living a lot more dangerously than he really does. Actually, he's an extremely introverted, cynical, asexual kind of man."

I asked how he would rate as a lover? "Well, he was a severe alcoholic in his mid-fifties so he wasn't that active, even though he continues to write about his sexual experiences." Still, she said coyly, "sometimes he was a good lover — I would give him a four-star rating." She giggled embarrassedly.

He was also very kind to her. When she called and wanted a ride at two in the morning, he would always come. When she needed to borrow money, he was there. He was also very fond of her small daughter: the three of them used to go on regular outings during the week — to the horse-races, to the Olympic auditorium to watch boxing.

Pam (these days known as Pam Brandes-Wood) thought for a moment when I asked her to sum up the man as best she could. She replied: "He's a very deeply scarred soul. He has a lot of gentleness. He portrayed me as an airhead in his book; he was very unfair, but he wasn't that way to me. The persona in the books is not him at all. But he's not an easy man to get close to. He's a misanthrope. I guess I'm contradicting myself. But he's also not really a misanthrope. He is reclusive; he values his privacy. He has experienced a lot of unpleasant things in his life. But he's really not a misanthrope. Once you get past a certain point with him, there's nothing he wouldn't do for you."

The Grand Old Man
Of L.A. Letters

T he grand old man of Los Angeles letters, Jake Zeitlin, invited me to lunch originally after reading my original book, *Literary L.A.*. When I showed the invitation to my librarian friend John Ahouse, he commented that I might want to hang on to it because a handwritten letter

Josephine and Jake Zeitlin

from Jake Zeitlin was a rare thing to have. I figured if a letter from the man was worth something, a lunch with him would be worth even more.

Jake has been gone from this earth for a while now, but when he was alive I often found myself driving past the striking red replica of a Pennsylvania Dutch barn on La Cienega Boulevard, just below Santa Monica Boulevard. But until I went inside to meet Zeitlin I had never been inside the quarters of Zeitlin & Ver Brugge, dealers in rare books, manuscripts and letters. The stuff of history was stored in book shelves that climbed up the second-story rafters of the building. It was also there in the lives of the man and woman who owned it. Josephine Zeitlin, whose maiden name was Ver Brugge, presided over the business office. Zeitlin, a stocky, handsome man even in his eighties, was the bookman incarnate.

After concluding business over the phone, he got up and we left, driving in Zeitlin's car to a Beverly Hills cafe nearby. During lunch, we talked about many writers, including Robinson Jeffers, Aldous Huxley, Thomas Mann, and Henry Miller. Huxley was the chief topic of conversation, however, because through my family connections, I had met the man and also got to know his widow, Laura Huxley. Zeitlin, through his association with the agent William Morris Jr., had introduced Huxley to Hollywood, hence to the City of the Angels, where the great British author spent the last two decades of his life. As an important figure in Huxley's Los Angeles history, Zeitlin had strong opinions about various people around the author. But before he would talk about these, he insisted that I not write what his opinions were — so I won't.

Zeitlin was also willing to share gossip without embargo as well. Stuff I loved. Opening his briefcase, he showed me letters from Frieda Lawrence, widow of D.H. Lawrence, whose estate — namely all the late author's manuscripts — Zeitlin once represented. One of the letters that Zeitlin showed cleared up a mystery that had always puzzled biographers of poet Robinson Jeffers — namely, what happened when Robinson and Una Jeffers went to visit Frieda Lawrence in New Mexico, leaving their Carmel home behind. The Jefferses were notorious for never leaving the stone castle that he had built above the rocks by the sea. Yet somehow Frieda Lawrence got them to leaving Tor House and come to live with her. Lawrence, it should be remembered, had a love life that was flamboyant and notorious. Lawrence was believed to have had hopes that Jeffers would stay and become the great poet of the Southwest. Instead what did happen was that Jeffers went into another room to talk with a Swedish woman friend of Frieda's, a woman with a dubious reputation. Convinced that Robinson had already fallen for this woman's charms, Una shot herself, crying out that since her husband needed her no longer, she was going to end it all. Over the next several weeks, Frieda nursed Una back to health. I read all this in a letter, with amazement.

For our next meeting with Jake, Nigey and I went over to the Zeitlins' for dinner. Zeitlin, you must know, was always much more than one of the world's great dealers in rare books and letters. He was a catalyst of Los Angeles's cultural community going back to the '20s, most of which was Bohemian, of course. Zeitlin had a providential meeting when he first came to L.A. in the '20s with Charles Lummis — Lummis had been the original Bohemian catalyst in L.A. and Zeitlin took his place afterwards.

Lummis had first sought Zeitlin out at the downtown Bullocks department store, where he worked in the book departments. Zeitlin had a reputation as a promising Bohemian poet himself, and Lummis always made it a point of meeting those young writers he thought were on the way up.

Zeitlin had arrived in Los Angeles in 1925, hitchhiking across the great Southwest — hitchhiking and hoboing. Zeitlin grew up in Ft. Worth, and he developed this thing in his family home — either early in the morning or late at night he would take off, "just disappear, sometimes for a week, sometimes for many weeks." He would get jobs during harvest season, and in the process he had collected a great many folk songs, which is why poet Carl Sandburg first developed a closeness to Zeitlin back in 1922 in Texas and why Sandburg later paid lengthy visits to Zeitlin in his redwood home in Echo Park in the '20s. Zeitlin's extensive knowledge of folk songs was also the reason Leadbelly, Alan Lomax and others came to pay their respects.

He learned the excitement of being a bookseller early on. Zeitlin used to drive a truck for his family's business, and one of his helpers was a fellow who had once worked at Saints & Sinners Corner, the rare book room at A.G. McClurg's Bookstore in Chicago. This peripatetic litterateur was a non-stop talker, and his talks had their effect on the 18-year-old Zeitlin, who decided that "the most wonderful thing in the world would be to have a book shop where people could come and browse and talk."

Zeitlin also decided that he did not want to stay in Texas with the family business — a family business that survived Zeitlin. His family had moved to Texas in 1905 when he was three years old, from Wisconsin, where he was born. The family first tried farming, "but what the boll weevil didn't get, the Johnson grass did. We were not farmers." Next the Zeitlins became fruit peddlers in "the way a lot of Jewish immigrants did. They deal with the things that the people who had made it didn't want to bother with." In this particular Russian Jewish family's cases, these things were vinegar, condiments and similar foodstuffs.

As a young man in Texas, Jake had quickly gained a reputation as a poet and literary critic — an early newspaper article claimed that Zeitlin looked like legendary Bohemian poet and character George Sterling, which Zeitlin today insists was a totally preposterous notion except, perhaps, for the nose — "We both had the same kind of nose."

Zeitlin of course ultimately headed for L.A., telling himself that he was coming to the big city to develop as a poet. The truth may have been something else. Zeitlin says that he didn't have the first prerequisite of a writer — an ability and talent to sit down and not get up. *Sitzfleisch*, says Zeitlin, was described by H.L. Mencken as the "ability to put one's rear onto a seat for a long period of time."

A bookseller, Zeitlin says, "can expend a lot of energy in a lot of different

Jake as a lean and hungry poet, 1925

directions and get a percentage of good results." And that's the kind of mentality he says he has — one that goes off in a number of different directions at once. Although Zeitlin once said he decided to go west instead of east by the flip of a coin back in his native Texas, he says that ultimately L.A. appealed to him because he was just a good "country boy" at heart; he never really liked big cities.

It was a happy meshing of personality and place. In 1925 Los Angeles was still a big enough city to impress a country boy — he had never seen so many people at the same time in one place. After a couple of false starts, Zeitlin located in Echo Park and stayed there from 1926 to 1938. During that time Echo Park was the locus of a flourishing Bohemian scene, and Zeitlin's various bookstores in downtown Los Angeles became a part of it. In fact Zeitlin's lifelong friend, Lawrence Clark Powell, the famed UCLA librarian and regional author, once wrote that the two flourishing Bohemian colonies in Los Angeles's literary history were Charles Lummis's at the turn of the century on the banks of the Arroyo Seco, and the Echo Park colony in the Depression, whose "downtown headquarters was a bookshop on West Sixth Street". Powell was of course referring to Zeitlin's place of business, next to the downtown library.

Zeitlin conceded that there had been such a flourishing Bohemian scene in Echo Park in the '20s and '30s and that it had even had its own peculiar book written about it.

It was a novel called *The Flutter of an Eyelid* by Myron Brinig, published in 1933. One of the novel's main characters is obviously meant to be a representation of Jake, except that if you know the man you know the characterization was simply not true.

Sol Mosier in Brinig's novel is a decadent Jew, a composite of every anti-Semite's catalog of cheap, hackneyed prejudices. Yet another of the characters was clearly based on Aimee Semple McPherson, the famed evangelist of the '20s who built her Angelus Temple next to Echo Park Lake.

The novel was written to shock, but in contemporary terms it reads like a pretentious effort to described a group of outlandish Bohemians set in a garish, surrealistic Southern California setting, that is destroyed, of course, by the Great Earthquake.

Among other things, Brinig's Zeitlin character decides to take a vacation from his sybaritic existence, and goes on the road in order to show that he can be a drifter and day laborer. After a couple of misadventures, Brinig's character decides that Jews apparently are not cut out for hard living and physical work and, giving up the attempt, returns to debauchery and drugs.

Brinig was Jewish, someone Zeitlin had befriended in his Echo Park days because the fellow seemed such a lonely soul — "a sulky baby elephant" who had "a certain way of winning your confidence."

Zeitlin did not particularly like Brinig from the beginning, he says. But he was very struck by another young writer, Carey McWilliams. McWilliams became not only an important California writer but also, for many years, editor of the *Nation*, one of the country's oldest and most distinguished political magazines. *Factories in the Field* and *Southern California: Island on the Land* were among McWilliams' classics — the latter volume is the foundational volume which every book on the subject since then has built upon.

I was surprised to learn from Zeitlin, although I shouldn't have been, that McWilliams rarely made money from his books; he always paid the bills with his job as a magazine editor.

McWilliams was one of the star writers of *Opinion*, published from October, 1929, to May, 1930, out of Zeitlin's bookstore at 705½ W. Sixth Street. He remained a close friend until McWilliams' death in 1980. Zeitlin believes that the period and the people around *Opinion* represented a Los Angeles renaissance.

After the nice dinner cooked by Jake's daughter Adriana, we all sat down to talk further into the night. I had read McWilliams' 1927 article in *Saturday Night* magazine that told how Zeitlin, a young poet from Texas and "protege of Carl Sandburg" had just arrived in Los Angeles.

Zeitlin immediately pooh-poohed his own poetry, saying that over the years he may have "flim-flammed" some people into believing he was a poet, but Sandburg was not really one of them. According to Jake, Sandburg wrote the introduction to a slim volume of Zeitlin's poetry not so much out of enthusiasm for the poetry, but because Sandburg "liked me."

In McWilliams' 50-year-old account of Zeitlin's life on the Echo Park Avenue hilltop there's a wonderful description of Jake gazing "down at night into a pool of liquid darkness, with flares of light in its shadow, while night odors and sounds drifted up the hill." The McWilliams article also includes some of Zeitlin's poetry; despite Zeitlin's modesty, while it may not have been the stuff of great genius, it was not at all bad and in fact is quite vivid and intelligent.

As we talked, Zeitlin seemed to get caught up in the memory of it all. Asked, after a while, why Bohemianism flourished in Echo Park, Zeitlin says the answer was simple: The rents were low, the shacks on the tree-filled hills afforded more privacy than flatland apartments did, and people could conduct their individual lives in peace.

"Bohemianism thrives on adversity. It's not a movement but a consequence of certain conditions. You have to have a concentration of people practicing their arts, people with superior endowments who don't necessarily fit into society, and who are, in fact, often engaged in rebellions against convention, creating a symbiotic society where not only can they go and eat at each other's houses when they're hungry, but where they can also spark each other and be each other's critical audiences. To such people, money is not the main motivation; they may like spaghetti and wine and women and conversation and not getting up in the morning to go to a job, but all believe in practicing something that is their justification for being, whether it be dancing, writing, sculpting or music."

Zeitlin then relates what is obviously one of his sweetest memories from long ago. "Someone had tied a long rope with a tire tied to one of the trees at the end of Echo Park Avenue, so you could stand on one side of the little canyon there, grab hold, and swing out over it, describing a sort of semicircle. If you were lucky you'd land back on the hill. One night when Sandburg came visiting, and the moon was bright, and we had imbibed a considerable amount of good wine, we went walking up toward the trees. I reached out and grabbed hold of the tire and swung out. I had no idea he was going to do the same thing — as soon as I got back, Sandburg gave a Viking war whoop, grabbed the tire, swung out over the canyon, and managed to get back to the other side without falling off."

On another drunken, full-mooned night, Zeitlin remembers walking along a ridge and seeing a naked woman coming toward him. He called out to her, but she dove off the side of the road into the bushes. He called her again, but she had disappeared. He continued walking toward the house from which the sounds of a party were emanating, and from which the naked woman had apparently come. Zeitlin recalls that one of the revelers at that party was director John Huston. Huston ran with a circle that included "a rather peculiar man who fancied himself a reincarnation of Edgar Allan Poe." His name was Ben Berlin — "an abstractionist of considerable originality." Berlin was part of a group called the Art Students League, an organization whose headquarters downtown on Spring Street, said Jake, "always smelled of rancid cabbage being cooked."

Jake says a number of important artists came from the glens of Echo Park — John Cage, the avant-garde composer; photographer Edward Weston (in fact it was at Zeitlin's bookstore that Edward Weston had his first show in 1928). Others who didn't necessarily hang out in Echo Park but were connected there because Zeitlin's shop hosted early shows for them include Rockwell Kent, who made magnificent woodcuts; and artists Paul Landacre, Peter Krasnow and Millard Sheets.

He talks again about the group who followed Berlin, who lived for a while in a house that belonged to Miriam Lerner, a woman who was active in the Young People's Socialist League at the same time she was private secretary to E.L. Doheny, the oil company mogul whose name was immortalized in the Teapot Dome scandal. Lerner had gotten the young Zeitlin jobs mowing lawns in Doheny's gas stations all over Southern California; sometimes he even mowed the lawn at the Doheny estate — where years later as a bookseller, he would be invited for tea.

Miriam Lerner was immortalized as "M" in Edward Weston's Day Books. She posed for a lot of Weston's pictures as well, and had a torrid affair with the photographer. Later on Lerner became secretary to writer Frank Harris.

So Echo Park in the '20s was a place that reverberated with Bohemia.

Sadakichi Hartmann, mysterious man of letters

One of Jake's most famous mementos of the time and place is a photograph of Carl Sandburg at the Edendale Red Car stop down the hill from the Echo Park neighborhood, taken either by Weston himself, or his partner, Margarathe Mather. Original prints of that photo now go for $5,000 and more.

One of the highlights of Jake's Echo Park years was meeting Sadakichi Hartmann, who had been the very archetype of Bohemianism in the early days of Greenwich Village. But by the time Zeitlin met Hartmann, at a dinner at a friend's house on Temple Street, Hartmann was no longer writing or being published.

"It was Sadakichi," Zeitlin says with a slightly wicked laugh, "who brought the disease across country." Hartmann came to Los Angeles, like so many other people in those days because he had asthma and his doctor had advised him to go west. Once proclaimed "The Most Mysterious Personality in America," Hartmann was physically a giant of a man, "a fascinating, ugly man, half-German and half-Japanese, who among other things had written the first good book on Japanese prints." Hartmann had also known and interviewed the painter Whistler, the wit and playwright Oscar Wilde, and poet Walt Whitman.

The son of a German consul stationed in Japan and a Japanese mother, Hartmann was educated in a German military school, against which he rebelled. Zeitlin says the result was a funny combination — he was very Germanic but then "he would suddenly break out and go absolutely wild."

When Zeitlin first met Hartmann, the latter had been reduced to earning a living not by writing but by playing a sort of buffoon-Bohemian role for the amusement of others. He did "strange, grotesque sword dances that scared the hell out of you," Zeitlin says, chuckling at the recollection. "He always celebrated his birthday at least four times a year, and always it was a benefit for Sadakichi Hartmann." Hartmann became even more of a professional Bohemian in his last years, says Zeitlin, when he was discovered by such Hollywood celebrities as Douglas Fairbanks, W.C. Fields, Gene Fowler and John Barrymore, who used to hire him to be a mascot and buffoon at their get-togethers. Along the way, Hartmann played the role of a magician in a Fairbanks version of "Sinbad the Sailor."

By the end, says Zeitlin, Hartmann had become a miserable character; alcohol was getting hold of him and he did not always present a pretty picture. That Zeitlin was intrigued on the occasion of his first meeting with the famed, aging Bohemian is no wonder. Sadakichi had approached the young Zeitlin at the dinner on Temple Street, after grabbing a loaf of bread and a bottle of wine from the host's table. He turned to Jake and said, "I want you to meet my good friend Aline Barnsdall." She, of course, lived in that magnificent place known today as Hollyhock House in Barnsdall Park, a place not actually designed as much by Frank Lloyd Wright as by his son Lloyd Wright, Zeitlin insists. Other Wright disciples like Robert Schindler and Richard Neutra also worked on the house, Jake adds.

Anyway, Hartmann and Zeitlin marched down Sunset Boulevard toward Barnsdall's house at one in the morning. The closer they got to the house the more Zeitlin protested that the time was wrong for such an impromptu visit. But no, Hartmann insisted, Aline Barnsdall was a good friend and surely she would welcome them. As they got to the front door, however, a guard burst forth and blinded them with a flashlight. The guard wanted to know what they wanted, and when Hartmann ordered the guard to wake up his "good friend," the guard replied that he would do no such thing; furthermore, he added, if the two men weren't off the property in five minutes, he'd call the police.

Zeitlin chortles at the memory of the two of them running down Sunset Boulevard afterward. "Imagine little me running alongside this giant, gawky Ichabod Crane figure. If the cops had seen him, they would have turned and run after them. But for all that, Hartmann was someone to be taken seriously. He knew a lot about art. He had been the very symbol of Bohemianism — and he infected the L.A. atmosphere with this terrible Bohemian disease."

Zeitlin did not stay a Bohemian poet for long. For one thing, he had a young wife and child. So he held a series of odd jobs, of which the truck driving and lawn mowing job Miriam Lerner had obtained for him was one. But then the inevitable happened — in his first year in Los Angeles he got a taste of the book business. He went to work at the Holmes Book Company, and although he was fired in a few weeks for "incompetence," he was set on his life's work. He came home with no job and took what little money the couple had, paid a month's rent in advance, laid in some groceries, and lo and behold, within a few hours their home was struck by fire. Enough of the kitchen was left to cook a meal by candlelight; but to sleep he and his first wife Edith had to find other quarters right away. It was at that dinner in the burned-out house that the future was decided. Jake and Edith and a friend who had come out from Texas to try his luck in Los Angeles sat down to their meal. The friend chewed meditatively for a while and then remarked as how he thought they had all given L.A. their best shot — now was the time to call it quits and go home. It was at this point that Zeitlin made what has been known ever since as "The Speech". He announced that he would never go home to Texas; rather, someday he would have his own bookstore, with the finest rugs hanging from the balconies, etchings by the likes of Rembrandt and Durer everywhere, and the best stock of rare books in all of Southern California.

Zeitlin had already begun dealing in books — but he wasn't making what anyone might call a living from it. It wasn't until 1928 that he got his first bookstore, a 12-by-15 foot hole-in-the-wall next door to the public library. Lloyd Wright had told Zeitlin that he couldn't keep selling books out of a satchel. He needed a shop where people could come to him. So Wright and Carey McWilliams helped him find, decorate and organize the first of his downtown bookstores. A year later he moved around the corner from Hill to Sixth Street; toward the end of the Depression in 1938, Zeitlin trekked west with the rest of the town — to Westlake Park. A decade later, after his marriage to Josephine he made his final move to the red barn on La Cienega Boulevard.

□

Over the years Zeitlin had earned a reputation as one of the world's top dealers in rare books and science manuscripts. Though Zeitlin had first announced himself on the Los Angeles scene as a poet, science is what he really loved. He had tried upon his arrival in Los Angeles to get a job at a museum; in Texas he had been a respectable local amateur birdwatcher who had even had publishing credits in the field.

These specializations haven't obscured his continuing involvement in literature, however. Early in Zeitlin's career a man wandered into his bookstore who would have a large impact on the city's intellectual life as well as Zeitlin's career. He was Elmer Belt, a doctor who may have been the consummate book collector of all time. Belt eventually would assemble the greatest collection of Leonardo da Vinci outside Italy, a collection that eventually wound up at UCLA. He was also the personal physician of evangelist Aimee Semple McPherson as well as of the "American Zola," Upton Sinclair, whose books he collected with fervor almost equal to that which he devoted to his hero da Vinci; the Sinclair collection is now housed at Occidental College. Among other things Belt was a prime mover in the founder of the UCLA Medical School.

Zeitlin told of his arrangement as Belt's primary da Vinci supplier in a eulogy he delivered at UCLA for Belt, who died at the age of 87 in 1980. Belt's office was across the street from Zeitlin's bookstore during the Depression, and the deal he made with Zeitlin helped immeasurably toward keeping the latter in business. Belt said he could afford to spend $200 a month on da Vinci, which Zeitlin admits was an important part of his cash flow in those days. But in return Belt told Zeitlin to go easy, not to overcharge him. "If you do, I won't buy anything else from you," he said. The relationship between Zeitlin and Belt proved to be lifelong and close.

□

Perhaps after all is said and done, Zeitlin's greatest impact on Los Angeles may have been through the books, resources and people he directed to UCLA, all of which helped him make it one of the greatest universities in the world. For a start, back in 1927, he sold many of the basic books that the university's new library would need; it was largely through Zeitlin's efforts that UCLA got Belt's da Vinci collection years later, and it was Zeitlin who "discovered" the man who would become UCLA's great librarian, Lawrence Clark Powell. Powell set out during the '30s and '40s to make UCLA's library as good as the great Bancroft Library on the Berkeley campus.

Dr. Elmer Belt, Zeitlin's patron

Powell came onto the bookstore a little late in the game, catching only the tail end of the original scene that emanated from Zeitlin's downtown operation. Powell was not a part of the inner circle that published *Opinion* in 1929 and 1930, for instance. But of greater significance than *Opinion* was the Primavera Press's emergence in 1928 from Zeitlin's shop. Through this publishing company Zeitlin became the first patron of the three great printers Los Angeles has produced: Saul Marks, Grant Dahlstrom and Ward Ritchie.

Powell first visited Zeitlin's bookstore in 1928. It was, he said, "a crack in the wall with a grasshopper sign on the window. There was no other shop in town like this tiny oasis where time relaxed its grip, an incarnate answer to Cobden-Sanderson's prayer, 'sweet God, souse me in literature!' — a place fragrant with oil of cedar, where purchases were wrapped in orange and black patterned paper."

Powell traveled to Paris during the first three years of the '30s. While there, Primavera Press commissioned him to write a biography of the poet Jeffers, who had grown to manhood in Los Angeles during the teens. When Powell returned to Los Angeles in 1933 his first volume was published. He went to work at the bookstore and moved into a house near Zeitlin's in Echo Park. The Jeffers biography sold out its first printing of 750 copies despite the fact it had appeared well into the Depression. Its popularity owed in part to the fact that it was illustrated by Rockwell Kent, but it was a good and interesting book about a then new and important figure. Three years later, however, the Depression was really beginning to take hold, and Primavera folded. Its tradition, however, was carried on for years after that by the printer Ward Ritchie.

□

It is hard to say where Zeitlin's influence on the intellectual life of Los Angeles was felt the most, for he seems to have brought together so many people for so many different reasons for so many years. But one way in which he certainly influenced the course of literature for this century was his efforts in getting the British author Aldous Huxley to move to Los Angeles. Huxley ended up living his last two decades, primarily in the Hollywood Hills, as well as the Mojave Desert.

Huxley wrote a lot about the town and place, and his ideas particular influenced the younger generation coming up during the '60s in Los Angeles. Zeitlin first met Huxley in the spring of 1938 at Frieda Lawrence's ranch, when he began the job of cataloging and offering for sale the manuscript of her late husband D.H. Lawrence. Zeitlin met Aldous and Maria and was close to both until their deaths. They became friends during several days spent in the beautiful New Mexico landscape, which included not only many long conversations, but also the viewing of Indian rain dances. "And it rained — it rained torrents," Zeitlin recalled. Zeitlin is particularly proud of the inscription Huxley once wrote to him at this point — "For Jake Zeitlin, our guide, philosopher and friend in the West."

Zeitlin convinced Huxley to come and work in the Hollywood movie studios, which paid well. Moreover, Zeitlin helped Huxley burn the first drafts he did of a screenplay, so bad was it. There was Huxley, pulling down $2,500 a week — in the late '30s, yet — but judging from his first effort, it appeared that he might never be able to write screenplays. Nevertheless, Huxley went on to eventually write good scenarios. His script for "Jane Eyre" is considered a Hollywood classic.

Zeitlin also brought his old friend Larry Powell, who was hungry and out of work, to do the job of cataloging the Lawrence manuscripts. In the process, Powell also became close to Frieda Lawrence and the Huxleys — friendships that would be important to the UCLA library Powell would one day develop. You can see why Powell would later write that "looking back, we see that the Depression nourished culture as it brought together artists, professionals and intellectuals. The catalyst was Jake, his shop the cultural heart of Los Angeles."

When Huxley made the keynote speech that opened Zeitlin's new shop in Westlake in 1938, he recognized the importance of Zeitlin's catalyst role. Writers were constantly attracted to his shop — William Saroyan wandered in once and tried to convince Zeitlin that he should publish something of his own, sight unseen. Zeitlin replied that he would be glad to publish something of Saroyan's, especially if he could see it first. You never knew who you might meet at Zeitlin's shop, said McWilliams. And it proved true with me. Zeitlin was full of great stories about his brushes with such noteworthy writers as Steinbeck, Faulkner, West, Dreiser and S.J. Perelman.

Zeitlin also knew Henry Miller quite well, although he was not an enormous fan of the man's writing or of the man himself, who he thought was essentially a rather commonplace and vulgar fellow, "a crumb" with no social consciousness, said Jake. Zeitlin's views are confirmed by Josephine as well. Zeitlin agrees that Miller obviously had an outsized writing talent. He took Miller to talk to Huxley over lunch in 1937, and while everyone was cordial enough, the chemistry wasn't there. Huxley later observed to Zeitlin that Miller reminded him "of a Sunday school teacher from the Midwest."

In the coffeehouse scene of the late '50s and early '60s, copies of *Air Conditioned Nightmare* were as much in view as *Tropic of Cancer* and *Tropic of Capricorn* had been on display in hip circles in the '30s, '40s and early '50s. That book, along with Kerouac, Ginsberg, Patchen and Ferlinghetti, were the true voices of the Beats.

It was getting late, and we had been talking for several hours. Zeitlin is blunt in his opinions, and I was anxious for him to venture more of them. For example, I told him that I thought his friend Powell had treated Upton Sinclair, one of my favorite writers, rather badly. And I suspected the reason was politics. What did Zeitlin think? Zeitlin replied that his old friend Powell may be a wonderful fellow — he and Powell communicated regularly right up to the end — but Zeitlin nonetheless said "he has no political sense. Never had. He even endorsed Nixon once."

Zeitlin had little patience with my impression that the great writers seemed to have vanished from the landscape. "I don't think writing has gone downhill. I think publishing has. There always were chambermaid romances and dime-store novels. And I think that Mr. McLuhan made more noise than sense," he adds, dismissing the late Canadian media philosopher who back in the '60s was predicting the end of literacy. "I don't think there's been a decline in literacy — although I don't know where the literates are anymore." He insisted that contemporary writers like Saul Bellow and John Updike must be taken seriously. "The writers of principle are still there, just as they always were."

I wasn't entirely convinced, but I listened when he said, "There's been a tremendous amount of ferment here, a lot of new enterprises, fortunes being made, and the material for a lot of crashes were also being made here. There's a tremendous intermingling of cultures. The legend of Los Angeles has grown tremendously, and people believe in legends, so much so they don't even compare the legend to the reality. Southern California has become a tremendously legendary place."

Zeitlin played a big role in that legend, for it is a legend composed of a very real river overflowing with waves of people and different ideas and books and institutions connected with books. People often look at the Los Angeles River, especially when it is dry in summer, and make jokes about it. They've done the same thing with the city's cultural life — they proclaimed it is a river that mostly runs dry.

I know what they are saying, yet the life of Jake Zeitlin alone absolutely disproves the notion.

Roots In The Garden
Of California Bohemia

Ever since I discovered "London House" in Hollywood, and told that story, first in the now defunct *Herald-Examiner* and then a decade ago in the original *Literary L.A.*, folks have been sending me all their yarns that link the fabled California Bohemian writer Jack London ever more deeply to the literary tradition of the City of the Angels.

London was the great schizophrenic — he had the disease of many Bohemians: he was half Socialist revolutionary and half Nietzsche superman. He used his pen to create a revolution that would result in a more humane and equitable society. Literally, millions of people were radicalized in the first part of this century by the writings of Jack London and another California Bohemian — Upton Sinclair.

Please understand that when one is called a Bohemian, it conjures up certain images that are only partly true. Upton Sinclair may have been linked in the public mind with debauchery as a result of the goings-on at Helicon Hall, on the East Coast, and the California Bohemia established by George Sterling at Carmel after the 1906 earthquake. Sinclair was a part of that — but in matters sexual, he ultimately became quite prudish.

In fact, none of the great California Bohemians — Mark Twain, Jack London or Upton Sinclair — were at their best when writing about the matter of sex and love. But oh were they linked with it.

In any event, "London House" was a great find for me. I once spent a rainy day by myself at Jack London's grave at his Valley of the Moon ranch, 50 miles or so north of San Francisco. When I stumbled across "London House" on La Vista Court, an alley just south of Melrose off Van Ness, I felt as if I was in the presence of a great totem, an actual physical link to San Francisco-born Bohemia.

My discovery of London House became all the more powerful when I saw in a windowpane an inscribed memento of Bohemia from George Sterling, which of course made the house completely Bohemian in my mind. Sterling actually spent time at the house in the last year of his life in 1926.

Everyone in Los Angeles has heard of Charles F. Lummis, L.A.'s "Renaissance" man from the turn of the century. While London House has not yet won any official affirmation as an historical monument, El Alisal, Lummis's incredible hand-built stone castle just off the Avenue 43 exit of the Pasadena Freeway, is an official state historical monument. Like London, Lummis was a 19th century man who left his mark — and Lummis and London did some

Lummis's El Alisal

tangling. Lummis, in fact, was one of London's first publishers.

London House was built as a sculpture studio in the early '20s by Finn Frolich, a good friend of London's and creator of the most famous sculptured images by which the writer is best remembered. Frolich's busts of London are at Valley of the Moon and at Jack London Square in Oakland. There's the same face, in bas relief, in front of London House. Frolich simply built his peculiar structure around a shack that is now part of the larger house. The shack was considerably older than the house, which was built shortly after London's death. But London may have lived in the shack when he came south to buy cattle in Los Angeles for his ranch in Northern California. London also may have hidden out at the shack to avoid "Lummis and his gang." London regarded them as bourgeois dilettantes. Lummis used to throw soirees on Saturday nights at El Alisal, among the sycamores on the Arroyo Seco. London used to come south not only to buy cattle on the land that was later made into Silverlake reservoir, but also to escape the hordes of people who were pressing in ever more at his ranch in Sonoma as he became more and more famous.

Lummis was not a great writer. He wrote books and articles that are important footnotes in a variety of fields, from archaeology to librarianship, especially as these subjects relate to the Southwest. Lummis ultimately must have been more a doer than a writer. He was a catalyst, giving Los Angeles a rich intellectual life at the turn of the century, when it was otherwise an intellectual desert. Lummis was given over to elaborate costumes. Underneath his corduroys he usually wore a great wide red sash in the old California style, sandals or moccasins, a sombrero or else a leather-banded cowboy Stetson, a red cravat, Navajo jewelry and almost always the big, pompous gold medal the King of Spain had granted him for his work in glamorizing the Spanish presence in old California. He was, some people have said, an elaborate poseur. But he was a genuine poseur.

He began building El Alisal in 1897. Then he conceived of the Southwest Museum, a rare cultural institution which is visible from El Alisal's kitchen windows — just as Lummis planned it. El Alisal is an unusual structure of huge wood beams — rail ties from the Santa Fe — and thick hand-crafted doors (the front door weighs a ton). Lummis built one of the grand doors to the dining room by modeling it on a Velasquez painting of an old Spanish castle. The house has 14-inch-thick, rock and concrete walls.

Lummis first came to the pueblo in 1885, when it barely had 12,000 souls. He was the first and last memorable editor of the Los Angeles *Times*. Illness took him away for some years, however, and when he returned for a second and final time to the pueblo it was just before the turn of the century.

Was he a Bohemian? Many, if not most, of the Bohemians had some sort of intellectual commitment to socialism; most likely Lummis never did. After all, he worked for General Harrison Gray Otis, the publisher of the Los Angeles *Times* and one of the most notorious Robber Barons of the era. Still, his love of the pastoral side of life, his love of literature, of art and ideas, that was Bohemian.

When the great San Francisco earthquake and fire of 1906 drove Ina Coolbrith from the city, Lummis was then the city librarian in Los Angeles. He asked her to join his staff, which for an unexplained reason she didn't. Coolbrith had been the head librarian at the Oakland City Library, and like Lummis, she was enough of a maverick and too controversial to keep the position forever. Coolbrith certainly has the distinction not only of having been close to Mark Twain and Bret Harte in her youth, but having been written about as the most fondly portrayed librarian in history in Jack London's autobiographical *Martin Eden*. He gave her the credit for having introduced him, a child of the slums, to the exalted world of books and ideas. The 1906 fire was a particular tragedy in Coolbrith's life — it destroyed a just-completed manuscript she had written on San Francisco's Bohemian scene, especially Twain and Harte, in the '60s, and the flourishing San Francisco Bohemia of the first years of the city.

Lummis died in 1927, far before my time. On the other hand, I did meet Dudley Gordon. In fact I was the last person to interview him before his death in 1982. Gordon had retired from his post as Professor Emeritus at Los

Angeles City College in 1963. As a boy back east, Gordon had been taken with Lummis's writings about the Southwest. But Gordon arrived in Los Angeles just a few months after Lummis had died. Though he never got to meet his hero, Gordon worked ever after to keep Lummis's memory alive. I visited Gordon in his pleasant home bordering the Silverlake Reservoir where London had gone to buy cattle. I asked Gordon to show me the corduroy coat he was famous for wearing when giving lectures on Lummis. It was Lummis's coat — given to Gordon by a Lummis daughter-in-law in the '40s. Gordon donned the suit, and we went on talking.

In a weird kind of way, it was as if I were talking to Lummis himself. Gordon probably knew more about Lummis than Lummis himself did. Gordon admitted that he felt some identity coming from Lummis to him when he donned the coat. He casually observed that he knew for a fact that Lummis wasn't as big as he said he was, for the suit fit him perfectly, and Dudley Gordon by his own reckoning was five feet, four inches tall. The corduroy material had been sent to Lummis by an admirer in Spain, where Lummis has been much better read than in his own country. It's a unique, wide-wale, heavy-weight, olive green corduroy. Gordon's book about Lummis is entitled appropriately enough, *Crusader in Corduroy*.

Gordon pointed out that some of London's earliest short stories were published by Lummis in his magazine originally called *Land of Sunshine* and then renamed *Out West*, which he edited for 14 years, beginning in 1894. Perhaps more than literature, Lummis's greatest accomplishments would certainly include founding the Southwest Museum, one of the largest and best Indian museums in the country today. Lummis was also the reason that many of the California missions were saved, including the venerable San Fernando Mission built in 1779. Lummis took a great many photographs of the Southwest — some of the most evocative are those of the San Fernando Mission, in ruins when he took pictures of it. It was a once great structure looking forlorn and abandoned, crumbling into obscurity. He used the photographs in his campaign to save the mission remains. He was also instrumental in the re-creation of Olvera Street near the site of the original pueblo in downtown Los Angeles.

Still, the magazine was his means of accomplishing many of his preservation and restoration projects. It was his power base. President Teddy Roosevelt said it was the only magazine that he took time to read. Roosevelt no doubt was more attracted by the conservationist message of the magazine than by its Bohemian aspects — although Lummis himself was very conscious of keeping the magazine in the tradition of Bret Harte's old *Overland Monthly*, which in fact merged with *Out West* after Lummis's death. The combined magazines even survived into the Depression years.

Did London hide from Lummis in the shack around which his good sailing friend Finn Frolich later built London House? Certainly Lummis was not used to taking "no" for an answer when he issued an invitation for one of his regular Saturday night soirees at El Alisal. Proud of his ability to spot future talent, he felt that he had done so by publishing London's early stories. But by the time London was traveling to Los Angeles, soon after the turn of the century, he was a well-established writer being besieged on all sides by a fascinated world. But Lummis was arrogant and egotistical. He might have expected London to pay tribute to him at his court — that would have been consistent with his personality. After all, hadn't the great Roosevelt himself visited London at El Alisal?

Roosevelt and Lummis had been old buddies at Harvard. When Roosevelt became the first president in office to travel by train to Los Angeles, he invited Lummis to meet him at the Grand Canyon and ride with him into Los Angeles. It must have been quite a sight — Lummis washing the dishes at El Alisal, and Roosevelt drying them. (Despite the warmth both men had for each other, and their mutual interest in conservation, they did not always see eye to eye. Lummis tried to talk to Roosevelt about using a big stick in this country's dealings with Latin America, but this was not Roosevelt's plan or temperament.)

But Lummis and London were not destined to ever be on the same wavelength, even though both could be said to belong to the California Bohemian movement. In 1905, Lummis asked London for help in forming a Los Angeles chapter of the American Institute of Archaeology, which was carrying on preservation work — photographing the remnants of Indian and Spanish civilization in the Southwest, and recording old Californio-period songs on Edison wax cylinders. London declined, not from a "lack of interest in your cause, but because of too great interest in my own Cause, which is the Socialist Revolution. Believe me," London wrote, "this takes all my time, to the exclusion of other and minor interests."

To which Lummis countered, "We can hardly compare the relative importance of causes; but the work of the Southwest Society has this peculiarity; unless this work is done right away, it can never be done."

London replied "You and I are both fighters, and single-purposed fighters, too. So I am sure you will understand my position. If I have ten dollars a year to spare, I'd soon put it into my fight than your fight. Besides, you can get capitalists to contribute to your fight, but I'm damned if we can get capitalists to contribute to my fight. I'm willing to give my countenance to your fight, but not to give my time or money."

In this exchange, there is much of the conflicts of the themes of Bohemia. Many of the Bohemians were revolutionary, but some like Lummis and Ambrose Bierce, were essentially conservative. What Bohemians all seemed to share was a love of wandering, which certainly Lummis had done, and often a love of nature.

Lummis had already done his share of traveling when he went to work for Harrison Gray Otis in 1885. In fact, he had trekked across the continent from Cincinnati to Los Angeles, battling wild animals, fighting off badmen, and even setting his own arm after breaking it. All these adventures and more are told in *A Tramp Across the Continent*. It's been suggested that some of his adventured sounded like the products of a fevered imagination — some even argue he never took the walk at all. Dudley Gordon dismisses this notion out of hand.

Lummis's first impression of the pueblo on which he would have so much effect was that "it was a dull little place," where the gringos were still out-numbered three to one. The following year Lummis spent three months wander-ing all over the Arizona territory, watching the U.S. Calvary looking rather silly as they chased down Geronimo, the great Apache warrior. Shortly afterward, Lummis, not quite 30, suffered a stroke. To recover, he went to live with the Indians in the pueblos on the Rio Grande for a few years, and against everything his doctors predicted, he recovered by fishing, hunting, and breaking horses. Then he went on some archaeological digs to Peru and Bolivia for five years. The most amazing archaeological achievement, besides founding the Southwest Museum, had to be the photographs he took of the Penitentes — the strange neo-Catholic crucifixion cults in the outback of New Mexico, who had rarely been observed. The Penitentes didn't stop Lummis from photographing them. He had a gun mounted on top of his camera, although, as it turned out, he didn't have to use it.

Lummis finally returned to Los Angeles to settle down in 1893, when he began editing *The Land of Sunshine*, then not much more than a booster magazine. The masthead of owners and contributors, however, soon came to include such bona fide Bohemians as Joaquin Miller, Charles Warren Stoddard, Ina Coolbrith, and the redoubtable Mary Austin, Lummis's troublesome protege. Five years after becoming editor, Lummis began building El Alisal, which became the intellectual meeting place in the city. One can easily believe the building will last a thousand years, as Lummis predicted nearly a century ago.

Trying to figure out what Bohemians are, one can note that they often share revolutionary politics — but not always. There is perhaps something that the California Bohemians share inordinately — a love for nature. Gordon, for example, pointed out that when he spoken before at a Sierra Club meeting, he was surprised that *they* were surprised that Lummis had been a close friend of John Muir, the great hero of the Sierra Club movement. Not only did the young Jack London get discovered in *The Land of Sunshine*, but so did a young, aspiring poet in Los Angeles named Robinson Jeffers, who, nearly a quarter of a century after Lummis began building El Alisal, moved to Carmel and built his stone Tor House on the rugged, storm-swept Pacific coast, where he wrote epic poems of man and nature that are unequalled anywhere.

Lummis was a chauvinist for L.A., which he envisioned as the capital of the great Southwest. Lummis, in fact, created the term "Southwest," just as he also invented the phrase, "See America First!" He saw the pueblo as a part of the large Southwest, whose tradition was both Spanish and Indian. He saw Indians as people who had once lived on the harsh but beautiful land in harmony with nature — and he saw himself as their champion. And, in fact, he was.

Perhaps there is something of the poseur in Lummis, but he was part of a voice that was important here. In prehistory, man lived in a magical landscape. Everything, from the rocks and plants and animals to the sky and rain, was imbued with a life of its own. In more recent times, that sense of landscape being alive and magical has diminished, except in literature. The fault, perhaps, is monotheism, which superseded pantheism, which it derides as superstition. That may be, but the essence of the work to come out of the California Bohemian movement was to give a strong sense of place, revealing where the animate spirits of things really dwell.

Lummis and some of the people around him rekindled the animus of the Southwest, which might otherwise have been lost. By settling in El Pueblo de Los Angeles after his various wanderings, Lummis strove to create a cultural capital here.

□

Most of the Yankee pioneers who came across this continent throughout the early and mid-19th century, hated both the land and its original inhabitants. People like Lummis were the exception. A couple of famous women California Bohemians were also involved with Lummis — with some evidence of romantic overtones. One was our old friend Ina Coolbrith, who to her great shame was one of Mormon leader Joseph Smith's many nieces. Smith had founded San Bernardino as a second Salt Lake City, and Coolbrith had come by covered wagon with the Mormon immigration to Los Angeles in 1885.

Coolbrith's was rather an odd story. The town had hardly had 5,000 souls, of which maybe 100 were gringos like herself. She attended the first class in the pueblo's first public schoolhouse at Second and Spring streets. She was not only the belle of the town during those years — she was its leading literary light; the Los Angeles *Star* published her verse regularly and said she had an international reputation, because some San Francisco newspapers had reprinted her poems.

Among other activities, she had led a grand march at a dance on the arm of California's last Mexican governor, Don Pio Pico. She was much sought out by the young men, finally marrying a successful young businessman, the owner of the Salamander Iron Works, who also was a part-time minstrel trouper. The husband was dashing and romantic and insanely jealous. Once he arrived home from a show in San Francisco, bursting in on his wife and her mother. He began calling Ina a whore, accusing her of having affairs with just about everyone in the pueblo. The husband found the kitchen knife and scissors that Ina and her mother had hidden. Dragging Ina toward him, he threatened to kill her, but nothing happened that day.

The next day, he returned with a six-shooter. Luckily for Ina and her mother, a gentleman passed by, telling the husband that "this was behavior unbecoming." Even after soldiers arrived, the husband went on shouting wild accusations. Finally, he took a wild shot at her but was stopped by a shot from Ina's stepfather, who had been standing nearby. This shot found its mark, for the husband's hand had to be amputated.

Affected by messy divorce proceedings, the possible death of a baby, and devastating rains in December, 1861, she decided to leave Los Angeles.

Years later, Coolbrith tried to recapture some of the old pueblo — especially the sounds of the Spanish speech from the '50s. In a nostalgic, romantic mood in the 1920s, just before she died, Coolbrith off-handedly asked Lummis to write her some Spanish love poetry. This he did. She sent Lummis a birthday poem in 1923. Two years later, both met for what they knew would probably be their last meeting. He sang Spanish songs to her, their eyes sparkled, and she rushed from the room crying.

□

Lummis was also involved with Mary Austin, who became his protege for a while. The first and most lasting of the 35 books Austin wrote was published in 1903 — *The Land of Little Rain*. It beautifully describes the interior valleys of Southern California, the northern boundaries of the Los Angeles basin that are also the start of the great Southwestern desert.

After the success of that book, Mary Austin went to Carmel and helped poet George Sterling establish the California Bohemian playground, which flourished there after the 1906 earthquake. There, Mary Austin had an ill-fated affair with Lincoln Steffens and knew Jack London, Theodore Dreiser, Sinclair Lewis, and Upton Sinclair.

While at Big Sur, she took to prancing around in elaborate costumes, wearing flowing robes and waist-length hair whenever she was in a classical Greek mode or felt like being an Indian princess.

Austin was actually a greater writing talent than Lummis. For a while, people compared her to Willa Cather, who had been a friend during their days in New Mexico. In her day, she was regarded as a weighty intellectual. In fact, Sinclair Lewis's female protagonist in *Main Street* had her origins in Austin's *A Woman of Genius*, and in Theodore Dreiser's *The Genius*.

Austin's first story was published in 1889 in the literary journal of the college she had graduated from in her hometown of Carlinville, Illinois. Entitled "One Hundred Miles on Horseback," it described the trek that Austin and her family made north to homestead 180 acres at Grapevine Canyon, near the Tejon Ranch, which opens into the San Joaquin Valley. Austin's interests, however, seemed to turn east, toward the great Mojave Desert and the Owens Valley, at the foot of the mammoth eastern escarpment of the Sierra.

The owner of the Tejon Ranch was originally General Edward Fitzgerald Beale, who had ridden east with Kit Carson in 1846 and delivered to the nation's capital the news of the conquest of California. Beale was much in love with the land, and, unlike other pioneers, respected the Indians as well as the vanquished Mexicans. Beale introduced Austin to the Indian folklore and coyotes and antelopes and Basque sheepherders; her first more-or-less professional story — "Mother of Felipe" — was published in the *Overland Monthly* in 1892. Another story is called "The Last Antelope," a beautiful tale about the region north of Los Angeles. When Austin first saw the Santa Anas sweep through the Tejon Ranch and Antelope Valley areas, she described a wind that "rises up again, it is pale gold, it seeks the sky."

Austin marched to a different drummer. For one thing, she did not always wear well on people. The folks around Independence and Lone Pine, in the Owens Valley, where the house she lived in is now a monument, were put off by her habit of roaming the countryside, flinging her arms about and expounding grandiosely on one subject or another. They were even more irritated by her apparent preference for the company of Indians and Mexicans. At Carmel, her odd posturing earned her the nickname of "God's Mother-in-Law."

It is good that Austin got to know the Indians. Before the white men came, California was home to more of the American Indian population than has been commonly assumed. Yet by the 20th century, Indians in California had nearly ceased to exist — basically as a result of genocide. Austin got to know the last surviving natives during her Tejon homesteading days, in the area just a few dozen miles north of modern-day Santa Clarita and Castaic. Although Austin and Lummis would have a falling out, they both tried to recapture their lost history.

Austin's book of pastoral sketches came out shortly after another masterpiece of the desert had made its debut, *The Desert* by John C. Van Dyke, also connected with the Lummis circle. Whereas Austin was more given over to magic and mysticism, the pantheism of the land and its original inhabitants, Van Dyke was a historian, naturalist and art critic. One day in 1898, he walked into the desert through the San Gorgonio Pass, near San Bernardino, living there for three years. He observed not only with a truly scientific eye, but he also explained the desert light and colors well, because of his art critic's understanding of these subjects. Both books rise far above mere prose; both are very poetical works, certainly of considerable regional importance.

☐

Jake Zeitlin admitted to me that he had not been much taken by Lummis. "He was a very picturesque man, a character, deliberately so. He liked nothing so much as being conspicuous; he was a rogue, and had a tremendous enthusiasm for women which got him into lots of trouble. But he did have talents — not as a writer but as a catalyst."

Zeitlin once took his friend Carl Sandburg to visit Lummis at El Alisal in 1926, only two years before Lummis died at 77 years of age. Lummis and Sandburg had a conflict of egos. Lummis saw it this way: "Zeitlin, a poet, benefited the most from the hour and a half visit because he was least full of himself.'" I asked Zeitlin whether he thought Lummis was part of the Bohemian tradition. He replied that he felt Lummis "represented something else," namely "the pastoral" part of the city's past. On reflection I decided I disagreed with Zeitlin. For all its socialism and sexual theory, Bohemians itself has strong pastoral, romantic ties. Like his boss at the *Times*, General Otis, Lummis may have been a reactionary about labor, but he was an early opponent of racism and a proponent of women's rights. Jack London, on the other hand, was a revolutionary about labor but reactionary about race. One of the plain facts about the California Bohemian tradition is that they were full of contradictions; so be it.

Jack London
May Have Slept Here

I t's been nearly thirty years since a friend who lived near Melrose and Wilton in Hollywood introduced me to one of the neighborhood's — dare I say the city's? — best-kept secrets. In an obscure alleyway called La Vista Court I caught my first glimpse of one of the most unusual-looking

Phil Stern's photo of London House

residences you'd ever hope to see. On its front, cast in the same plaster as

71

was the house, was a bas-relief portrait of my favorite writer, Jack London. Beneath the portrait was the enameled inscription, "Jack London slept here."

For a couple of years my friend and I used to walk past the place and talk about it and about Jack London, and wonder what the history of the place was. Then, in the mid-'60s, I got my first newspaper job in Pismo Beach, nearly two hundred miles north of Los Angeles. On the last night before I left town, I decided to knock on the door of the house and find out what it was all about.

The man who came to the door was not at all upset at my interest in his place. His name was Robert Gary and he invited me up the narrow stairs to a second-floor apartment. This was the main apartment of London House, Gary explained, and he lived in it. He was also the landlord of four other apartments in the building. Gary's apartment had a two-story-high ceiling, capped off by a large skylight. There was also another set of narrow stairs going from his apartment to a third-story penthouse bedroom that towers over the other buildings on La Vista Court; you can clearly pick out London House from nearby Van Ness because of the third story.

That first night, Gary and I talked late into the night, discussing Jack London as well as a number of other things. But Gary insisted that he did not want his house to be written about. Although the place was historical, he also lived in it. I remember going away from the house feeling that I had been lucky to have discovered London House, which nobody had ever written about. I spent the rest of the decade as a wandering newspaperman, more in the northern part of the state than the southern. When I eventually resettled in Los Angeles, it was not long before I was showing my friends the front of London House in La Vista Court in Hollywood every time I got a chance. If I couldn't write about it, by God, I was still going to make people aware of an unexpected piece of Los Angeles literary history — namely that the great Jack London, who was known as a Northern California writer, had also been something of an Angeleno.

Over the years I avoided knocking on the door of London House to talk to Gary, but I noticed that London House was looking more and more down on its uppers than it should have. The bas-relief of London had been knocked a little askew, whether by earthquake or just plain settling I didn't know. The blue-enameled "Jack London slept here" sign that had so intrigued me at first was gone. A car had knocked another bas-relief sculpture of a sailing ship off the front of the house, although most of the various satyrs and nymphs adorning the house seemed to have withstood the ravages of time. The ship's lantern on the second floor seemed less red than it had been, and part of the block-and-tackle over the large two-part barn door on the second-floor apartment had come down. The stucco looked decidedly shabbier and even the external redwood pegs between the floor and ceiling seemed to be aging poorly.

On a hunch, I knocked on the door again. Gary wasn't there, but I made arrangements to see him. As it turned out, Gary remembered me. And as I suspected, he was now in a worse position than he'd been in the first time I met him. Although he's been pouring a good part of his salary into keeping up the house, it needs more and more work all the time. Ultimately, the place is going to require massive rebuilding, maybe $50,000 worth, estimates Gary. It needs an entirely new foundation, for instance. Gary explained that he had been trying to do the work because he loves the place and thinks it has great historical importance, but none of this is easy. For the last four years, the Internal Revenue Service has called him in every year, demanding that he explain his rebuilding. "They don't care if it's an historic house; my economics just don't fit their computers. They think I take in too little income for the amount I'm spending on it," he says a bit ruefully. "If this were just a piece of real estate I guess that would be true," he adds.

Here I should explain that in the fifteen years between my first two visits to the inside of the London House, the details of its history had taken on the warm, indistinct glow of a fantasy — most of it going back, I think, to the intriguing blue enamel sign that said "Jack London slept here." This fantasy was partly based on what I thought I had remembered during my first visit with Gary in the mid-'60s. I think Gary himself had subsequently learned more about the house than he had known on the occasion of my first visit.

Throughout most of the '70s, I showed many people the square, three-story structure that stands tall and looks so much different than anything else in the neighborhood. And I told them what I believed to be the information I had gotten from Gary on my first visit. I always said that the house dated back to 1870 or so. No one who ever saw the place doubted that it had to be at least a hundred years old. I had remembered Gary's saying that London House was originally the ranch house of a cattle ranch that extended from Hollywood past where City Hall is now, in downtown L.A. Jack London — or so the story went — would come to this ranch house, which had been renamed in his honor by the friend who now owned the ranch, to buy live-stock for his own ranch fifty miles north of San Francisco.

My impression, in other words, was that the London House had a noble and untold past as a sort of Bohemia South. I imagined great scenes occurring at the London House, where London and his companion George Sterling and other such greats got together for extended conversations. Over those fifteen years, I had often thought of the one piece of evidence that really linked

London House to this imaginary Bohemia South: an inscription, on an inside wall of Gary's apartment, from Sterling, who was famous in his own right as a California poet laureate as well as being London's close friend.

Like many writers since London, I first felt the call of the literary arts after reading his great, autobiographical *Martin Eden*. It was, of course, *The Call of the Wild* which first brought Jack London fame and fortune right after the turn of the century. He became the most successful and popular writer the world had ever seen, the Skid Row bestseller who was far bigger in his day than any movie or rock star has been since. He was also the bastard son of an eccentric spiritualist and an itinerant Irish astrologer and writer. London's harsh childhood was spent in the slums of Oakland and environs, and sometimes on farms. It was a childhood of poverty and defeat. By the time he was ten years of age, he was working nineteen-hour days in waterfront factories to help support his family. By the time he was out of his teens, he had been a king of the San Francisco Bay oyster pirates, a sailor around the world, an adventurer to the Yukon, a hobo, a famed revolutionary socialist, an alcoholic, and most of all, a writer.

There is no more compelling version of a writer's trials and tribulations than those described in *Martin Eden*: cranking out his manuscripts, spending his last few cents on postage rather than food, seeing each day's mail bring more and more rejection slips. After a while, he replaced his wallpaper with rejection notices. Yet when London struck it big, during the few short years that remained of his life, he had produced more than fifty books as well as countless articles and short stories. Not only did he write the greatest adventure stories, but he also produced such powerful social protest works as *People of the Abyss*, *The Iron Heel*, and *South of the Slot*.

The last years of London's life were spent on Glen Ellen, his ranch in the Valley of the Moon, north of San Francisco. The hobos and sailors and drifters and criminals, working men and hangers-on he had met in his world travels knew they were always welcome at Glen Ellen, for London was a generous man. It is said that Glen Ellen typically had as many as five hundred visitors a day. And, if a man wanted a job at a good wage, London tried never to turn him away.

Glen Ellen also was the meeting ground for some of the most famous men of San Francisco's Bohemia. London was the great star of a distinguished literary set that included such other famous characters as Ambrose Bierce, George Sterling, and Joaquin Miller. London actually hated Bierce, though it was Bierce who spanned the careers of both London and Mark Twain. It is probably not just coincidence that both Twain and especially London were instrumental in introducing the notion of realism to the then all-too-genteel world of letters. London's influence on later 20th-century writers as diverse as Hemingway and Kerouac was pronounced.

Just before my most recent visit with Gary, I re-read Irving Stone's biography of London, *Sailor on Horseback*. Stone appropriated the title from an auto-biography London never got around to writing. I was looking for evidence that London had indeed slept at London House. I thought I had found it when Stone mentioned that, in 1906, London came to L.A. to buy livestock and stayed in the home of a sculptor friend named Felix Piano. I remembered vaguely something Gary had said, that the man who owned London House was a sculptor friend of London's. London had lived in Piano's house in Oakland as well — the Piano house there was said to be adorned with a profusion of bas-reliefs of satyrs and nymphs, as well as nudes on pedestals. Surely, I figured, Stone was talking about London House on La Vista Court, in Hollywood.

Yet I wasn't so sure when I went back into old issues of the Los Angeles *Examiner*, which had interviewed London during his 1906 trip. For one thing, my dream that Jack London sat on the roof of London House and saw no houses all the way to the original pueblo just could not have been true. By 1906 — it was apparent from the pages of the old *Examiner* — there were more than a quarter of a million people surrounding the old pueblo.

So the first thing I asked Gary was — and I assumed his answer would be yes — were the bas-reliefs and the house built by Felix Piano? Gary laughed. No, he said. He had thought that, too. But the fact was, the house had been built by Finn Haakon Frolich, a sculptor and sailor friend of London's who was, as a matter of fact, a much closer friend than Piano had ever been.

I looked around the place and suddenly realized why it felt so much as though Jack London had been here. The narrow steps, the cabin-like bedroom, everything about the place gave one the feeling of being inside a ship. It was a subtle thing, but that was what Frolich had done with London House. In *Sailor on Horseback*, Stone describes Frolich as London's "court jester and sculptor" at Glen Ellen. It is Frolich's bust of London, for instance, which adorns the entrance to Glen Ellen, which today has been made into a state park and the Jack London Museum. And it is Frolich's bust of London that was cast in bronze by the Oakland Port Authority when it built Jack London Square.

Frolich was very much a part of the San Francisco Bohemia of which London was the star — and he was very much an intimate of London's. Frolich had a tremendous, booming laugh and loud voice, by all accounts. And he had been one of London's friends who witnessed the final disintegration of London during his last days at Glen Ellen.

London committed suicide in 1916 at the age of 40. In some haunting words, Frolich described the change in his friend. "He didn't do the sporting things he used to do — wrestle, play, didn't want to go into the mountains riding horseback any more. The gleam was gone from his eyes." Of course in the forty years of his life, London lived more lives than a hundred mortals combined. Interestingly enough, London predicted his own suicide in *Martin Eden*, written at the height of his career several years earlier. He said that *Martin Eden* had been written to show the folly of extreme individualism — but if London was anything, he was a great individualist as much as he was ever a socialist.

How about the inscription on the wall I had seen from George Sterling? Gary pointed to the wall — the inscription is still there. But it wasn't carved into the wall, as I had remembered; it was a decal, dark and opaque and hard to read except under a very strong light. The words were woven into a latticework of the nymphs and satyrs London's Bohemian friends all seemed to cherish. Gary said the decal had originally been sandwiched between two pieces of glass in an old sash window in the back bedroom. "The window was so rotted out I had to replace it," he explained. "Here's what it says," he added, swinging open the top part of the large barn door on the front of London House to catch the sunlight. "'The young in heart shall find their love and laughter anywhere.'" The words around the bottom of the decal are harder to make out. "'He only in Bohemia dwells who knows not he is there,'" he added. "Dedicated to Finn Frolich by George Sterling." He paused again. "And there's a date," he slowly added. "It is 1924."

I asked Gary to repeat the date of the inscription. If Sterling inscribed the decal to his friend Frolich in 1924, and Frolich was one of the regulars at Glen Ellen during the last year of London's life, the sculptor probably didn't come to Los Angeles and build what, after all, was really his studio until after London's death. To my direction question — had Jack London ever slept in London House? — Gary was a bit evasive. He said that this was what had been rumored. "We found a basement downstairs, six feet square. Probably a wine cellar. We found a few things." Gary showed me a rusted metal toy locomotive. "We found this and some paper matchboxes from the '20s and some handmade bottles down there," he said. "A friend of mine suggested we keep digging because we'd probably run across some bottles London himself drank out of." But Gary said he wasn't even sure when the house was built — he estimated sometime between 1900 and 1920, "although it looks older than that, I know." Gary said he was sure London House had been the only structure in the neighborhood when it was built.

Gary suggested I contact Frolich's son and daughter, one of whom he believed lived in Hollywood and the other in San Francisco. Whatever the connection of London House and Jack London, he added, he definitely knew the house was rich in Hollywood lore. Gary ought to know — he works as a script supervisor on films and television serials. La Vista Court, he said, used to be called McDougall's Lane, and McDougall's Lane sloped into a pond. Most of the scenes where a car runs into a pond in the Keystone Kops movies were shot in the alley, he said. The rest of the Keystone Kops pictures were usually shot on nearby Larchmont, which runs only a few blocks between Melrose and Third Street, Gary said.

"I've heard both Tony Quinn and John Carradine lived here. I know my friend Dick Beymer, who was a big star for some years — he was in 'West Side Story' — lived here. And my friend Victor Buono almost always stays here whenever he's in town working on a movie," Gary added.

Hefty Buono? I ask. How does he get up the steep, narrow stairs? "With difficulty," Gary replies. "He always says gravity is his enemy." Gary goes on: "You know, Jack London was really one of the first writers for movies — his *Sea Wolf* was one of the first silent films. It was remade as a talking picture later with Edward G. Robinson, but Hobart Bosworth, the famed silent-screen star, played in the original *Sea Wolf*. I have a picture taken here in the house, of Frolich and Bosworth admiring Frolich's bust of Bosworth."

Gary bought the house from Frank Lopez, a pioneer Chicano activist who has since died. "Everyone who has had the house was somehow on a line from Jack London. Lopez was a friend of Frolich in part because of their politics. Frank was an incredible landlord. Never pried into your business or raised his rents. I became very attached to the place, so when he wanted to sell the house in 1957, I purchased it from him." Because London House is named after a man who had a reputation as a flaming socialist, Gary keeps his rents low, and refuses to engage in real-estate speculation. That would mean tearing down the house and building apartments or breaking up old houses into bootleg apartments as Gary says some of his neighbors have done.

Virginia Forstad, Frolich's daughter, lives today in Hollywood, an old woman surrounded by mementos of the past, including pictures autographed for her by Jack London. She's not very clear about early details of her life.

Gilbert Frolich says that his sister lived with London and Frolich, all right, but it was at the Glen Ellen ranch, in Northern California. There's a famous picture of London and Virginia, who is four years of age, and Gilbert, at one-and-a-half years. The kids are nude and not in entirely respectful postures in the presence of the great author, who is wearing a black bathing suit, typical of the day, with a fishing pole in one hand, and the other arm over his wife Charmian.

Gilbert is very precise in his recollections. Since his father's life was so mixed up with California's early Bohemian and literary history, he's made a hobby of researching his father's background. Gilbert says his father brought his children to Los Angeles from Northern California in 1920 in a Model T.

He remembers that the trip, for unexplained reasons, took three months. Shortly after he arrived here, Frolich bought the land on McDougall's Alley and began building his house and studio there. Although Gilbert says he realizes that Frolich's studio was widely known as London House, "he dedicated it more to himself than to Jack London." He says the bas-relief of London wasn't even finished until the middle of the Depression.

So Gilbert rules out the possibility that London ever slept at London House, even though Gary used to get mail delivered to "London House, La Vista Court, Hollywood" for many years. Gilbert, however, said he's pretty sure George Sterling slept there.

Gilbert remembers Sterling sitting on the porch of some friends, crying over a lost poker game, not very far away from his father's sculpture studio. In some ways, says Gilbert, Sterling was a greater man than London. Or at least a greater character, if not a writer. London wrote about Sterling as Brissenden in *Martin Eden*.

Gilbert adds he's sure that John Carradine lived there. "Mom and I came down from Oakland to put Carradine out for not paying the rent in the middle of the Depression." Carradine called the cops on Gilbert and his mother, Gilbert explains, because they were keeping a bust Carradine had made of Cecil B. DeMille. Carradine, who had been a good sculpting student of Frolich's, wanted the bust because he said he was going to "break into Hollywood" with it. Gilbert mother finally relented and returned the bust to Carradine, who later did indeed present it to DeMille.

"My mother said Carradine was such a good actor that he was almost, but not quite, the only tenant ever to talk her out of collecting the rent," Gilbert says.

Gilbert says he's been writing a detailed history of the house to send to Bob Gary soon, but a couple of heart attacks have slowed him down.

Because the house was then in such terrible condition, Gary had nightmares about the house being torn down. The most vivid nightmare he ever had involved the proposed Beverly Hills Freeway. "My nightmares used to go like this: I look out the barn door windows and I can see that the bulldozer has knocked all the other houses on La Vista Court down, and now it's making a U-turn at the end and is headed at London House," Gary said with a shudder. When Jerry Brown was elected governor, he eliminated the route.

But Gary has been trying to turn his troubles with London House to the good. He's been working on a screenplay about a young writer who moves into the London House. One day the writer's girlfriend asks him if he's ever read Jack London. The young writer says no. But he begins to read London, and that changes his life and his writing — an effect which London had on many people. Gary sees the movie as a chance to do a London biography as both a documentary and a piece of fiction. Gary, who casually mentions that he's distantly related to Mark Twain, says of London: "He was the first writer who wrote about life in the raw and didn't try to sweeten it up with sugar."

Gary says that even though he's broke, he's still dedicated to saving London House, although he's not sure a historical society would be interested in helping him. "I'm so angry I might just turn London House into the Church of Jack London. People will be ordained. The Bible will be Irving Stone's *Sailor on Horseback*, and we'll argue about different things London wrote. I'll take a vow of poverty and give my house, car, and income to the church in exchange for it supporting me. Just the way the Catholic Church does. I won't have to pay taxes that way. If I have to do that to restore London House, I will."

We talk some more. He discusses some of the things that have been broken off or stolen from the front of the house when he brings up the matter of the sign that had first attracted me to the house. Frankly, I had forgotten about the sign. Before I can ask Gary how that sign came to be affixed to London's bas-relief, he is explaining it.

"In London, England, you know, all the houses where famous writers lived have little enamel plaques. Well, a friend of mine made one of those to go under the bas-relief in front. It was just like the ones I've seen in London. It was enamel blue with white letters. It was really authentic looking."

"What did it say?" I ask, getting excited again.

"Oh my friend just made it up, I think. It said, 'Jack London slept here.'"

Jack London bas-relief

Just Passing Through

L os Angeles is a town of never-ending motion — rootless, transitory. Here today, gone tomorrow. But passing through — not permanence — has become a major part of the human condition in the 20th century. They say that if you turn America on its end, everything loose slides into L.A.; well, a few of our great literary artists happened by, too, and began writing major works before moving on.

I first became intrigued with the idea of writers "just passing through" years ago, when I was caught up in a minor mystery surrounding one of the greatest and most truly American of American writers, Mark Twain. Back in the late '60s, when I went to work as a reporter on the Newhall *Signal*, one of the first persons I met was the town historian, Arthur B. Perkins. Newhall is only thirty-five miles north of Los Angeles City Hall, and it is beginning to look more and more like any L.A. suburb, but down by the Saugus train station, and Hart Park, it still has some of the feeling of an old Western town. Perkins had his office in the back of the Chamber of Commerce, right across the courtyard from the Newhall *Signal*. On hot summer days, when things got slow and everyone kept the doors open, I got in the habit of wandering across the courtyard and through Perkins's open door. Perkins was still tall and imposing and only a little shaky for a man in his nineties. For a young reporter trying to learn all about a town during the first weeks on the job, Perkins was a wonderful find. His cussedness and literate intelligence somehow branded him as the old New Englander he was, but it also seemed as if he had lived in Newhall forever. There was hardly a thing in the town's history that he hadn't meticulously researched.

I never forgot his telling, one afternoon, how Samuel Clemens (also known as Mark Twain) had come to Newhall in the 1860s. The stagecoach stop in Newhall then was called Lyon's Station, and Twain was coming to visit nearby Placerita Canyon, where in 1842 a Franciscan friar named Don Francisco Lopez had, while plucking some wild onions sitting under an oak tree, discovered flecks of placer gold on the roots. California gold, contrary to what is generally thought, was not first discovered at Sutter's Mill near Sacramento in 1848, but rather in Placerita Canyon. (That oak was later officially described and commemorated as "The Oak of the Golden Dream.") By the 1860s there were regular commercial mining operations going on. And not far away, in Pico Canyon, oil seeping through the ground was being used to keep the lights burning in the San Fernando Mission. Recently, I checked Perkins's thoughts on Mark Twain with Ruth and Tony Newhall of the Newhall family who ran the newspaper then, and neither of them could verify the Twain story. But I was able to find a long piece by Perkins that the Southern California Historical Society had published in 1958. If Twain did come to Newhall, Perkins apparently discovered it after he wrote that article, which was entitled "Mining Camps of the Soledad."

I was perhaps too eager to place Twain in the same town I was starting out to cover. I would have dropped the notion forever but for the fact that over the years my friend Monty Muns — the former coffeehouse entrepreneur, journalist, poet, and title searcher in downtown Los Angeles we've already mentioned — kept telling me about the strange old 330 N. Broadway Building. It was replaced by a parking structure several years ago, but if it were still standing, it would be located next to the Hall of Justice. Muns's job took him into the building almost daily, for the place was used as a repository for records of probate cases. One day Muns asked the veteran clerk there why the building had so many strange, narrow stairways, cubbyholes, and private rooms. The clerk replied that the building had been a "hotel" at the turn of the century. More specifically, it had been a whorehouse. Mark Twain was once a regular patron of the establishment and even had his own room there, the old clerk contended. Other regulars, he added, were Hart Crane and Bret Harte.

Since Twain died in 1910, the "hotel" story is rather questionable, but it is true that there has been a curiously unexamined relationship between a surprising number of great writers and the City of the Angels. While New York has maintained a persuasive claim to being the nation's literary capital, it was in California that the frontier character of this country found its most expressive voice. The frontier influence was eloquent and rough-hewn; New York felt uncomfortable in its presence. In the aftermath of the San Francisco gold rush, men of letters didn't turn to New York for guidance; they were much more influenced by the Paris Bohemians of the 1840s. During his California days, Mark Twain was known by his San Francisco newspaper colleagues, not always affectionately, as the "Sagebrush Bohemian."

☐

An important writer in Bohemian George Sterling's charmed California circle was Theodore Dreiser. When Dreiser came to Los Angeles for a three-year stay in 1919, he had not yet written his most famous and successful work, *An American Tragedy*. Dreiser was living with his cousin and companion of many years, Helen Richardson, whom he didn't make Mrs. Dreiser until the end of his life. About midway through their L.A. stay, Dreiser and Richardson went north to meet Sterling. Being like-minded rebels and pessimists, Sterling and Dreiser quickly took to each other. Sterling also took to Helen, whom he amused by taking off his clothes and swimming into a lake to retrieve some dripping water lilies.

Born in 1871 in Terre Haute, Indiana, Dreiser was as well known for being the brother of songwriter and Tin Pan Alley mogul Paul Dreiser — for whom he wrote the lyrics to the song, "On the Banks of the Wabash" — as for his novel, *Sister Carrie*. *Sister Carrie* had been a controversial book when it was published in 1900, and hadn't done well. Dreiser was an extreme mechanist who thought that everything was determined by biology and environment. He wrote in a hard, cheaply journalistic style at times, for he had made his daily living as a newspaper and magazine writer. In recent years Dreiser has fallen out of favor with American critics and readers, but the scope of his storytelling and his unremitting realism gave him a place in America's literary pantheon which no one can take away.

Nonetheless, his life was often messy. When Dreiser left Gotham to come to L.A. in 1919, he was doing so to avoid his wife (from whom he was separated) as well as publishers anxious to know how his writing — for which they had advanced him money and then seen very little — was going. Dreiser wouldn't even give his close friend H.L. Mencken anything more than a post office box address in Los Angeles. At first, he and Helen lived in a rented part of a private home on Alvarado Street. After that, according to W.A. Swanberg's biography, *Dreiser*, the couple moved often. They lived in a bungalow on Sunset Boulevard and a cottage in Glendale. Helen, an actress, was speculating in real estate, like almost everyone else. Mencken despaired of ever seeing his friend again. He wrote, "Dreiser's is in Los Angeles. What he is doing there I don't know. I have heard that he is being kept by some rich wench."

In fact, Helen was not doing all that badly. She had a couple of supporting acting roles, including one in Rudolf Valentino's first flick, "The Four Horsemen of the Apocalypse". Dreiser seemed bored and resentful of her success. He called L.A. "the city of the folded hands." He was flagrantly unfaithful to Helen. After three years in L.A. Dreiser was convinced that the city was no place for an artist. He had, however, put aside *The Bulwark* and tentatively begun *An American Tragedy*, his big book.

When he returned to New York, with Helen abandoning her career to follow him, he finished *An American Tragedy*, but then had a long fallow period. By 1935 he wanted to go back to L.A. again. He had a close friend, George Douglas, who worked on the Los Angeles *Examiner*. He moved in with Douglas, and Helen rented a room nearby. After a while, Dreiser and Helen rented an apartment on Rosewood and moved in together again. They didn't stay there long, however: they returned to New York. Dreiser wanted to go back to Los Angeles the following year, but Douglas had died. It wasn't until 1939 that Dreiser and Helen got back together and moved permanently to L.A., taking an apartment at 253-A West Loraine Street in Glendale.

The second time Dreiser made Los Angeles his home it did not help him out of his fallow period. He continued working on *The Bulwark* and *The Stoic*, books he had begun much earlier in his career. But the going was rough, and both books were only published after Dreiser's death here in 1945. Los Angeles had helped him out of a bind once before, but Dreiser and Helen were not living well at the beginning of the second L.A. years. For a while they had an apartment at 1426 N. Hayworth, just off Sunset Boulevard. Dreiser was so ashamed of that place that when his old friend Sherwood Anderson came to town, Dreiser didn't invite him back to the apartment. He took Anderson out to eat in a restaurant near the Figueroa Hotel. Later, things improved a bit; the couple moved to a place they had purchased at 1015 N. Kings Road, near Santa Monica Boulevard, and they added a new couple to their social life — Charles and Oona Chaplin, who also were good friends of Upton and Mary Sinclair.

Dreiser, however, suffered from deep intellectual confusions. One day he drove out to Torrance to consult a fortune teller. Another evening he and Helen went to a seance in Pasadena at the home of the Sinclairs. The political conflicts of the day inflamed him: he was as bothered by corruption in City Hall as he was by the bad news from the Spanish Civil War. On the one hand he became a member of the Communist Party; at the same time, like such other mystics as Aldous Huxley and Christopher Isherwood, he was serious about yoga and contemplated a trip to India. He was no longer able to produce a single, powerful vision of things. Perhaps this was because he wasn't a 20th-century writer so much as he was a writer who bridged the two centuries. And perhaps it was because he was such a Bohemian.

☐

Usually when people talk about Bohemian writers in Los Angeles, they think of the Garden of Allah, where F. Scott Fitzgerald, Robert Benchley, and Dorothy Parker drank and partied and lived through some of the Depression years while earning fabulous salaries from the nearby Hollywood dream factories. Writers like Somerset Maugham, Dashiell Hammett, and S.J. Perelman were frequent visitors to the Garden of Allah. Hemingway met Gary Cooper there, and they became great friends. Had he been around in those days, Mark Twain could easily have been the king of the roost there, for Hollywood was attracting people from all over with its own kind of gold rush: a celluloid rush. But Twain, of course, was dead by then, and the Garden of Allah is no longer to be seen, except as a model display near the vault of the savings and loan that displaced the famed residence-hotel at the corners of Sunset and Laurel Canyon boulevards.

Twain would probably have been uncomfortable at the Garden of Allah anyway, since it was primarily a hangout for Eastern writers who regarded the natives as baboons and yahoos. This eastern chauvinism would not have been Twain's cup of tea at all, although oddly enough the worst of the Eastern chauvinists was the most Bohemian of the writers there, Dorothy Parker. Parker, in fact, was the most Twain-like of the group. She was a great wit, the star of the Algonquin Hotel circle from the '20s in New York City. In retrospect, it appears that her greatness as a writer was underestimated because of her wit, and this also happened to Twain. Parker left no novels; her output was composed mainly of literary essays, short stories, and very quotable and funny poetry. Yet those short works, which have been reissued by Viking Press as *The Portable Dorothy Parker*, show that her writing compared favorably with Hemingway's. Despite this, it seems as if her reputation will forever record her a originator of the line, "Men don't make passes at girls who wear glasses." At her husband's funeral, when an acquaintance asked her if she needed anything, she snapped, "Yes. You can get me another husband." The acquaintance was shocked, and asked Dorothy Parker if she really had meant that. Parker's reply: "Then get me a ham sandwich and hold the mustard."

Her wit as quick against her friends as it was against her enemies. She lived much of her life in a New York Bohemian milieu, and many of her friends were undoubtedly "authors and actors and such." Yet in her poem "Bohemia" she wails that "People Who Do Things exceed my endurance; God, for a man that solicits insurance."

To Dorothy Parker, Hollywood was a zoo in which she happened to have lived for nearly two full decades, off and on. She regarded her bosses in the studios as cretins, which they probably were, so she had funny things to say about Hollywood. And very true things. But the Garden of Allah was more interesting than important in Los Angeles's literary tradition.

In 1976 Tom Dardis wrote *Some Time in the Sun*, which put forth the revisionist theory that ultimately Hollywood didn't do so badly by people like Fitzgerald, Faulkner, West, and Huxley. He also noted that these and other writers made their contribution to Hollywood in such classic films as "The Big Sleep," "Jane Eyre," "The African Queen," "To Have and Have Not," and "Pride and Prejudice."

Dardis argued that Hollywood aided these men financially and creatively. His argument about Fitzgerald is worth considering. Fitzgerald's last years in Hollywood were not as bad as they have been portrayed, Dardis maintains. Fitzgerald's reputation and creative powers had plummeted by the middle of the Depression and it was only after he had come to Hollywood that he finally found "something new to write about." *The Last Tycoon* was his California book, and his publishers were every bit as excited by it as they had been during his glorious days in the '20s. Dardis does not deny that

Fitzgerald was drinking, but even that has been exaggerated, he argues.

Dardis says that the "ultimate source for all those 'ruined, shattered man' descriptions" of Fitzgerald was Budd Schulberg, of *What Makes Sammy Run?* fame. Schulberg had worked with Fitzgerald on movie jobs, and had drunk with him; Fitzgerald had also recommended Schulberg's book to Random House. But Fitzgerald did not think that Schulberg was talented, and Dardis suggests the latter might thus have had some motivation to paint Fitzgerald as a failure.

To my mind, Dardis is a little less convincing in the case of William Faulkner. Over a period of time Faulkner spent more than four years in Hollywood. His best known effort on a script was "The Big Sleep," and his main influence here seemed to be the addition of a Southern feeling to a Southern California setting. Considering that a good part of L.A.'s population emigrated from the South, he might have been onto something. Faulkner, however, did not take his writing duties in Hollywood as seriously as did Fitzgerald, for example. He wasn't paid as well, either. He couldn't afford to stay at the Garden of Allah, so the great Faulkner lived in shabby hotels and took long, solitary walks on downtown L.A.'s grubby streets. And he drank like crazy, for he wanted to go home to Oxford, Mississippi. Dardis argues, however, that ultimately the Hollywood money enabled Faulkner to write his great books, and that the Hollywood influence is to be seen in some of them.

Then there was the case of Evelyn Waugh, who spent a short while in Los Angeles and went back to England to write *The Loved One*. Dardis didn't write about him, but we will here. Waugh was a rather typical English gentleman who took his Church of England background so seriously that he later converted to Catholicism. On his short visit to the City of the Angels, what he was most taken with was the L.A. way of death, at least as it was represented by Forest Lawn. As one Waugh biographer put it, *The Loved One* was a satire on "the decline of religious belief and practice in the twentieth century, as evidenced in the California burial customs Waugh had observed while in Hollywood." To my mind *The Loved One* is a rather good book, but falls short of being a major contribution to literary Los Angeles. It's been suggested that Aldous Huxley did a better job on the themes of death and California in his *After Many A Summer Dies The Swan*.

It was not the muse of the movies that drew John Steinbeck to Southern California at the nadir of the Great Depression. Steinbeck was not yet a successful writer when he moved to the L.A. area at the beginning of the 1930s. But not too many years later, he would don the mantle of the great California writer with such books as *Tortilla Flats*, *Grapes of Wrath*, and *Cannery Row*. Steinbeck grew up in the Carmel-Salinas area, which became known as "Steinbeck country." Yet at a point in his life, perhaps when he was still looking for the muse, he moved south.

His novel *Cannery Row* is about Monterey, but there is a chapter in it about Tom and Mary Talbot, a writer and his wife, which was actually based on two periods of Steinbeck's life when he had moved away from the Northern California coastal region in which he grew up.

In *Cannery Row*, Mary is always trying to keep Tom's spirits up when the rent is overdue and the electricity is about to be turned off and there is no money in sight. Mary's gaiety is infectious and usually keeps her husband from getting despondent. "We're going under," Talbot says. "No, we're not," she replies. "We're magic people. We always have been. Remember that ten dollars you found in a book — remember when your cousin sent you five dollars? Nothing can happen to us."

Talbot was, of course, Steinbeck, and Mary was Steinbeck's first wife, Carol. They were married in Los Angeles in 1930. Steinbeck described their "shack" at 2741 El Robe Drive in Eagle Rock as a "cheap place to live." They paid fifteen dollars per month for the place, which had, among other things, a thirty-foot living room with a giant stone fireplace, and a sleeping porch. Steinbeck enjoyed having people come and visit him, and he wrote to his friends from out of town suggesting that they come and "sit in front of a fire and talk, or lie on the beach and talk, or walk in the hills and talk." Later he would write a letter to a friend: "Remember the days when we lived in Eagle Rock? As starved and happy a group as ever robbed an orange tree. I can still remember the dinners of hamburgers and stolen avocados."

According to Mike Spencer, who worked as a publicist for the Lung Association, Steinbeck was doing clerical work at the Association to keep alive. He was broke and not yet famous, yet still working on his second book, *To a God Unknown*, which didn't do well when it was finally published.

Steinbeck's stay in L.A. began in January of 1930 when there was plenty of rain and cold, which made the fireplace an object of worship. But by August, not only was the electric-company about to turn off the juice, Steinbeck was also complaining that it was "pretty hot down here now and my mind seems more sluggish than it usually is." The crowning blow came when the landlord, admiring all the fixing-up the Steinbecks had done on the house, evicted them so that he could give it as a wedding present to his daughter. At this point, all the Steinbecks could think to do was get in their car and drive as far as their gas would get them. They ended up going back to Salinas, where Steinbeck's father and mother lived. His father gave the couple a small living allowance and a house in nearby Pacific Grove.

Three years later, Steinbeck had apparently forgotten the August and September heat of the Southland. He and Carol moved back to another outlying L.A. community — this time they lived at 2527 Hermosa Avenue in Montrose. By then, Steinbeck was working on the final drafts of *To a God Unknown*. Again the time came when the rent was due and the utilities were about to be turned off. Now, however, Steinbeck's mother became very ill, so the couple went up north for the final time. Steinbeck would later write magnificently of the poverty of the Dust Bowl Okies in *Grapes of Wrath*, but his own bottom-of-the-Depression stories took place in Los Angeles.

Hollywood — the movie industry, that is, not the town — played only a minor part in drawing Henry Miller to Los Angeles. Miller, of course, spent the first and most productive part of his writing career as an expatriate from Brooklyn living in Paris during the Depression. On the eve of World War II he came back to his own country and his place in it, a process described in his book *The Air-Conditioned Nightmare*, which was about an automobile trip across the country. The book expressed Miller's rather dismal view of American culture, but it also indicated his belief that California was the only place where he saw any hope. Critics do not now regard *The Air-Conditioned Nightmare* as one of Miller's great books, but in Los Angeles of the 1950s and '60s it was one of the treasured books of the young disenchanted intellectuals. Miller's philosophy was a curious combination of apolitical anarchism and resolute devotion to joy and happiness. His zest for life was expressed in his style, no matter how negative his intellectual perception of things.

Miller arrived in Hollywood in 1941 and began his early drafts of the book during his stay at the Gilbert Hotel, a seedy fleabag that is still there. He wasn't happy during his Hollywood stay, and he ended up going back to New York to finish the manuscript. But it wasn't long before he left New York forever to return to California. Here he discovered Steinbeck's biologist friend in Northern California, Ed Ricketts. In Southern California he met the famous British author Aldous Huxley and had as close friends the not-so-famous artists Margaret and Gilbert Nieman, who lived in a rundown place on Bunker Hill. Miller liked visiting the Niemans, from whose porch he swore downtown L.A. looked like Paris — at least at night. Miller also used to hang out with the artist Man Ray in the Villa Elaine apartment house across the street from where the Hollywood Ranch Market stood on Vine Street for years.

When Miller returned to California for good, he lived for a while in L.A.'s Beverly Glen Canyon. Then he moved up to Big Sur, where he lived for some years. In the early '60s he returned to the Southland, purchased a house in Pacific Palisades, and spent the last two decades of his life there, writing books that were mostly published by Capra Press, a smaller press in Santa Barbara.

Although Miller lived in L.A. a long time, it must be admitted that much of his important work was done in the first part of his life. *The Air-Conditioned*

Nightmare represented a bridge, and in the chronicle of his drive westward we are getting more than a simple travelogue.

The most interesting person he met in those travels was an old desert rat from the Barstow area. The desert rat talked a lot about automobiles, which he said were not only senseless killers, but had changed the country — in some ways for the better, but mostly for the worse. The desert rat talked about living in the desert with the stars and the rocks, "wondering about creation and that sort of thing." He uttered words that Miller obviously regarded as prophetic in 1941. "I figure," he said, "that when we get too close to the secret, nature has a way of getting rid of us." Miller anticipated a lot of '60s consciousness when he wrote about the Indians of the desert, whose life he contrasted favorably with the mundane, commercial, trivial and brutal culture of white America.

In Barstow it was too hot to go on right away. Miller discovered, however, that he couldn't just linger in a restaurant without ordering food or beverage, which had been his habit in Paris. So, realizing that it was Mother's Day, he went to the railway station to send his mother a telegram. That completed, he sat under a tree at the railway station that he had seen in 1913 when he made his brief visit to the Southland. That was the time he ended up in Chula Vista, "burning brush all day in a broiling sun," and in San Diego hearing a speech by Emma Goldman. It was a speech that changed his life, he said. He also spent time during his 1913 visit looking for a job as a cowboy on a cattle ranch in the San Pedro area.

By the time he got to Burbank, these memories of Southern California not long after the turn of the century had been doused. "I tried to summon a feeling of devotion in memory of Luther Burbank, but the traffic was too thick, and there was no parking place. Perhaps they had named it after another Burbank, the king of soda water or popcorn or laminated valves." (Actually, Burbank was named after a dentist who was one of the city's founding fathers.)

The first night in Hollywood, Miller ended up at a millionaire's party. He didn't like the assortment of businessmen, aged strike-breakers, football players, and flag wavers he met there. One drunken, garrulous lout especially annoyed him. The lout asked Miller how he liked California. So Miller went on and on explaining that this wasn't his first visit to the Golden State. He said that he'd been here once before, doing a stretch at San Quentin for attempted murder. He explained that he hadn't known the revolver was loaded when he took a potshot at his sister and luckily missed her. He complained that the judge hadn't understood the circumstances of the shooting and had sentenced him to prison. As Miller's story got more and more bizarre, the lout got more and more uncomfortable, and finally disappeared. Not much later, Miller was walking north on Cahuenga Boulevard toward the hills, "looking up at the stars when a car came up behind me and ran into a lamppost. Everyone was killed. I walked on 'irregardless,' as they say."

Interesting to ponder is the encounter between L.A. and Jack Kerouac, who was the very soul of the restless wanderer in the 1950s. Kerouac was known as the King of the Beats, although it was not a title he had sought out and, in fact, he tried to reject it. Restlessness was a hallmark of such California writers as Jack London, Mark Twain and Robinson Jeffers. But usually they came to terms with their wanderlust and found a piece of the planet with which to identify at the end. Kerouac never did. He was the eternal wanderer.

The most clear-cut influence on Kerouac was California's own Jack London, who wrote a book of hoboing experiences called *The Road*. The book that made Kerouac famous was *On The Road*, published in 1951. In *Lonesome Traveler*, which appeared in 1961, Kerouac was still writing about wandering. *Lonesome Traveler* begins with a description of Kerouac coming into Los Angeles on a freight train in 1951, and *The Dharma Bums*, published in 1958, with Kerouac riding a freight train away from Los Angeles. In both cases he was riding the "Zipper" — the fast Southern Pacific night freight — but one was southbound and the other northbound. Although he was cold, riding as a hobo in an open car, Kerouac felt a tremendous sense of aliveness and even health as the Zipper flew past Santa Barbara, past Surf, and onward to Guadalupe and Oceano. In *Lonesome Traveler*, Kerouac was riding in the Zipper's heated caboose, legally, because he had worked as a brakeman in the Southern Pacific's Texas division; but he was suffering from a virus. As he headed toward L.A. he was so miserable that he was unable to "appreciate a good ride" as the train "flashed past the snowy breaking surf caps at Surf and Tangair and Gaviota on the division that runs the moony rail between San Luis Obispo and Santa Barbara."

When Kerouac arrived in downtown Los Angeles in *Lonesome Traveler*, he checked himself into a hotel on Main Street and treated himself nicely by taking "bourbon lemon juice and Anacin" for twenty-four hours and looking out the window at the "hot sunny streets of L.A. Christmas." After a while he bestirred himself and checked out the pool halls and shoeshine places on Skid Row, just to kill time. He was due to go down to the L.A. harbor at San Pedro, to meet his friend Deni, who was due in on the S.S. *Roamer*. (It is probably not coincidence that Jack London owned a boat called *The Roamer*.) Deni had promised Kerouac he could get him a job on the S.S. *Roamer*, and on the strength of that, Kerouac had come across the country to Los Angeles for this evening.

It was Christmas night, 1951, in San Pedro. The *Roamer* came in and

Deni got off. Deni first wanted to go up to Hollywood and see the stars and have some fun. "After a fast hike of about twenty minutes along those dreary refineries and waterskeel slaphouse stop holes, under impossible skies laden I suppose with stars but you could just see their dirty blur in the Southern California Christmas," Kerouac and Deni arrived at the Red Car tracks, where they would be whisked up to Hollywood.

First, however, Deni wanted to go into the hotel in downtown San Pedro across from the Red Car stop. "Someone was supposed to meet us with the blonds," Deni told Kerouac. "The hotel had potted palms and potted bar-fronts and cars parked, and everything dead and windless with the dead California sad windless smokesmog," Kerouac noted. Kerouac's further descriptions of the hotel indicated that the vacuous young men and women of today's glitter generation were with us even then. So were the "hotrod champion sons of aircraft computators of Long Beach, the whole general and really dismal California culture."

They decided to look for a quick beer. Deni warned Kerouac to avoid places with lots of Mexicans: "They're *pachucos*, they just like to beat up on people for the hell of it." Kerouac replied that when he was in Mexico it didn't seem to him that the Mexicans were that way. Deni agreed that Mexicans were different in Mexico, but somehow turned it around so he was accusing Kerouac of being the kind of person who worried about the starving multitudes of Europe.

Then Deni realized they had better catch the last Red Car if they were going to see the "glitters of Los Angeles if possible or Hollywood before all the bars closed." The last train, however, had just pulled out. Deni insisted on hiring a taxi to catch up with it, but the taxi driver wasn't fast enough. The Red Car clipped along at over sixty miles per hour "toward Compton and the environs of L.A." and also seemed to tow the reader on into the next chapter and yet another installment of the Kerouac cosmos.

Deni — predictably enough — had no job for Kerouac aboard the *Roamer*. And no money to lend Kerouac. As the *Roamer* pulled out of San Pedro harbor, Kerouac watched it go and didn't seem terribly sad at its departure without him. For suddenly he had a strong vision of the *Roamer* as a floating metal prison. He shrugged and headed down Mexico way.

Kerouac's view of L.A. was obviously that of someone just passing through. But there is something of the "just passing through" quality in Steinbeck's and even Miller's encounters with the place. Perhaps there was a kind of synergistic relationship between L.A. and writers; the combination of restless authors an ever-changing, transitory town helped produce a new vision in American literature.

Down And Out At The Brown Derby

Malcolm Lowry
Late of the Bowery
His prose was flowery
And often glowery
He lived, nightly, and drank daily
And died playing the ukulele.

(Malcolm Lowry's self-composed epitaph)

The eruptions of Mount St. Helens a decade ago or so reminded me of a terrifying, powerful book called *Under the Volcano*. Malcolm Lowry's masterpiece is a nightmarish, hallucinogenic vision of a man's descent into purgatory. The book's main character is a self-destructive drunk in Cuernavaca, Mexico, who is flung into the abyss, literally under the volcano Popocatepetl.

Lowry's protagonist — a figure who is almost entirely autobiographical — is called simply "the Consul." The Consul had been serving as a British diplomat in Cuernavaca, but by the Day of the Dead in 1939, England had broken off relations with Mexico. The inevitability of the coming World War pervades the book, and the story is not only of one man drinking himself to death: it is about a whole world plunging into the abyss.

Malcolm Lowry lived in Los Angeles during that fateful year of 1939. And while most of the action was written in Vancouver, Canada, and the action takes place in Mexico, there is a strong Los Angeles connection in *Under the Volcano*.

When Lowry died in his native England in 1957 at forty-eight years of age, little of his work had been published since *Under the Volcano* in 1947. *Dark As the Grave Wherein My Friend is Laid* is a thinly fictionalized version of a trip Lowry took from Canada back to Mexico in the last days of the Second World War. Lowry's alter ego in *Dark As the Grave* is taking his wife Priscilla back to Cuernavaca. (Priscilla's real-life model was Margerie Bonner, Lowry's second wife, whom he met in 1938 during his longest stay in Los Angeles, where he landed after being ejected by the Mexican authorities on his first visit.)

During a longish stopover at the Los Angeles airport in *Dark As the Grave* we find the Lowry alter ego thinking about Los Angeles, and his thoughts are not flattering. He thinks of the "barren deathscape of Los Angeles, and yet it was in this hell they met." He's impressed by how Los Angeles has changed through the war years, while he has been away in Canada with Priscilla. Other cities had big new airports, but "it was that the mode of travel on this great new scale was new itself, and no airport could have absolutely expressed this newness better than Los Angeles, than this huge gray-sounding place with its tremendous sense of junction, to north, east and west."

At another point in his musings, the Lowry figure admits to having hated Los Angeles "so violently" that on occasion "all he could think was that it was a hell, the sort of hell his spirit would have wandered to had he killed himself." To Lowry, L.A. was a junction between heaven and hell — although more hell than heaven.

Lowry was at his greatest, of course, in writing about hell, since his life was lived in one. To UCLA English professor Richard K. Cross, whose *Malcolm Lowry: A Preface to His Fiction* had been published by the University of Chicago Press, "Lowry saw Los Angeles as the dissolving edge of civilization. He did not like Los Angeles."

Cross says that Lowry, whose reputation has been growing since his death, wrote one of the eight or perhaps ten best novels of the century in *Under the Volcano*. Cross says that Lowry's book puts him on a level with such twentieth-century masters as Thomas Mann, James Joyce, Joseph Conrad, and Franz Kafka. "Lowry was an important writer," Cross told me, "who just couldn't do it again."

Lowry was born in Cheshire, England, in 1909. His father was a prosperous international trader, but Lowry felt more identity with his Norwegian sea-captain grandfather on his mother's side. The books of Jack London inspired Lowry to join the merchant marine as a young man. He was driven to his ship's side in a Rolls Royce limousine, which of course made it difficult for him to be accepted by the other seamen. Lowry recorded these adventures in his first novel, *Ultramarine*, which was published in London in 1933. The book had an indifferent success. The rest of his life, Lowry labored in obscurity, except for the brief flurry of attention that came his way because of *Under the Volcano*, the only other book of his to be published in his lifetime.

He gained a reputation as a genius and a drunk early on, especially among his peers at Cambridge. Nearly everyone who came into contact with this short, barrel-chested man — a man who couldn't find his way in a city, who was given to constant mishaps and misadventures — sensed that they were in the presence of genius.

Lowry met his first wife Jan Gabrial in Paris in 1933, in the home of his mentor, the writer Conrad Aiken. Like the second wife he was later to find in Los Angeles, the first was an American. But Gabrial was not at all like the faithful and adoring Margerie, who helped her helpless husband function. Rather, Gabrial complained about the poverty of their life, and wondered why they were poor if everyone was convinced that Lowry was such a genius. It was a stormy marriage from the beginning. Lowry kept drinking, and Gabrial left for days and even weeks on trips with other lovers, which only drove Lowry to more drinking. Jan obviously became the "bad" part of Yvonne, the Consul's former wife in *Under the Volcano*, who came back to Mexico to save her husband but also makes love with Hugh, the Consul's communist half-brother, and M. Laruelle, a friend of the Consul and a washed-up filmmaker.

Much of what is known about Jan Gabrial came from Aiken, who said she had a "strong social conscience" but was, on the whole, a rotten woman. Aiken, however, was hardly an objective third party — he too had been her lover, and in *Ushant* portrayed her as the lover of both men. It fell to an old Cambridge buddy of Lowry's, the critic John Davenport, to tell Lowry that Gabrial was involved with a lot of old writer friends. (Davenport, incidentally, was the one who went to Los Angeles and convinced Lowry he ought to go there too. But that was later.) "Malc simply couldn't cope with a woman like Jan," Davenport said. "His deep sense of sexual inadequacy — a characteristic of the Consul too — probably stems from the situation with Jan."

Finally she left Lowry in Paris and went back to her native New York. But Lowry, who seemed really to love her, soon followed. Perhaps Lowry would inevitably have come to the New World, in any event. His biggest loves, after drink, were jazz (he played the ukulele, as his epitaph noted, and had even published some songs in London) and Herman Melville.

Had other things been equal, Melville alone might have attracted him to the New World. Melville and Lowry not only labored in obscurity to produce one great masterpiece, but both attached great symbolic importance to things: in Lowry's case it was a volcano, in Melville's a whale.

Lowry successfully reunited with Gabrial in New York, but he also was treated in Bellevue for his worsening alcoholism. After Bellevue, they decided to make a new start elsewhere — so they took a bus to Los Angeles.

At the same time Lowry's old friend Davenport was going to Los Angeles by train to take a studio writing assignment. Davenport left telegrams scattered across the country at strategic bus stops, telling Malcolm and Jan they could stay with him when they got to Los Angeles — which they did, for a couple of months.

Lowry's ending up in Los Angeles was not as unexpected as it might have seemed. *Under the Volcano* has been called the most cinematic novel ever written. Lowry was fascinated by films, and badly wanted to work in Hollywood, according to Davenport. But there was no work in 1936. Years later Margerie would insist that Malcolm had indeed worked on a number of scripts during his first stay in Los Angeles, but was unhappy with the mediocrity that was expected, and abhorred team-writing. Davenport said that the only work he knew of Lowry doing was work he himself gave to Lowry. So perhaps it was economics that drove Malcolm and Jan to leave San Pedro and arrive in Acapulco on the Day of the Dead in 1936. Living was cheaper in Mexico than in Los Angeles, which mean that father Arthur O. Lowry's dole would go a little further there.

Whatever the circumstances of Lowry's first departure from Los Angeles, his going to Mexico proved to be fateful for him. "Like Columbus I have torn through one reality and discovered another," Lowry wrote in a letter to a friend toward the end of his infamous two-year stay in Cuernavaca, under Popocatepetl and its twin volcano far to the east, Ixtacihuatl. As Professor Cross says in his book on Lowry, "It was by no means the last of Lowry's perilous voyages, but it was undoubtedly the most decisive, as crucial for him as the journey up the Congo had been for Conrad."

Malcolm and Jan were undoubtedly attracted to Cuernavaca partly because there were lots of foreigners there already, and many were literary types. But another attraction had to be the abundance of tequila and mescal. A Lowry biographer described Cuernavaca as both a "drunkard's paradise and hell." After two years there, Jan was gone, and Lowry himself was not-so-gently escorted from the country — although it's not clear if he was officially deported, since he made a second trip back after the war, with equally disastrous results.

Although Lowry saw Mexico as an "age-old arena of racial and political conflicts," and even mentioned how the great California Bohemian writer Ambrose Bierce found his death there, the Mexico Lowry wrote about was as much his own "inner landscape" as an objective reality. Alcohol undoubtedly added to his paranoid visions. Still, the reality of Mexico then was that it had a leftist president named Cardenas who had kicked out the foreign oil corporations and was trying to help the poor, while at the same time the military and police were being infiltrated by Nazi agents from Germany who sought a means of threatening the United States.

Plainly Lowry was finding echoes of the Spanish Civil War in Mexican politics of the time as well. Lowry had lost some of his friends from Cambridge, who had fought with the Loyalists in Spain against Franco. It was not just coincidence that at the end of the Day of the Dead in *Under the Volcano*, the Consul is killed by the local military police because they think he is a Jew, a communist, and a spy. He is, of course, none of these things.

It was obvious later to various of his friends who saw Lowry in Mexico that he was living the life of his Consul. Jan disappeared with her lovers for days on end, and finally she just packed up and went back to Los Angeles. Meanwhile Lowry was drinking — once he drank for twenty-four hours a day for three days and two nights without sleeping. Yet somehow he also got a start on the manuscript of *Under the Volcano*, and had a forty-thousand-word manuscript completed before he returned to Los Angeles in July, 1938. In his alcoholic perambulations, however, the first draft was lost before he got back to L.A. (Lowry would lose more than one manuscript in his life through various and sundry mishaps — indeed he would eventually lose his life through mishap. The original draft of his first novel, *Ultramarine*, had been lost by an editor, so he had to recreate it in a hurry, and was never happy with the result. In fact, Lowry barely recovered one of the last drafts of *Under the Volcano*, which was finally published in 1947, from a fire which destroyed his home.)

Aiken was one of those who saw Lowry in Mexico, and he noted Jan's cold indifference to Lowry's plight in *Ushant*. Lowry, said Aiken, was becoming less and less the lighthearted mystic and more and more a fanatic one. He was obsessed with cabalistic structure, and his novel is clearly built around the cabalistic tree of life. He kept his trousers up with a necktie knotted around his waist; his face was becoming red and rounder. Toward the end of his stay in Mexico, Lowry was forever being thrown into dingy jails in the interior in order to dry out, only to be released to drag himself to the closest cantina to order his beloved, hallucinogenic mescal.

Finally the Mexican authorities decided to get him out of the country. At one point, as he was being held in prison before his deportation, he was asked by prison authorities who he was, and the answer he got became a famous line in *Under the Volcano*. "You say you are a wrider," Lowry quoted the authorities as saying to him, "but we read all your wridings and dey don't make sense. You no wrider, you an espider, and we shoota de espiders in Mexico." Lowry said he took the word espider to mean spy.

Toward the end of his stay Lowry wrote his father, trying to make the worse appear the better. "We had a good deal of bother lately," he wrote in a cheerfully vague manner, "what with our house being robbed and leaving Mexico...so we decided each to get jobs, Jan going to Los Angeles for a bit, I on assignment here of an innocent nature." His "assignment" was his drinking himself to death, of course.

Arthur Lowry's lawyers took charge. Malcolm was put on a train in Mexico City by his father's agents and changed trains at Nogales, Arizona, for Los Angeles. He was met on his arrival in L.A. by his father's attorney here, Benjamin Parks, and immediate taken to the Hotel Normandie near Wilshire Boulevard. He was declared an incompetent by the State of California. Parks paid his hotel bill and gave him a tiny bit of money for food and cigarettes.

At the same time, Jan accepted a "sizeable cash settlement" in lieu of divorce alimony, according to Douglas Day in his biography *Malcolm Lowry*. She took the money and ran, with a lover, to Santa Barbara. But she turned up in Lowry's life a few more times before disappearing from view forever. Once she wrote a letter to Lowry, after he had moved to Canada with Margerie, saying she'd like to get together for old times' sake. Lowry tore up her letter and never answered it. She also wrote a thinly-veiled fictional account of what had happened in Mexico; it was published and apparently hit home with Lowry, who was depressed by it.

But that was all later. For the moment, Lowry had settled down to writing at the Hotel Normandie — writing poems about Mexico, and possibly working on a new draft of *Under the Volcano*. A woman down the hall was said to be typing the new version. It has long been a mystery just when and where Lowry began this second draft, which is really the first extant draft of *Under the Volcano* and was finished in Canada in 1941. "No one really knows," says Professor Cross, "where it was begun. It's anybody's guess."

What is known for sure is that he was lonely most of the year he spent in Los Angeles. His old English friends Davenport and Arthur Calder-Marshall had left Hollywood. He wrote long letters to people around the world. To Nordahl Grieg, the Norwegian novelist who was almost as much a mentor as Aiken, he wrote from the Hotel Normandie: "I have been married, lost my wife, and been importuned by fascists. I had a terrible sojourn in Mexico. I am but a skeleton — thank God — of my former self." To Aiken he wrote that Jan had left him a sort of Lear of the Sierras, dying by the glass in the Brown Derby, in Hollywood. "I don't blame her, I was better off in the Brown Derby."

One of his only friends during that period was another tenant of the Hotel Normandie, one Jack King. It was King who changed Lowry's life by introducing him to Margerie Bonner, of whom Lowry would later say that he "had unlocked her from the prison of Los Angeles."

Margerie Bonner was a true child of Hollywood — her mother brought her and her sister Priscilla to Tinseltown from Michigan. Priscilla was just starting to play starring film roles (opposite comedian Harry Langdon, for example) when her eyes were blinded by klieg lights, cutting short her career. Margerie then began to find some success in playing young horsewoman roles in westerns, and when she was not working as an actress, she was churning out scripts either for radio or for Disney cartoons. She also had some of her detective novels published. So she was indeed a professional writer.

There's long been a raging debate, however, over how much of *Under the Volcano* she wrote. She certainly rewrote and edited Lowry's later works, which were issued after his death. At one point in Canada Malcolm wrote

Priscilla a letter describing how "we" are working on a book — the book he was referring to was *Under the Volcano*.

Both Margerie and Priscilla lived in Beverly Hills. At seventy-five Margerie Lowry had a severe stroke, which left her unable to talk. Priscilla says, with regard to her sister's feelings for Lowry, "I think she blocked out the horrors and kept the good parts. There's been a great deal said about his drunkenness, but there were long periods, especially when they lived in Vancouver, when he was industrious and sober. Those were the happiest years of her life."

Priscilla said that Lowry's friend at the hotel, Jack King, a salesman for a pharmaceutical house, had known Lowry from China during the latter's sailing days. One day he called Margerie, who was a friend, and announced that he could recommend this gentleman most highly, he was an Englishman and so forth, would she have dinner with him?

According to King, as reported in the biography *Malcolm Lowry*, it was a case of love at first sight. Malcolm called Margerie on the phone first, and they agreed to meet at the corner of Western and Hollywood. Lowry took a bus to the meeting. King was a few seconds late. By the time he arrived, they were embracing — and still embracing several moments later.

Two weeks later, in what was surely not a coincidence, Lowry was ushered from the Hotel Normandie by attorney Parks, no doubt on Arthur Lowry's insistence. Parks told Lowry he had to get ready to leave Los Angeles right away, that he had to go to Canada to renew his visa. He wouldn't even allow Lowry to go down the hall to the typist who was working on *Under the Volcano*, although he promised that he would fetch it and mail it to Lowry, which he did. Lowry's biographer, Day, says that Lowry really didn't have to go to Canada — most likely the senior Lowry was unhappy at the money he had to settle on Jan Gabrial, and wasn't anxious to have his son become involved again.

Margerie was in Lowry's room when Parks arrived. As Lowry was driven away from the hotel, he hung out the rear window of Park's car, yelling to her that he would be back. And he did try.

After a few days in Vancouver, Canada, Lowry boarded a bus headed back to Los Angeles. A poem about that experience — admittedly not a good one, Lowry said — can be found in *Dark As the Grave*:

> *A singing smell of tar, of the highway,*
> *Fills the gray Vancouver Bus Terminal*
> *Crowned by dreaming names, Portland*
> *New Orleans,*
> *Spokane, Chicago — and Los Angeles!*
> *City of the angels and my luck —*

The trip back to Los Angeles was another typical Lowry misadventure. He got drunk, and when he got to Blaine, Washington, the immigration authorities turned him back. After that, Lowry started to go into a rapid decline. But Margerie quit her job as secretary to Penny Singleton, Hollywood's "Blondie," and was with him within a month of his leaving the Hotel Normandie.

Lowry was not an easy person to live with — he had frequent rages, black moods, childish tantrums, and later, when he went back to serious boozing, he became violent and threatening. Because of his experience with Jan Gabrial, he would never fully trust even Margerie.

At first Lowry hated Canada; he wanted to take Margerie back to Los Angeles. "Margerie is American, helpless and utterly without money," he complained in a letter to Aiken, "and were she deported to Hollywood she would have nothing to live on, and moreover she would be, for many reasons, in an untenable position and also could not stand being without me." But they persevered in Vancouver — they found an uninsulated, poorly heated squatter's shack in the country outside of Vancouver. The nearest bar was ten miles away.

By 1941, the "second draft" of *Under the Volcano* was completed and was, in turn, rejected by a host of publishers. Lowry went back to improving it, and by 1946, he found both an English and an American publisher. Critics compared Lowry to James Joyce and Thomas Wolfe when the book was published the following year. He even made the cover of the *Saturday Review*. Lowry responded to the adulation by drinking more.

The book sold thirty thousand copies, which was good but not stupendous. The last ten years of his life became more and more difficult — at one point Margerie had a nervous breakdown. Still, she stuck by him, even after a doctor warned her that if she didn't leave him he would kill her, much as the Consul kills Yvonne in *Under the Volcano*.

During his last days in England, Lowry dreamed of going back to Canada, which had begun to claim him as its greatest writer. There had been good times in Canada for both the Lowrys. Once in Vancouver, for instance, there was a telling meeting between Lowry and his old friend, the great Welsh poet Dylan Thomas. "How is ruddy old Malc?" Thomas had asked before the meeting. Then when they met it was a simple warm clasping of hands. "Hullo Dylan," Malcolm said, and Thomas replied the same shy way. Not much later, of course, Thomas would die from his alcoholism, just as Lowry would. The poet and the novelist were men who lived under the same volcano, but nonetheless were possessed of an incredible creative ferment. Perhaps it was the combination of the transcendent qualities of mystical inebriation and their natively outsized talents that produced the great works of each.

Both were hopeless drunks — in Lowry's case not even the love of

Margerie could save him. He went through apomorphine aversion treatment in London before the doctors simply gave up on him. He was locked in a tiny cell illuminated only by a red bulb, given injections of apomorphine, and allowed all the alcohol he wanted to drink. The combination produced nausea and vomiting, and supposedly builds a conditioned response against ever drinking again. Most patients can't survive five days of this torture, but Lowry was going strong after twenty days. And within forty-eight hours of his release, he was back drinking in a pub.

After his death in 1957, Margerie worked to complete his manuscripts, although much of the paradise part of Lowry's intended *Divine Comedy* was lost in a fire that destroyed their Canadian shack — the same fire that almost consumed *Under the Volcano*. She never remarried. "She would have never remarried," her sister told me, "for she was married to Malcolm for eternity, at least as far as she was concerned."

Just how much of *Under the Volcano* is L.A.? If you were counting even only Margerie, the answer would be quite a bit. But another big ingredient was Hollywood, for despite his disdain for Tinseltown, *Under the Volcano* was more influenced by cinema than any single novel. In Vancouver, the Lowrys had worked on a movie script of Fitzgerald's *Tender is the Night*, with the hope that it might be used by MGM. It wasn't used, but it is said to be a brilliant script.

A more direct line to Los Angeles was the influence on *Under the Volcano* of Russian filmmaker Sergei Eisenstein's "Thunder Over Mexico". That film was the result of Charlie Chaplin's introduction of Eisenstein, who was then looking for work in Hollywood, to Upton Sinclair, who agreed to produce the movie. *Under the Volcano* obviously owes a great debt to *Thunder Over Mexico*, particularly the powerful imagery of the Day of the Dead.

There are scenes toward the end of *Under the Volcano* in which Yvonne remembers her early days as a starlet in Hollywood. She attempts a comeback after being a child star. "She received promises, and that was all. In the end she walked down Virgil Avenue or Mariposa beneath the dusty dead shallow-plant palms of the dark and accursed City of the Angels without even the consolation that her tragedy was no less valid for being so stale."

No, Lowry knew something about Los Angeles in the late '30s, something that may not have been all pretty, something that may have been his own private hell as much as it was the real city, but still something real. Although Lowry hated Los Angeles, it was inevitable that he come to Los Angeles, as inevitable as everything in the Consul's life. Death was the bottom of the cabalistic down-cycle that had to come before life. The plunge into darkness taken by both the Consul and the world in 1939 is best summed up in the last words of *Under the Volcano*. They are: "Somebody threw a dead dog after him down the ravine."

The Day Of The Locust

On a hot summer day, if you walk up the steep incline on Ivar Street just north of Yucca, it might seem as if nothing much has changed since Nathanael West sat in a dingy room in the Parva-Sed Apta apartment hotel in 1935 and began writing the greatest Hollywood novel of them all — *The Day of the Locust.*

The Parva-Sed Apta

The automobiles look different, of course, and a couple of places that are on the hill now obviously weren't there during the middle of the Depression.

But the Parva-Sed Apta, which translates from the Latin as "small but suitable," probably doesn't look very different now than it did then — at least from the outside. A cross between Tudor and Black Forest cottage, it has an important-looking though shabby facade. "Parva-Sed Apta" is emblazoned on the door glass, complete with the hyphen, which was a common affectation of the '20s.

The Parva-Sed Apta was the oldest building on the hill, even older than the Alto Nido, which sprawls on the hilltop above it. There's still a remnant of all the stained glass that was in the building when West lived there. The glass is believed to have come from an old church when the building was built in 1923.

Once you get past the lobby, the building looks like any other shabby Hollywood rooming house. West put it this way in *The Day of the Locust*: "Another name for Ivar Street was Lysol Alley." And in case that doesn't make the point, he explains: "The rent was high because it included police protection, a service for which he (West's protagonist) had no need."

West used the inhabitants of the Parva-Sed Apta as models for many of the characters in *The Day of the Locust*, although his physical description of the San Bernardino Arms is modeled on another nearby building. The movie version of *The Day of the Locust* used one of the fancy buildings over on Rossmore.

Today you will find many of the same kinds of people living at the Parva-Sed Apta as were there in the mid-30s. James Udall Sr., the Westwood estate agent who was the building's leasing agent when West lived there, says he remembers most of the inhabitants as "clerks" and so forth. But how many self-proclaimed writers and actors and musicians admit these kinds of aspirations to landlords? The building's owner, Dr. Frank Pierce, who has had it in his family since the early '30s, suggests that it certainly has had its ups and downs, as witness the fact that he had to remove much of the stained glass to his own house in Beverly Hills in order to save it from tenants intent on tearing the place apart. But the Parva-Sed's manager, when I went there, was a bright-enough-seeming gent named Michael Leo Michaud, who hands you a business card that announces that he's not a property manager but an assistant cameraman. To listen to him, things at the Parva-Sed haven't changed all that much from the way West said it was, back in the old days.

While Michaud is dealing with what looks like either an eviction or a landlord-tenant controversy of some dire sort, and at the same time keeping tabs on a young woman who looks like she's done a bit of heroin in her time and whom he obviously doesn't want around his building, he explains that most of the inhabitants are "filmmakers." You assume by looking around at the place that they have not yet become successful filmmakers, but suddenly a fellow on the front porch starts talking rather intelligently and knowledgeably about Upton Sinclair and Sergei Eisenstein.

West, no doubt, would have understood Michaud — West was a hotel manager and night clerk himself, in New York, before he got his first job in a Hollywood studio. He came to Hollywood in 1933 for a job writing scripts, on the strength of his sale of *Miss Lonelyhearts* to Twentieth Century-Fox for four thousand dollars, even though the novel itself had sold poorly. He stayed only a few months.

It was when West returned to Hollywood from the East Coast in 1935 that he moved into the Parva-Sed Apta. He said he did it in part because he wanted to live in a genuine Hollywood rooming house so that he could research his next book. In *The Day of the Locust*, West was not writing about the movers and shakers of Hollywood, as his good friend F. Scott Fitzgerald was in *The Last Tycoon*. West was writing about the lower depths, the sea of hopefuls from which the chosen few emerge. Unlike so many writers who came to Hollywood, West was rather good at separating his life's work, writing novels, from his hack work, which was grinding out scenarios, mostly for "B" movies.

Hundreds of novels have been published about Hollywood; one estimate is that there have been at least fifteen hundred titles. Naturally, only a few of these have been very good. Certainly the ranks must include Evelyn Waugh's *The Loved One*, Raymond Chandler's works, *The Last Tycoon*, and perhaps even Budd Schulberg's *What Makes Sammy Run?* But many critics contend that the elusive essence of Hollywood was best captured in West's novel.

To many who are familiar with that vague section of the Los Angeles area called Hollywood, *The Day of the Locust* captures its apocalyptic mood, a mood that doesn't seem to have lessened that much in the last half-century. It isn't just that one is reminded at every corner that the creation of fantasy on celluloid is the primary enterprise here; it is also the fact that so many of the apartment buildings are unreinforced masonry doomed to extinction when the inevitable big earthquake strikes. The orgy/riot climax of West's novel seems metaphorically to pinpoint this madness.

To some, however, it is a book about a Hollywood that no longer exists. One view of how Hollywood has changed comes from Ken Hense, a real-estate appraiser and a keen observer of the Hollywood cultural scene. After seeing the movie and rereading the book he offered the view that back in West's time "there was still a lot of hope as well as innocence" about Hollywood. He suggests that this is no longer as true, that the Hollywood population has gained a substratum that has no aspirations to glamour. That's gone.

Not so for West in that summer of 1935, when he became involved in the lives of the Parva-Sed's tenants, characters he described not as "clerks," but as aspiring actors and actresses, seedy comics, prostitutes, broken-down vaudeville performers, stunt men, technicians, and a particularly repulsive dwarf.

Understand that although a Depression was on, Hollywood was a boom town when West first arrived, almost in the manner of San Francisco during the Gold Rush. The early '30s were especially good for writers, because talkies were still coming in, and there was a big need for scripts. Films were becoming a major industry in the country during the Depression — one of the nation's top ten industries, in fact. And it was an industry centered in Los Angeles.

West had come from an affluent family that was wiped out financially by the Depression. West's sister Laura, however, had married his old college chum, S.J. Perelman. Perelman became not only West's lifelong admirer but also his patron. During West's Parva-Sed days it was only as a result of Perelman's generosity that West was able to survive even in a modest manner. Even if he had been able to get work, it is doubtful he would have been able to do it. He was ill during part of his stay at the Parva-Sed.

For days on end, West didn't leave his room. He felt that he was building up a giant debt to his brother-in-law which he'd never be able to pay, that he was a failure as a writer who'd never get a job. It's understandable that West felt this way; his imagined problems were being compounded by real physical ones. Not only was he suffering from gonorrhea, no doubt obtained from another tenant in the Parva-Sed, but he was also suffering from a flare-up of an old prostate problem. He was in terrible pain, for which the doctor gave him morphine. He was losing weight, and looking more and more like a scarecrow. He couldn't sleep, and could hardly sit on a chair for more than ten minutes.

Some critics have professed to have great insights into *The Day of the Locust*, based on their interpretations of West's sexual nature. But in fact his circumstances were not conducive to a healthy appreciation of sex during that period of his life. He was floating in a sea of characters who somehow seemed to sum up the human condition; they were like characters out of paintings of the damned. *The Day of the Locust* reads like a painting in many ways, and that's not accidental. West was something of an artist himself, and like his protagonist, Tod Hackett, he had been an art student. Moreover, the novel has his strong sense of the surreal, the absurd, the ironic, and the perverse.

For example, West owned a car while he was at the Parva-Sed, and he often lent it to the prostitutes so that it would be easier for them to conduct their business. This tickled West immensely.

It is, of course, no surprise that the language of the madam and prostitute, the aspiring actresses, the race-track enthusiasts, and the out-and-out con artists was so beautifully incorporated into the book.

In *The Day of the Locust*, the whole creative mechanism of Hollywood seemed to be lubricated by dope and sex and other assorted cheap thrills. One day, someone asked West to store a suitcase. He stored it, but several weeks later he became suspicious, opened it, and found it full of marijuana. He disposed of the dope through his underworld connections.

His room at the Parva-Sed was "quite horrid," consisting mainly of a Murphy bed and a kitchenette. The summer heat was tremendous, and sometimes as he lay in bed, West felt as if the whole of Los Angeles were an inferno. Not only was it summertime, but the rim of the sky above the "ugly" but "almost beautiful" Hollywood Hills was filled with smoke. The air rang with the sounds of fire trucks going up and down the canyon. At night, unable to eat or sleep, West watched the glow of the flames complete the picture.

Throughout the book Hackett is working on a painting called "The Burning of Los Angeles."

West was not always on his back dreaming burning nightmares in bed at the Parva-Sed. When West was well, he loved to cruise Hollywood Boulevard and he was a perennial fixture in front of Musso & Frank's Grill, where he would stand chewing a toothpick, assessing the surroundings intently. He was an acclaimed cohort of the many celebrated writers who gathered there, and also next door at Stanley Rose's bookstore, now gone. Those writers may have been in Hollywood only because of movie work, but when they gathered they did not talk movies, they talked literature. Among them were John O'Hara, Erskine Caldwell, William Saroyan, William Faulkner, F. Scott Fitzgerald, and Dashiell Hammett.

In 1936, even though he was working again and had left the Parva-Sed, West still sought sleaze. In his pursuit of the underworld, he became a fixture in the pressrooms downtown. He got to know police-beat reporters and went out on calls with them. He was particularly intrigued by domestic murders, which usually were over money. He enjoyed Filipino dance halls, and he was an inveterate cockfight attender — one of the greatest scenes in *The Day of the Locust* is the cockfight scene in a garage in Beachwood Canyon. West may in fact have attended such a cockfight, but he usually went to Wilmington or even as far away as Pismo Beach, nearly two hundred miles up the coast.

Another Los Angeles phenomenon West found fascinating enough to describe in *The Day of the Locust* was Sister Aimee Semple McPherson's temple (officially called the Angelus Temple, which still overlooks Echo Park Lake; it probably is not merely coincidence that L.A., which has long been known to writers and readers as Lotus Land, houses the nation's biggest lotus collection in Echo Park, a gift from the mystic East, given by Sister McPherson in the '20s). West was also fascinated by Grauman's Chinese Theater and used to go there to watch premieres. The last scene in *The Day of the Locust* occurs at "Kahn's Pleasure Dome," which is, of course, a combination of the pleasure dome in Coleridge's "Kubla Khan" and Grauman's Chinese Theater.

All West ever made from his four books, during his lifetime, was a little more than eight hundred dollars. Yet "it's fair," his biographer, Jay Martin, insists, "to put him in the category of Hemingway and Fitzgerald — perhaps he wasn't as great a writer as Tolstoy or Faulkner or Malcolm Lowry. His was a very condensed kind of writing, directly connected to human psychology, rather than a representation of society, manners or morals."

In a very basic sense, West was out of step with his age, which might well account for the fact that his books didn't sell well until after his death. Like so many during the Depression, West was a Communist sympathizer and even a political activist. He went on to become one of the founders, for instance, of the Screenwriters Guild. But many of his leftist friends were uncomfortable with his unrelieved pessimism. West even tried to please them by putting politics into *The Day of the Locust*. But it just didn't work. The original ending of the book was far more explicit in its politics than the version West finally sent to the printers. In that first version, Tod is taken to his friend's house, where they argue about class warfare. West wanted *The Day of the Locust* to be a Marxist morality play. He wanted to say that proletarian politics offered hope. But he decided against this ending. Ultimately he was saying "Nothing redeems, and there's no promise of redemption," Martin says. Black humor and unmitigated pessimism didn't become popular until the '50s, when the West revival began.

It is clear that West could most certainly be counted as the first Jewish writer in America to achieve entry into the ranks of the nation's great writers, even if Nathan Weinstein did change his name to the oh-so-English-sounding Nathanael West. Martin suggested to me that West's pessimism "probably had its source in his own personal sense of marginality as a Jew and a writer, but the nation was marginal too." His abandonment of his heritage without anything to replace it helped to mold this "complicated, bizarre, eccentric person," as retired UCLA Librarian Lawrence Clark Powell described him. He was uniquely attracted to the bizarre and absurd. He loved the story, which he would constantly retell, of the famous Hollywood mogul who had even hired someone to wipe his behind. More than one critic had noted that although West derided Hollywood as a place for a real writer to be, Hollywood was bound to be the place where West's jaundiced view and taste for the extreme would make the most sense.

West's family had been well-to-do builders and craftsmen in their native Lithuania. Then, like so many other millions of Russian Jews who had fled the Czar's pogroms, they proved quite adept at becoming builders in New

York City. West was never outstanding in school, but by fudging his academic records he went to college and enjoyed the life of the pampered collegian that Fitzgerald wrote about. The Depression, however, began in the late '20s for West's family. The Weinsteins lost nearly everything, and it was only because of the family's remaining business connections that West was able to get a job as a night clerk in a couple of New York hotels. Several of his broke writer friends from Greenwich Village had roofs over their heads only because of West. Dashiell Hammett, for instance, finished *The Maltese Falcon* because West sneaked him into a room. Yet during West's Parva-Sed days, Hammett, who was in a position to help West, lent him a little money but extracted a heavy emotional price for it. Among the writers indebted to West were Quentin Reynolds, Erskine Caldwell, and James T. Farrell.

West helped pay for a private publishing of his first novel, *The Dream Life of Balso Snell*, in 1931. He also rather light-heartedly changed his name for the occasion, inspired in his choice of a new name by the saying "Go West, young man." His *Miss Lonelyhearts* was published in 1933 by the prestigious firm of Boni & Liveright. Unfortunately, the prestigious firm went bankrupt a week before President Roosevelt declared a bank holiday, and the books hardly got into the bookstores. Not that anyone was buying them.

A year later, however, F. Scott Fitzgerald's *The Great Gatsby* was reprinted by Modern Library. In his new introduction for it, Fitzgerald mentioned West as an up-and-coming talent. Later, when West applied for a grant from the Guggenheim Foundation, Fitzgerald, Malcolm Cowley, Edmund Wilson, and George S. Kaufman wrote letters of recommendation. However, the Guggenheim, in its wisdom, declined to sponsor West, although ironically enough, when Jay Martin wrote his biography of West he did it on a Guggenheim grant.

West wrote his third novel, *A Cool Million*, after his first visit to Hollywood in 1933. It didn't do well. He returned to L.A. in 1935 to make a living and write about Hollywood, but it wasn't until the beginning of 1936, after he had moved out of the Parva-Sed Apta, that he took a job. Then he began a modestly successful career as a screenwriter, which lasted the rest of his short life. West was, as was mentioned, pragmatic about screenwriting, and did not regard it as being very much different from hotel night-clerking. The difference was money — $50 a week versus $250, and finally, $350 a week. West worked at Republic Studios in Gower Gulch, off Sunset Boulevard. The studio was mainly known for making films no one ever remembered, and for the most part West's stuff was pretty much like everyone else's there.

During the time West was laid up at the Parva-Sed with his various ailments, another young writer whose first books had achieved critical acclaim but little commercial success, William Faulkner, was also desperate for work in Hollywood, and would have taken a job at fifty dollars a week. Both Faulkner and West made fairly good money later, in the studios; and they went hunting together in the Tulare marshes of the San Joaquin Valley or in the Santa Cruz area. Supposedly both enjoyed a passion for hunting and didn't bother talking about writing during their jaunts.

Fitzgerald and West met again in Hollywood — after the incident with the Guggenheim — and toward the end of both of their lives they became close. In April 1939 West sent Fitzgerald galleys of *The Day of the Locust*, telling him how difficult it had been to write in between "working on westerns and cops and robbers." When the book came out that year, it sold fewer than fifteen hundred copies. It didn't even make back the paltry five-hundred-dollar advance West had been given.

West was not, of course, happy about this, but friends report he was becoming far less pessimistic because of his marriage in 1939 to Eileen McKenney, the "Eileen" of the popular book, *My Sister Eileen*, written by her sister Ruth. The couple purchased a handsome house, then only four years old, that stood until recently at 12706 Magnolia Boulevard in North Hollywood. Fitzgerald lived nearby in Encino with Sheila Graham. The two couples became very friendly, and were frequent visitors in each other's houses. The two men often showed and discussed works in progress.

Yet it was the timing of their two deaths that linked them in a startling way. Fitzgerald suffered his fatal heart attack on December 21, 1940. West and Eileen were on a hunting trip in Mexicali, but they may well have never heard of his death. It was the following day that West, never a terribly attentive driver, plowed into another car at an intersection near El Centro. Eileen died before she got to the hospital, and West died soon afterward.

The newspapers wrote more about her death than his because of the current fame of *My Sister Eileen*. West was described, not as the author of four obscure novels, but as a lowly screen scenarist. A further irony was that the bodies of West and Fitzgerald ended up in the same mortuary in Los Angeles. Later, Fitzgerald's body was shipped to Baltimore, and Sheila Graham left Hollywood to go east on December 26 on the Santa Fe Super Chief. S.J. Perelman was aboard the same train, taking West's body home in a casket.

It was more than a decade before West was rediscovered, and it wasn't until Martin published his *Nathanael West: The Art of His Life* in 1971 that much was known about him. Martin says he suspects that one of the effects of his book was to "diminish the mystery of West's life." Nonetheless, a virtual industry of West criticism has grown up and still prospers in academia. Martin also says West's works are still being discovered in other parts of the world — for instance, West was published in Russia for the first time not long before *glasnost*.

To a limited extent West's work foreshadowed that of such Jewish writers as Philip Roth and Saul Bellow. To a great extent Joseph Heller's *Catch-22* was influenced by West's black humor and sense of the absurd.

When Jay Martin's biography of West appeared in England, such famous British critics as C.P. Snow and Anthony Burgess suggested that West had been a greater writer than either Faulkner or Hemingway. Even if this is hyperbole, it has made me look at the old Parva-Sed Apta with more than a little awe. It's made me look at all those old Hollywood apartment buildings with new respect, because of the tales they could tell, and in the case of the Parva-Sed (with some help from one Nathan Weinstein) did tell.

Faustus In The Palisades

I became obsessed with the twentieth century's most famous musical and literary controversy simply because one afternoon back in the '50s I was hit over the head with a viola case by the son of Germany's greatest living writer.

I was sitting with my mother in the back seat of the family Hillman Minx

Thomas and Katia Mann

going south on Overland Avenue, and we had just cleared the hill on the way down to Venice Boulevard. My father and Michael Mann, son of the

Nobel Prize-winning German author Thomas Mann, were in the front seat. We were on our way to USC, where Michael and my mother were going to give one of the concerts broadcast every Sunday on radio station KFAC.

My mother and Michael had just finished a piano-viola duo tour throughout Europe. Now another, bigger tour was lined up; but all that was about to end. For just as we came off the hill on Overland, Michael turned around, threw the viola case at me, and lunged at my mother with a knife he had been concealing. He cut her right above the eye. Then he jumped out of the car and ran. Later, after a visit to the hospital where my mother needed to be stitched up, Katia Mann — Michael's mother and wife of the writer — called us in West Los Angeles. You have to understand that the Mann presence was perennial in those days. For one thing, Michael spent a lot of time around our house on Pelham Avenue. I remember being awed at the quantities of cheap red wine he consumed many nights, and the earnestness with which he imbibed it; the more he drank, the more he sulked and scowled. I also know that my mother had been reaching the end of her rope with the Mann family, and this latest incident convinced her this was it.

Katia and, I presume, Thomas himself, were anxious to patch things up. Later, in fact, they were afraid my mother was going to sue them for the ruin of the upcoming world tour. My mother said she had no intention of suing; she just didn't want to have anything more to do with the Manns.

Katia began the conversation a little huffily, saying that my mother must have "done something to upset Michael," and added something to the effect that one should never upset a Mann. Katia said that what had happened to my mother was not such a big deal; he used to do that all the time to *her* when he was a child. My mother acidly replied that "a Mann had tried to kill a Menuhin," and she didn't want to have anything more to do with them. When Michael called her many years later to attempt a reconciliation, she again told him she did not wish to renew the friendship.

"That had been the way Katia gave in to the moods and demands of her husband, just as she did with the children," my mother said during a recent phone interview from London, where she now lives and concertizes. "There was this demonic force in Thomas Mann. He seemed to be very gentle and mild on the outside — he was always very courteous with me — but anybody who wrote the things that he wrote was not a gentle, melancholy mess after all."

In my mother's opinion — which, she is the first to admit, is far from objective — Mann was a highly overrated writer, even though some critics have called him the greatest writer of the century and *Doctor Faustus* his greatest work. To my mother, the fact that his books are so pessimistic and offer no hope of optimism invalidates them.

"He was like a Tolstoy, an idealist for the world, victimizing his family into sharing the life he felt was right. He considered himself the champion of freedom, but at home there was a lot of tyranny."

Thomas Mann was the most famous of the many famous refugees from Hitler's Germany who sought out the untroubled blue skies over Los Angeles, so far away from the Holocaust in Europe. Primarily because of the chamber music often played there, our front room on Pelham Avenue was one of the salons where they frequently gathered. It was a small, incestuous world, all these famous names in European literature and music in Los Angeles. Many of the greatest personalities, as well as egos, had come to L.A. to escape Hitler. Some were Jews, of course, but many, like Mann and Stravinsky, were not. Some were quite left-wing; others were conservative. Yet they clung together, mostly in desperation, for they did not sense then that Los Angeles had any great appreciation for their presence.

Among the results of all this were some rancorous arguments as well as warm social scenes. Undoubtedly, the most famous of all the ideological and personal battles to hit the community occurred between Mann and Arnold Schoenberg over the publication of Mann's *Doctor Faustus*. It was a battle with literary, political and musical implications that have not been resolved to this day.

To my mother, however, the ideological battles weren't half so important as the reality of the individuals themselves. She tends to see things on individual rather than grandiose, ideological levels. To her, the whole Mann family reminded her of one of the elder Mann's novels. "No boundaries were set. There was no understanding of any normal, natural relationships," she said. She did not feel comfortable, for example, with Mann's fascination for the "homosexual thing" that was typical of the period in Germany before Hitler. "It was supposed to be a much higher form of love," she said, "than that of the normal bourgeois who married a woman and had children. It was a protest against convention."

Talking of the debate over *Doctor Faustus* between Mann and Schoenberg, she says that she has sadly had to conclude that the exiles were "scarred in a way, damaged by their experience. They all demanded total loyalty from their worshippers. If you talked to them about anything they couldn't explain or that might throw a shadow on any of their ideas, they immediately reacted with the old Nazi idea of 'we're superior and you don't understand us.' I mean Nazi in the sense that one is supposed to accept the word of one who knows best, without any kind of protest. They never understood there was space for all of them. It was idol worship really," she says, adding that she believed the refugees were marked by a "mixture of melancholy, resentment and even a strain of the victimizers."

It is ironic that my mother never actually read *Doctor Faustus*, even though she sometimes saw its creator on a nearly daily basis, because Mann's work addresses itself to the very things she does. She read other of his works, but not *Doctor Faustus*, which, ironically, he was actually working on when she first came in contact with the Manns. She knew, for instance, that Michael Mann, who was a member of the San Francisco Symphony when she first met him, was helping his father with the musical passages in *Doctor Faustus*, and that was a lot of help, for music is what the book is about.

Furthermore, one of the most powerful characters in *Doctor Faustus* is Nepomuk, or Echo, an angelic child who appears in the last pages of the book. When I was reading *Doctor Faustus* and came across Echo I had the odd feeling that I knew the lad. He seemed very familiar — I don't know if it was because Michael Mann's son, Thomas Mann's favorite nephew, was the model for Echo. "You remember Michael's son, who gave me the mumps that time, don't you?" my mother asked. "He was such a nice, quiet boy; today he is a theologian in Germany. I saw him not long ago in Zurich."

I must admit that, on listening to her recount all these things, I could see why I felt at least vicariously involved in the great battle between Schoenberg and Mann over *Doctor Faustus*, which occurred quite literally on our sun-drenched shores in the Pacific Palisades, where Mann lived at 1550 San Remo Drive.

At this point, it would probably be appropriate to mention that *Doctor Faustus* is the "biography of the composer Adrian Leverkuhn, as told by a friend," who is, not so incidentally, a parody Mann wrote on himself. *Doctor Faustus*, however, is much more than just a purported biography (the book is, after all, fiction). *Doctor Faustus* is the story of a nation's descent into the maelstrom of total barbarity — what happened in Germany between her two defeats in World War I and World War II.

Mann tells the story of his beloved nation's descent into bestiality by the parallel story of Leverkuhn, an avant-garde composer who, by the time *Doctor Faustus* was supposedly written, had achieved some degree of sanctification. Leverkuhn was conceived by Mann as the ultimate anti-Beethoven figure. Beethoven, of course, was Germany's greatest artist, the representative of hope, optimism and democracy. Leverkuhn was quite the opposite.

One of the last conversations Leverkuhn has with Zeitblom, the narrator who is supposed to be his friend, reveals the fullness of his misanthropy. He blurts out, "I find that it is not to be."

"What, Adrian, is not to be?" Zeitblom responds.

"The good and noble, what we call the human, although it is good and noble. What human beings have fought for and stormed citadels, what the ecstatic exultantly announced — that is not to be. It will be taken back. I will take it back," replies Leverkuhn, pointing out that these were the things

Beethoven had in mind in his great "Ode to Joy" in the Ninth Symphony.

In its various biographical details, the figure of Leverkuhn was not Mann's neighbor, Arnold Schoenberg, who lived not far away from the Pacific Palisades in Brentwood, at 116 N. Rockingham. Leverkuhn is more like the famed German philosopher Nietzsche, who died after a prolonged period of insanity brought on by syphilis, a disease Beethoven is believed to have suffered from as well. But the musical system that Leverkuhn invents as part of his deal with the devil, the system of musical composition that enables Leverkuhn to make the "artistic breakthrough" composers from the turn of the century were looking for, is almost wholly borrowed from Schoenberg. And this is where things got tricky between the two exiles sequestered on Los Angeles's golden shores.

There could be little doubt that Leverkuhn was the inventor of the same method of "composing with twelve tones" as that of Schoenberg. After all, until Schoenberg, composers hadn't even considered inventing a system of composition in order to make music. Musicality was regarded as something innate; technique was primarily a tool for getting the music down on paper. Schoenberg, however, "constructed" music using a mathematical system of his own devising. From the beginning, the results this system produced were highly controversial. So when Mann had Leverkuhn invent a musical system, there could be little doubt about what system he was talking about.

"If I were Schoenberg with his esoteric musical theory and I sat down to read *Faustus*, I would be a little disturbed, too," declared Steve Willett, a former professor of literature at Northwestern University and a graduate of Los Angeles's own Occidental College. Willett is particularly interested in Mann and German literature, and he has had long conversations on the subject with Erich Heller, regarded as the foremost Mann authority in the world today.

Willett went on to say, "While Schoenberg could say that he and Leverkuhn were not the same, for Mann had indeed written burlesques of specific composers in previous books, I would see some rather serious implications in *Doctor Faustus*. Were I Schoenberg with my twelve-tone system, I wouldn't like at all the esthetics Mann had hooked me into."

Even though most of Schoenberg's increasingly strident objections to *Doctor Faustus* centered on what he called the theft of his intellectual property by Mann, Willett points out that more to the point is what Mann was saying the Leverkuhn-Schoenberg system represented. In fact, Michael Mann himself — who later quit music and became a professor of German at UC Berkeley — said he thought Schoenberg was really upset because ofdthe political and historical implications his father was making.

Leverkuhn, after all, is hardly an attractive character. He is a man literally possessed by purgatory, a sickly man with demonic drives, whose musical system expressed and helped lay the ground for the triumph of the well-ordered barbarism that was Nazism. Leverkuhn's system creates a music that eschews melody and harmony in favor of a "collective polyphony" reminiscent of earlier times: Mann certainly must have been aware that the same sort of criticism had been leveled at Schoenberg's system as well.

Mann stoutly denied that Leverkuhn was Schoenberg, yet he inscribed a copy of *Doctor Faustus* to Schoenberg saying that he was "the real one." Furthermore, although Leverkuhn's life is in a few ways like Schoenberg's, Leverkuhn is one of the strangest characters in twentieth-century letters; in almost no place in the book is he given much of a physical presence. One hardly knows what he looks like; and that is as Mann intended. Leverkuhn was the embodiment of an *idea*, the great anti-Beethoven figure.

It is surely not coincidence that in 1908 Schoenberg set to music some poems by Stefan George as songs for voice and piano. Schoenberg regarded this work as his "breakthrough" — melody and harmony almost completely drowned out by atonality — and he believed that he had finally succeeded in his (and Leverkuhn's) claim of emancipating dissonance with his work. In *Doctor Faustus*, at about the same time in history, Leverkuhn completed his Brentano songs, and called it his "breakthrough" work.

Also, the whole background of Stefan George suggests the brutality of the intellectual satire Mann may have been committing on his neighbors and acquaintances. Stefan George, with whom Schoenberg was so enchanted, died in 1933. He is today regarded as the spiritual father of Nazism. Blood and uniforms, little boys dressed up in Greek robes, diabolical rites; these were among the things that excited this strange man. A lot of his poems were overwritten paeans to the beauty of various young men, for George was a rather flamboyant, decadent, aristocratic type of homosexual, whose poems didn't make much sense except to the Illuminati.

Like Schoenberg — and Leverkuhn — George was a dedicated member of the so-called avant-garde, which was always searching for a "higher order." George was proud and overly sensitive and no doubt felt very misunderstood. His inner vision was not meant for all mankind, as Beethoven and the poet Schiller had intended the "Ode to Joy" to be. George's work was done for an elect few, as was Schoenberg's. Schoenberg felt, in fact, that only his musical peers had a right to pass judgment on his works — and, interestingly enough, Schoenberg's music has continued to draw more enthusiasm in academic circles than among the regular crowd of music lovers.

Schoenberg felt that his music would find wide acceptance a few decades down the line. But this has not happened. What has happened is that he has achieved a kind of sainthood in contemporary music schools. There is a Schoenberg Hall at the University of California, Los Angeles, since he taught there. And there is Schoenberg Institute across town at the University of Southern California. Yet to those who find that his compositions sound more like cacophony than music, it's a mystery why academics get so excited over Schoenberg. Steve Willett points out that the avant-garde has similarly suppressed the traditional narrative structure in literature, just as melody has been dismissed as "too sweet" in academia, where atonality has become the status-quo. "The works which seem to be major landmarks in 20th-century culture," Willett says, "are marked by what the devil gave Leverkuhn; an enthusiasm for evil, madness and mental disorder."

Although this commentary may seem strong, similar language has been used by others who are less than awestruck by Schoenberg. The critic and writer, Louis Untermeyer, was reported to have left a performance of Schoenberg's "Pierrot Lunaire" harumphing, "Moonlight in the sickroom."

Although Schoenberg may have run in circles that provided the intellectual and artistic soil for the Third Reich that was later to emerge from post-World War I Germany and Austria, he himself was not loved by the Nazis. This was because he was born a Jew. He converted to Christianity in his youth, but he later rediscovered his Jewishness when Hitler gave him no choice, and fled Europe, ending up in Los Angeles with the likes of composers Stravinsky and Mario Castelnuevo-Tedesco, the latter who dismissed Schoenberg's work as "composition by slide rule."

Ernest Gold, who came from Schoenberg's native Vienna and now lives in Pacific Palisades himself, told me that he regards Schoenberg as a second-rate talent who couldn't write a *good* melody, and so decided that music should have *no* melody. Gold has written both serious music and successful movie music, including the Oscar-winning score for *Exodus*. "Besides," says Gold, "look at his odd relationship with that Nazi, Hauer."

Joseph Matthias Hauer was a contemporary of Schoenberg's who also claimed to have invented the twelve-tone method. He and Schoenberg tried on more than one occasion to get together for the common cause of atonality. But they would usually fall out, primarily because even in the great cause of their esoteric innovation, Hauer couldn't bring himself to work side by side with a Jew.

Schoenberg was a notorious autocrat. Once when his wife was enjoying a knitting circle with some friends in the kitchen, Schoenberg told the women to stop because they were distracting him, when it would have made more sense for the composer to have moved. But then Mann, apostle of Democracy, needed constant attention to his every whim from his wife Katia, too. "She would have killed the children so he could do his work undisturbed," Yaltah told me, adding that she was sick of the stridency of the old arguments that ran through the refugee community, and sicker yet of all the competing egos.

Katia Mann blamed the flap between her husband and Schoenberg on Alma Mahler-Werfel, who had once been married to the composer Gustav Mahler. Katia said that the former Mrs. Mahler, then remarried to Franz Werfel (author of *The Song of Bernadette*), was malicious, mean and drank too many sweet liqueurs. The Manns and the Werfels were much closer than the Manns and the Schoenbergs. Katia insisted that it was the former Mrs. Mahler who brought to Schoenberg's attention the whole Leverkuhn parallel. Katia wrote in her *Unwritten Memories* that "she gave her former husband Gustav Mahler a very difficult time. She alienated him from all his friends and made him break off with his female admirers. Mahler died young. I think she was rather too much for his nervous system."

In those same memoirs, Katia also makes it clear that she wasn't much fonder of the Schoenbergs. But she was particularly appalled with the Schoenberg offspring, one of whom is now a judge in Beverly Hills. She said they were terribly "ill-behaved."

Katia also tells a fascinating story, during her diatribe against the family, about how Schoenberg died. Her point was that Schoenberg was not only an unpleasant man, but a superstitious man as well. It seems that Schoenberg had long been sure he was going to die on the thirteenth day of the month. On on July 13, 1951, Gertrud Schoenberg sat up with her husband, holding his hand, just as she had done on previous occasions when it was the thirteenth midnight of the month. She was worried about his nervousness because he was seventy-six and suffered from a heart condition. Nonetheless, on this July night it appeared that he had lived through another 13th, so Schoenberg went upstairs to bed while Mrs. Schoenberg, as was her custom, stayed downstairs in the kitchen to make him a hot drink. When she took his drink upstairs he was dead — and the clock downstairs in the bedroom was just turning midnight. She decided that the clock *downstairs* had killed him by being fast. When he had come upstairs by himself and seen it was actually still the 13th and not yet midnight, the shock had killed him on the spot, Gertrud reasoned.

In fairness to Schoenberg — some of whose critics have suggested that his interest in numerology shows that his system was more a system of metaphysics than the science of music he claimed it was — Mann was also fascinated by numerology. How else could he have written *Doctor Faustus?*

Doctor Faustus is not an easy book to read; it supposes a certain knowledge of music. The book has particularly intrigued musicians and musicologists alike, for Mann accomplished an amazing thing. The musical system, and indeed the musical works he created only in words, made such sense to people, it was as if they could hear it. In a very real sense, Schoenberg could be said to have accomplished not so very much more, because his music is still more talked about than listened or played.

If Mann was parodying Schoenberg's intellectual system, he was attracted as well as repelled by it. In a sense, *Doctor Faustus* has an appearance of being "constructed." Mann rarely made up people and events; he almost always took them from real life. More than his powers of imaginative storytelling, Mann's greatness was in his perceptions and his ability to synthesize. Especially in *Doctor Faustus*, he saw where the patterns of culture and history came together. His writing sometimes seemed musical, as if his works had melodies and harmonies, yet he was himself only an amateur pianist. His son was the only real musician in the family.

The controversy among the two exiles did not remain on the lovely, smogless shores of Los Angeles. As the *Saturday Review* noted in 1949, "*Doctor Faustus* has occasioned one of the most notable literary controversies of our time."

Schoenberg complained in a letter to the *Saturday Review* that Mann had stolen his "intellectual property" in order to lend "the hero of his book qualities a hero needs to arouse people's interest." He went on to state that Mann had done this "without my permission and even without my knowledge." Schoenberg then blamed a former acquaintance, a musicologist and philosopher, Theodor Wisengrund-Adorno, who had studied the system. In fact, Schoenberg was right: Mann had consulted Wiesengrund-Adorno at some length in the writing of *Doctor Faustus*.

Schoenberg and Wisengrund-Adorno had had some sort of falling-out; no one was sure just what caused it. However, it was known in L.A.'s exile community during the writing of *Doctor Faustus* that Mann was working on a novel that borrowed heavily from Schoenberg's musical system. In fact, once when Mann and Schoenberg were together at a barbecue at the Werfels', Mann pumped the composer for musical and biographical information.

Schoenberg's letter to the *Saturday Review* further complained that Mann's dedication of *Doctor Faustus* had read, in German, "To A. Schoenberg, the real one." Schoenberg said he took this to mean that Leverkuhn "was an impersonation of myself." He pointed out that he was not a lunatic, "and I have never acquired the disease from which this insanity stems. I consider this an insult." Schoenberg further alleged that when Mann was confronted with evidence indicating that he had borrowed wholesale from his neighbor, he replied, "Oh, does one notice that? Then perhaps Mr. Schoenberg will be angry?"

Mann's reply to Schoenberg in the *Saturday Review* was to say he was "both astonished and grieved." He pointed out that the two had already exchanged letters on the subject, and he thought the composer had been mollified with the note penned at the end of the English edition of *Doctor*

Faustus, which more or less admitted that Schoenberg and not the fictional Leverkuhn was the inventor of the twelve-tone system.

Mann suggested that Schoenberg had never read the book, that he knew it only through "the gossip of meddling scandal-mongers." He argued that he was certainly not trying to steal Schoenberg's system, which everybody knew Schoenberg had invented. Mann then tried to explain what he meant by his inscription to "the real one." He was trying to say to Schoenberg, "Not Leverkuhn is the hero of this musical era; you are its hero." He protested that his respect for Schoenberg was profound, that he thought of Schoenberg as a "bold and uncompromising artist." He stated flatly: "The idea that Adrian Leverkuhn is Schoenberg, that the figure is a portrait of him, is so utterly absurd that I scarcely know what to say about it."

Mann pointed out that, in many details, Leverkuhn's life was closest to Nietzsche's, and to some extent his own. He suggested that Schoenberg should have accepted his book with "a satisfied smile" that "testifies to his tremendous influence on the musical culture of the era" rather than regarding *Doctor Faustus* as a "rape and an insult." Said Mann, with perhaps only a hint of courtly sarcasm: Schoenberg should "rise above the bitterness and suspicion so that he may find peace in the assurance of his greatness and glory."

Perhaps Mann's cordiality was, in part, fully serious. It seemed that the more he protested that he did not want to become Schoenberg's enemy, the more the composer was galled, and rallied his supporters to the fight. After all, they had been friends. Mann had complimented Schoenberg once on what good coffee he made — something very important to the Viennese. And Schoenberg had dedicated a work to Mann. Mann had even given Schoenberg a copy of his *Magic Mountain* with the inscription, "From somebody who also tries to build music — Thomas Mann."

Bombs are falling on a defeated Nazi Germany as *Doctor Faustus* ends, and it is symbolic that Leverkuhn is in an advanced state of syphilitic madness. Schoenberg and Stefan George were in their heyday long before Nazi Germany arose. Yet Mann traces the rise of fascism from their milieu.

Mann's message is not a simplistic one. He is not saying that everything avant-garde was bad. To Schoenberg and others, at the turn of the century in Germany and Austria, it appeared that music had reached a dead end — in fact, not just music, but all of the arts. Wagner had pushed melodies and harmonies to such a point that he had left nothing for composers who followed him. Thus, most of the music after Wagner does seem like parody. Sometimes, as in the compositions of Hindemith, the form became ever more elegant and complex. Mahler struck many people as only a second-rate Wagner. Compared with the works of Beethoven, the first romantic, who emphasized so many rich melodies, music seemed to have little content any more. The new composers were using the old forms and saying nothing new. Much of their music seemed hollow.

What to do? That was the question that concerned artists at the turn of the century and into the Weimar Republic. The avant-garde believed that the solution was to change the form of music, not to find new content. Part of the deal the devil makes with Leverkuhn is this promise: "You will lead the way, you will strike up the march of the future, the lads will swear by your name, who, thanks to your madness will no longer need to be mad."

The Leverkuhn system took music-making away from individual expression and returned it to the tribal polyphony of earlier, more barbaric times. Composers would no longer be able to make music that had their own distinctive melodies and harmonies if Leverkuhn's system triumphed. The clear suggestion was that composing music by his system was a very totalitarian thing. Steve Willett insisted that the whole point of Leverkuhn is that he represents pure expression of feeling, unconscious tribal feeling, untroubled by logic or reason, the peculiarly human qualities that ultimately are our only improvement over the animals on this globe. As Willett said this, however, he pointed out that others might have a different interpretation. "You understand," he said, "you are getting yourself into this vortex, this quicksand of Faustus criticism, which is endless."

The matter was not just of academic interest to me. After all, I had been initiated into this whole matter of *Doctor Faustus*, an incredibly ambitious work that ties culture and history together, with a hit on the head. The critics have been arguing ever since the book was published about just how well Mann connected the two. Certainly the most surprising thing about this most ambitious and profound of 20th-century works is that it was rooted in a saga that unfolded on Los Angeles's golden shores as well as in the musty halls of European culture.

You can see that the work Thomas Mann created here was indeed a major saga in literary and musical history; so was the saga of his battle with his neighbor over it, for it revealed at least part of what Mann was talking about.

The critics have long argued about the effects of Los Angeles on Mann. Usually, musicians fare better in exile than writers. Writers need to read and hear their native language; they need their audiences and their familiar surroundings to write about. Mann, however, was famous enough so that he could try to transcend the lack of this infrastructure in Los Angeles.

Some have said that *Doctor Faustus* turned out all the better for Mann's being in exile in Los Angeles. He was alone and cut off. He worried about his homeland and hated it at the same time. He was not at all comfortable among the natives of Los Angeles, any more than *any* of the exiles were. That's why they clung together so tenaciously. Yet against adversity and ill health (Mann was sixty-six when he came to Los Angeles in 1941), Steve Willett asserts, Mann's German developed a purer, deeper, and perhaps more classical turn, which is part of the reason *Doctor Faustus* is regarded as his masterpiece.

Mann was not himself avant-garde, either in his own art or in his personal taste. *Doctor Faustus* may have been intricate at times, but it had a traditional narrative form. Mann far preferred the late romantics, such as Wagner, to the likes of Schoenberg.

Here is how the seclusion in L.A. might have helped: First of all, the Pacific reminded everyone of the Mediterranean coast. A source of obscenely easy money in the Hollywood dream factories was close by.

Surely if Mann had not come to L.A. and had not had Schoenberg as a neighbor and friend, he would not have written *Doctor Faustus*. And I'm absolutely sure that had Michael not hit me over the head with his viola case, I would never have gotten around to reading Thomas Mann at all, and I might have missed the book that some critics have hailed as the greatest novel of the 20th century. It was written in Los Angeles.

Aldous Huxley's Strange Passage To The West

O nce when a reporter asked Aldous Huxley why he had lived the last third of his life in the Los Angeles area, the great English writer replied he had merely stopped there on his way to India and ended up staying because of "inertia and apathy."

I remember counting myself lucky to be an L.A. resident the day I shook

Aldous Huxley in L.A.

hands with the great man not too long before Huxley's death on November 22, 1963, the same day President John F. Kennedy was assassinated. Upon the same occasion I also met Laura, Huxley's second wife, not realizing, of course, that nearly two decades later, she would again cause me to remember and contemplate the ghost of that tall willowy man, by getting me involved in a strange adventure out in the Mojave Desert.

On the second occasion, when I met only Huxley's widow, I had been told by my uncle, Yehudi Menuhin, to put myself in the good hands of Laura Huxley. Yehudi had played the Bach Chaconne on his fiddle at the December 17, 1963, memorial gathering for Aldous in London. Yehudi had been very close to both Aldous and Laura, and it was because of Yehudi, of course, that I had been privileged to shake Huxley's hand so many years previously.

Yehudi remained on close terms with Laura. Both he and Laura had been prodigy violinists as children. Also, Laura had dedicated her life to carrying out the mystical prescriptions by which her husband wanted ultimately to be remembered. My instructions from my uncle were to put my life in Laura's hands, and she supposedly would mold me according to Huxleyan principles.

It was not just coincidence, I'm sure, that a few weeks before Yehudi entrusted me to the care of Aldous Huxley's widow, Huxley himself had been the topic of a curious discussion. It started early one evening and ran well into the next morning in the Denny's coffee shop on Highway 14, where the Mojave Desert starts, just past the last outpost of Saugus.

Huxley lived in the high desert throughout most of World War II. Although the landscape north of the San Gabriel Mountains is quite different than the city south of the mountain range, both are in Los Angeles County. Usually, one does not think of L.A.'s cultural history as coming from the area north of the L.A. basin, but at the end of World War II Huxley wrote *Ape & Essence*, a novel about L.A. in the year 2018. It was far more grim than his more famous novel, *Brave New World*.

At the Denny's coffee shop on the edge of the Mojave we — my wife Nigey Lennon and I, and Don Van Vliet, best known as the rock-and-roll cult hero Captain Beefheart — talked of many things, finally leading up to a possibly apocryphal Beefheart story about Huxley. We had been discussing drugs, the '60s, and the high desert. Beefheart was talking about how people who live in the desert (where he was reared) are often far more eccentric than those who live on the L.A. side of the San Gabriels.

Once, as a young lad growing up in the desert, Beefheart had a part-time job selling Electrolux vacuum cleaners in Pearblossom, which wasn't very far from Llano and Wrightwood, the desert communities that Huxley lived near. Beefheart explained that it was known that the famous author lived in the desert, so when a tall, gangly customer came into the store where Beefheart was working, Beefheart recognized him immediately.

Van Vliet remembered being impressed by how down-to-earth Huxley was. Huxley explained that his wife Maria (for Huxley's first wife did not die until the mid-'50s) had sent him out to look for a vacuum cleaner. Huxley asked Van Vliet if he could recommend one. Since Beefheart was selling Electroluxes, it was, of course, an Electrolux that Huxley bought. Then they talked a bit, according to Beefheart.

It is quite likely that this was while Huxley was writing *Ape & Essence*, in which case the great author must have been under the spell of some darkly powerful ruminations there in the high desert. During the conversation at Denny's, Beefheart said that Huxley had seemed to him a man who was looking for something, that he was an eccentric among the eccentrics who inhabit the desert. It is no doubt significant that Huxley described L.A. in that gloomy work created on the high desert as "the world's largest oasis," for it was as if he were viewing L.A. from the perspective of the desert.

The first time Huxley saw Los Angeles was on a quick trip through in 1926. At the time, he dismissed the place as hopelessly uncivilized. Six years later, Huxley published his famous *Brave New World*, the first of three utopian novels he would write. *Brave New World* was published in England in 1932, but Huxley's two other utopian novels, *Ape & Essence* and *Island*, were written during his twenty-four years in the Southland.

Although Huxley wrote scores of novels and books of essays, these three books show quite clearly the logic of his life. *Brave New World* was written as the end of his first period, while Huxley established himself as a writer of great intelligence and graceful style. His early works, such as *Crome Yellow* and *Antic Hay*, had a tone of amused bewilderment with the human condition; the release of the writer's pain came in an outrageous, almost scatological, sense of humor. But his disillusionment with technology in *Brave New World* was the last of his good-natured, British works. *Ape & Essence* would mark the end of Huxley's second period, for its pessimism was extreme. It made *Brave New World* (and George Orwell's *1984*), seem like a picnic by comparison.

Aldous was from the most famous literary and scientific family in England. He and his brother, Sir Julian, were grandsons of Thomas Henry Huxley, the famed agnostic and the scientific colleague of Charles Darwin. Yet Aldous began showing a mystical, if not a religious bent, as early as 1936, in his *Eyeless in Gaza*. The next year, Huxley took his first wife Maria and their son Matthew and left Europe. As he became more and more a part of the Southern California landscape — especially after the *Ape & Essence* period — he became more and more mystical, with results that were controversial to his reputation.

Later in life, it was almost as if he were disavowing his past. In the post-

Victorian period in England, Huxley had been one of the bright, cynical, witty, and properly rational young literary figures. But as the drift in world events seemed more and more to point inevitably in the direction of yet another, terrible world war, he became more and more the hopeless pacifist.

Huxley's strengths and weaknesses as a writer came out of his Olympian view of things. Few of Huxley's characters ever seem to hold nine-to-five jobs, or worry about ordinary things like money. They are mostly successful in their careers. Perhaps this was to be expected from a member of such an intellectually elite family. But perhaps some of his aloofness may also have been traceable to his near-blindness. He had lost his eyesight in 1910, at the age of 16, possibly because of inadequate, if not incompetent, medical care in school. He had enormous enthusiasm later in life, especially in California, for such unorthodox medical treatments as homeopathy, as well as the Bates Method, which claimed that eyesight could be improved through exercise, without the use of glasses.

There was always a controversy about how well Huxley could see. His most strident and uncritical admirers told many stories showing that he really could see quite well. Others were less convinced that Huxley had solved his vision problems as well as he thought he had. My own impression was that he was practically blind. Yet one of the reasons he loved the high desert and lived there for much of the Second World War was that he had an incredible eye for detail of flora and fauna. And he was able to drive on back dirt roads in the desert without known mishap. His wide knowledge of nature stood him in good stead during his many hikes and drives in the desert.

His growing mysticism, no doubt, also drew him to the desert. He was partial to the Eastern, as opposed to the Western, religious view of nature. Huxley felt that when man tries to dominate nature, it tolerates the intrusion only for so long before it rebels.

In Europe, Huxley had not been known as a man who had any great attachment to one place. He may have been somewhat fond of Italy, but mostly he liked to travel, and he was a fine travel writer. Still, when Huxley left Europe with his family there was little reason to believe that he might be going for good.

The primary reason for Huxley's visit to the United States was to see Frieda Lawrence in Taos, New Mexico. She was the widow of D.H. Lawrence, and Lawrence and Huxley had been closely allied through different periods of their lives. There was something of the British gentleman in the additional reasons Huxley gave for his visit to America. He said, for instance, that he wanted to find a good college for his son in the United States. He was also interested in the unusual educational and psychological experimentation then going on in the U.S. which was not happening in Europe.

The Huxleys stayed with Frieda in Taos for a few months, while Huxley finished *Ends & Means* there. Although the New Mexico landscape was astonishing and beautiful to Huxley, he said he did not enjoy it. He found the landscape alien and somehow "hostile to man." Huxley was not known to have had that reaction to the Mojave — if he did, it may have been on the subconscious level. Maybe that had something to do with the extreme pessimism of *Ape & Essence*.

The next stop after New Mexico was Los Angeles. Huxley wasn't necessarily planning on staying when he rented an apartment here in 1937. But soon there was a whirl of things to keep him here. For one, there was his good friend from England, Gerald Heard, the mystic. Huxley and Heard hit the lecture circuit together. Huxley also made it clear that he was willing to entertain fantastic offers from Hollywood, which did, in fact, start coming his way.

During his first years in the Southland, Huxley moved around, from West Hollywood to the Pacific Palisades to Beverly Hills. But he fell in with good and entertaining company — people who'd do crazy things, such as having picnics on the bottom of the Los Angeles River or outdoor parties at the Farmer's Market.

Some of his friends and acquaintances included authors Christopher Isherwood and Anita Loos (*Gentlemen Prefer Blondes*), Edwin Hubble, the Mt. Wilson astronomer who was an early proponent of the expanding universe theory, the Great Garbo, and Charlie Chaplin. Upton Sinclair was sometimes part of the circle, and the composer Igor Stravinsky was also very close to Huxley.

Huxley accomplished some good work in the movie studios, for which he was indeed well paid. He adapted such classics as "Pride and Prejudice" and "Jane Eyre." He wrote the script for "Madam Curie." And the movie "A Woman's Vengeance" was made from his own short story, "The Gioconda Smile."

Huxley's relationship to Los Angeles was curious. On the one hand he was appalled by the vacuity on the faces of the natives he saw riding on a department store escalator; on the other hand, he was genuinely attracted by the cheap, fantastic, glimmering lifestyle of the area. He lived for a while in a house in the Pacific Palisades, rented from a man who had painted rather tasteless orgy scenes on the walls, which seemed to amuse Huxley somewhat. He was appalled, however, when he saw his first small towns in the Southland on the drive in from New Mexico. What bothered him was that so few of the towns had monuments or outdoor cafes with terraces.

He discovered that the research library at UCLA was second to none. Former UCLA librarian Lawrence Clark Powell remembered Huxley as a courageous, distinctive, curious, and amiable man, often stopping his labors at the card catalog, to sign an autograph for a student.

In 1939, Huxley published the first of the two novels he wrote that had a Southern California setting. *After Many A Summer Dies the Swan* was a good novel, but that year also saw the publication of some other great California novels, Powell points out — there were *The Grapes of Wrath*, *The Big Sleep*, and *The Day of the Locust*.

After Many A Summer Dies the Swan was modeled on California's then-most famous citizen, newspaper tycoon William Randolph Hearst. You might remember that a young filmmaker-actor named Orson Welles was making his immortal "Citizen Kane", also based on Hearst, that year. The plot revolved around Kane's desire for immortality. The book, of course, was full of satire on Hollywood and included in its scenery a castle like Hearst's San Simeon — only instead of being located in California's midcoastal region, it was set in the San Fernando Valley.

Huxley spent three or four good years on the West Side, near the Pacific Ocean, before moving to the high desert behind the San Gabriel Mountains. Even in those prewar days, there were hints of the smog that was to come to L.A., and part of the reason the Huxleys first thought of living in the

Phil Stern's picture of Huxley's house at Llano

desert was that the air was clean and dry there. They thought this would be good for Huxley's eyesight as well as for Maria's lung problems.

They moved to the Mojave Desert in 1942, to a place on the site of the old utopian colony, Llano del Rio. The heat in the summer was unbearable. Water shortages were regular events. Electricity was far from reliable. The "shack" the Huxleys purchased was constantly being worked on, and was makeshift at best. Huxley's study had a canvas ceiling propped up by a pole, for instance. When Christopher Isherwood came visiting, he remembered Maria Huxley asking him to read by candlelight because if he turned on the electric light, that would start up the noisy gas-engine generator outside.

Perhaps much of the grimness of *Ape & Essence* may have come from the fact that life on the high desert was sometimes too secluded full, too full of the joys of nature. During the war Huxley's royalty checks from England were gone, and gas, tires and spare parts were hard to come by. Eventually he would have to abandon the desert because he was finding more and more of his income in the studios. Certainly no city ever had a more gloomy prophecy created for it than Huxley created for L.A. in that book written primarily in the Mojave.

Yet Huxley loved the desert. He loved the Joshua trees, the wildflowers and the rattlesnakes. In 1945 the Huxleys moved from Llano to Wrightwood, further up the mountains. A landscape of pinewood and sagebrush, which Huxley turned out to be terribly allergic to, surrounded them. A raccoon adopted Huxley, and it would come out of the hills every night to be fed. Huxley even reported meeting a bear on one of his walks at Wrightwood.

The move to Wrightwood came the year the atom bomb was tested and subsequently dropped on two Japanese cities. After the horrors of the Second World War in Europe, where Huxley still had many friends and relatives, the Nuclear Age thoroughly horrified him. In 1945 he wrote a friend, "Thank God we are to have peace soon," but went on to say that he thought it would be a disquieting peace at best, since "atomic bombs would be hanging overhead" L.A.

"National states armed by science with superhuman military power always remind me of Swift's description of Gulliver being carried up on the roof of the King of Brobdingnag's palace by a gigantic monkey: reason, human decency and spirituality, which are strictly individual matters, find themselves in the clutches of the collective will, which has the mentality of a delinquent boy of fourteen in conjunction with the physical powers of God," he wrote.

The terrible pessimism that began to clutch Huxley from the late 1940s until the time in the 1950s, when he discovered psychedelics, dates from the advent of the atom bomb. He began *Ape & Essence* at his Wrightwood home in 1947. The idea for the book was to be that of a "post-atomic-war society in which the chief effect of the gamma radiation had been to produce a race of men and women who don't make love all the year around, but have a brief mating season. The effect of this on politics, religion, ethics, etc. would be something very interesting and amusing to work out," Huxley told Anita Loos.

Ape & Essence is not an easy novel to call amusing, unless, of course, one is amused by torture, brutality, degradation and other unspeakable horrors. Huxley wrote *Ape & Essence* with his considerable wit and satire, however, so it is not totally without humor.

On the 22nd of February, 1948, Huxley walked into the kitchen at Wrightwood and told his wife he thought he had finished the book. The survivors in the book were mutants. The original inhabitants of L.A. had been killed long ago, in "those three bright summer days" of the Third World War. The physical city still stood; the wars had not scored a direct hit on L.A., but the radiation had destroyed most of the crops as well as finishing off the human population. Thus the handful of mutants, a few thousands at best, lived in and among various familiar Southern California landmarks — the County Museum and Coliseum in Exposition Park, Pershing Square and the Biltmore Hotel across the way, USC and UCLA and so on. The outlying neighborhoods were still there too, only they were not inhabited. The gas stations were rusting.

The community center of the mutant survivors of L.A. was in Pershing Square. The mutants were oddly dressed, because their clothes came from corpses dug up from nearby graveyards. They drank from skulls of the corpses, which had been fashioned into cups. Heat for the communal baking ovens in Pershing Square was provided by burning the books in the nearby public library. Water was carried in goatskins to be stored in earthenware jars kept in Pershing Square. Between "two rusty posts hung the carcass of a newly slaughtered ox and in a cloud of flies a man was cleaning out the entrails."

Across the way from this charming scene in Pershing Square was the mutants' temple — in the old Biltmore Hotel. In the book, the clergy lived there, chief of whom was "His Eminence the Arch-Vicar of Belial, Lord of the Earth, Primate of California, Servant of the Proletariat, Bishop of Hollywood." His aides included the "Patriarch of Pasadena" and the "Three-Horned Inquisitor."

The main event of the year, which was held in the Biltmore, was a two-week period of wild, enforced, orgiastic copulating, for sex was outlawed the rest of the year. The women wore flaps over strategic parts of their bodies that had the word "No" emblazoned on them. Nine months after the orgy there was a corollary event: Belial Day, a mass, sacrificial slaughter of the deformed offspring born from the main event. Women were called vessels to signify their uncleanness. In the book, most of the children the vessels had were offered to the sacrificial fires of Belial Day.

Unlike other Europeans who lived in L.A., Huxley did not leave the

Southland after World War II. But in 1949, he did abandon the desert and mountains and moved to 740 N. Kings Road, in West Hollywood. No doubt the fact of his proximity helped direct the attention of young intellectuals to his work. *Ape & Essence* was an especially popular book on Southland university and college campuses during the early '50s. In 1952 *The Devils of Loudon* was published, from which Ken Russell would later make the movie, "The Devils". Not long afterward, Huxley began dabbling with psychedelics because he found the chemical substances gave life to his admittedly intellectual mystical ideas. His *Doors of Perception* and *Heaven and Hell* in the mid-'50s made Huxley a major influence in his adopted town during the '60s with the psychedelic set.

Huxley was also active, with Christopher Isherwood and his friend Gerald Heard, in the Vedanta Society of Southern California. But it was the psychedelics that seemed to make Huxley a somewhat happier man than he might have been during the last part of his life.

After the death of his first wife, Maria, in 1955, Huxley did not produce much literature of lasting value. He seems to have become much less pessimistic, however, and his life with his new wife Laura saw him veer more and more toward mystical directions. His last novel, *Island*, the manuscript of which was saved from the clutches of a fire which destroyed one of his homes in the Hollywood Hills, was his optimistic work. Here he attempted to show how human life could be lived ideally. Unfortunately, many critics and readers found it rather dull, because in it, Huxley's customary critical facility seemed to have been suspended.

Although Huxley gave L.A. some fine literary presents, topped by *Ape & Essence*, he remained ever the Englishman. It is fitting to note that he himself, when hearing a recording of his voice, commented on how terribly English-sounding he remained, despite living in the physical and intellectual desert around L.A.

The Lost L.A. Years
Of Robinson Jeffers

Then what is the answer? — Not to be deluded by dreams.
To know that great civilizations have broken down into violence,
and their tyrants come, many times before.
When open violence appears, to avoid it with honor or choose
the least ugly faction; these evils are essential.
To keep one's own integrity, be merciful and uncorrupted and
not wish for evil; and not be duped
By dreams of universal justice or happiness. These dreams will not be fulfilled.
To know this, and know that however ugly the parts appear the whole
remains beautiful. A severed hand is an ugly thing,
and man dissevered from the earth and stars and his history...
for contemplation or in fact...
Often appears atrocious ugly. Integrity is wholeness, the greatest beauty is
Organic wholeness, the wholeness of life and things, the divine beauty
of the universe. Love that, not man apart from that, or else you
will share man's pitiful confusions, or drown in despair when his days darken.

—ROBINSON JEFFERS

One day in the late '70s I ran into John Harris, the proprietor of Papa Bach Bookstore, the late distinguished West Los Angeles emporium of the printed word whom we met in an earlier chapter. Harris is also a poet and a publisher, the closest thing Los Angeles has to a literary Renaissance man.

I respect Harris, and I listened when he mused aloud: "I don't know why no one has written about Robinson Jeffers as an L.A. boy. He spent his formative years here. He's a very important and great poet, the last of the great narrative poets. The tradition of narrative poetry, which is all but dead now, went back to the Greeks, and Jeffers was the last in the tradition. I also never understood why his poems weren't made into movies; they seemed such naturals."

Jeffers is best known for his association with the Big Sur coast, where the California Bohemians went to play and work after the San Francisco earthquake of 1906. Jeffers and his wife Una moved to Carmel in 1914, but his poetry was so strongly linked with Big Sur it seemed as if he had always been there. In fact, most of the Jeffers scholars who sift through the poet's early work looking for clues to the mature work written in Carmel, do so in Los Angeles.

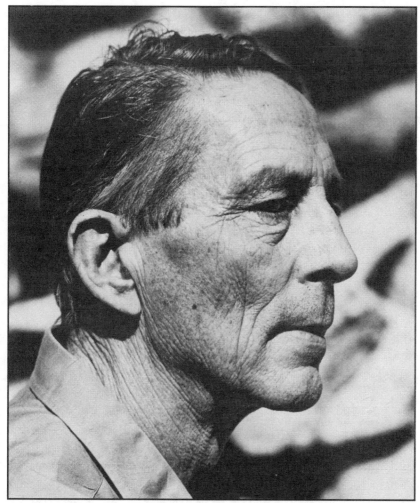

Epic Poet Robinson Jeffers, later in life

In an effort to trace the characters in Jeffers' poems geographically, Harris actually went to Big Sur and also wrote letters to everyone who might have known Jeffers. Harris gave me a packet of his research — including a letter to Harris from the astronomer Hamilton Jeffers, the poet's brother. There was an essay by Harris called "Testaments and Revelations: A Study of Robinson Jeffers as an Historian," which pointed out again Jeffers' link to Southern California. "The years before Carmel," Harris wrote, "had seen Jeffers devote his wide-ranging interests to the study of such subjects as literature, religion, philosophy, languages, geology, medicine, forestry, zoology and the law."

Harris makes the point even more strongly. "It wasn't only his academic studies, which were prodigious at both Occidental and USC. He acquired his love of nature in the nearby San Gabriel Mountains, and he first fell in love with the Pacific not at Carmel but in Hermosa and Manhattan beaches."

I discovered Jeffers's poetry in the mid-1960s when the Sierra Club and Ballantine Books issued *Not Man Apart*, which included photographs of the Big Sur coast, matched — in a sometimes fragmentary way — with poems from Jeffers. A lot of my old buddies and I were in the habit then of leaving L.A. in the morning and sleeping on a Big Sur beach that evening. There was no better way to escape the city — which so many of us seemed to want to do — than by walking down through the fog and mist of a wet, green Big Sur canyon in the dark to a moonlit beach, where we'd sleep overnight. Then we'd awaken the next morning, letting the sense of the place bathe us with something very eternal. Jeffers captures that eternal something in far less prosaic words than my own.

The first time I opened *Not Man Apart*, it was in anticipation of seeing Edward Weston's famed photographs. But it was Jeffers' poetry that side-tracked me. I do not think I had ever read words so powerful, so full of a sense of the apocalypse mixed with such a strong sense of the cosmos.

I heard of Jeffers again when I became a writer-in-residence in 1971 at Villa Montalvo, and began to learn something about the legend of the place which said that U.S. Senator Phelan apparently had a penchant for fancy women as well as the finest in the fine arts. The legend of Montalvo took in the fact that Phelan used to stage both poetry readings and orgies there — the place seems a likely site for both or either. Legend also has it that Jeffers was the star of these affairs, although Jeffers scholars in L.A. have assured me it is unlikely that Jeffers would have partaken of the joys of orgies.

I originally knew of Jeffers only as a great poet of Northern California. Yet it was from Southern California that Jeffers and his wife Una emigrated when he began building their granite Tor House in Big Sur in 1914. Jeffers was then twenty-seven. During the previous decade, he had been developing and maturing as a young man in Los Angeles, but it was in his stone tower "on the continent's edge" that he found his voice.

By the time Jeffers's career began to flourish in the 1920s, people had forgotten that he had grown up in Los Angeles, so identified with Carmel and Big Sur had his work become. Perhaps Los Angeles never properly celebrated Jeffers as one of its own because Jeffers's career declined so precipitously in the 1950s, just when Los Angeles was beginning to grow up and collect its own legends.

In fact, Jeffers achieved, if not a great literary reputation, certainly some notoriety in Los Angeles before his move to Big Sur.

Jeffers burst on the world poetry scene as the author of epic narrative poems, full of melodrama, storm, and fury. They were modern-day Greek dramas — his themes were sexual and brutal. They dealt with such acts as fratricide, adultery, incest, and bestiality. His greatest epic poems were novels in poetry, shocking works, such as "Roan Stallion," "Tamar," "Give Your Heart to the Hawks," "Thurso's Landing," and "Cawdor." Jeffers's characters followed their tragic and inevitable paths to doom against a beautiful but totally inhuman backdrop of primeval nature in the form of Jeffers' Big Sur landscape. This backdrop was Jeffers's reality and his cosmic view, and it was the most distinctive quality of his poems.

His works were still selling well in the 1930s, but his increasingly anti-Roosevelt stance hurt his public image. He was culturally, as well as politically, a very conservative and traditional man. He was a staunch Republican, which was an unusual stance for a poet.

It was Jeffers's political isolationism in the 1940s that really finished him off. Except for the efforts of a few Jeffers fanatics, he might have been forgotten in the 1950s, although he was still appreciated in Europe. Only a few years after his death, in 1962, did his reputation again began to grow. Undoubtedly, the very popular *Not Man Apart* volume has much to do with this.

I walked out of John Harris's bookstore carrying not only Harris's personal files on Jeffers, but some rare, prized editions by and about Jeffers from Harris's own collection.

I next sought out Robert J. Brophy, professor of English at California State University at Long Beach, who had not only written a highly respected volume on Jeffers — *Robinson Jeffers: Myth, Ritual and Symbol in His Narrative Poems* — but also was editing the *Robinson Jeffers Newsletter*. Brophy and his gang of Jeffers fanatics have spent long hours retracing Jeffers's life in Los Angeles. "We're always looking for letters, pictures, old buildings, and so on relating to Jeffers," Brophy explained.

When talking about Jeffers's Los Angeles period, Brophy observed: "A Freudian analyst would be delighted with the material of Jeffers's early life. I mean, Jeffers's dad was a very strange bird, twice the age of Jeffers' mother, who had lacked a strong father image in her childhood. Jeffers's father was very stern. Jeffers's mother turned her emotional life onto her son. And there was a lifelong antagonism between father and son."

Brophy said that Jeffers's father forced his son to study such a prodigious amount of Latin and Greek and other classical subjects that the boy developed headaches. The young Jeffers was finally sent away from his native Pennsylvania to private schools mostly in and around Zurich. Even in the Alps, Jeffers was not safe from his father, who would show up every six months or so and move his son to another school. Consequently, Robinson Jeffers became very

Jeffers's house in Highland Park

shy and did not learn how to make friends.

In Los Angeles, however, Jeffers "seems to have gone through a freeing period. He seems to have made an amicable break with his father, to have lived a lot on his own. He had lots of love affairs, did lots of drinking, his father would not have approved of. It was a real maturing period for his intellect," Brophy declared.

Jeffers's father was a minister, a distinguished professor emeritus at a Presbyterian seminary, intellectually a rather liberal man for his day, but personally a combination of eccentricity and strictness. In the small suburb of Pittsburgh where Jeffers spent his childhood, he never had a chance to make friends. This was because whenever he'd start to get friendly with anybody, his father would react by moving the family to the outskirts of town. The elder Jeffers wanted his son to study, and he told his wife to take careful note of Robinson's development because one day, the information would be needed by biographers.

One day in 1903, the minister retrieved his son from Switzerland and moved his whole brood to California, where he kept up his curious habit of restlessly moving from place to place. The first house the Jefferses had in the Southland was a cottage in Long Beach — no one remembers exactly where. Soon, however, the good doctor found a lot in Highland Park. The elder Jeffers liked the location because he wanted Robinson to attend nearby Occidental College, then a small Presbyterian college with a student body of some two hundred. In 1904, he spent four thousand dollars to have a two-story frame house built. The house still stands at 346 W. Avenue 57.

Jeffers, just entering his manhood in Los Angeles, began to shed some of his shyness at Occidental. He became the editor of the literary magazine, in which he published many of his early poems, mostly about the joys of exploring the San Gabriel Mountains. Occidental College still maintains an extensive collection in its Robinson Jeffers Room, and the college librarian, Tyrus G. Harmsen, is a leading authority on Jeffers.

Jeffers's infatuation with nature was legendary among his Occidental class-mates. Those who went hiking with him say his vitality was simply incredible; he walked with a magnificent stride that few could equal, reciting verse from Tennyson and Homer. When it was time to make camp, Jeffers was always willing to pitch in and do more than his share. He simply never tired. And during the days on the trail, he didn't mind carrying more than his share on his back.

Not long after the Occidental period, Jeffers became familiar with and began to love the ocean. Jeffers's father was getting restless again, and so in 1905, when Robinson, at the age of eighteen, graduated with honors, the Highland Park home was sold. The Jefferses first moved to a house a block south of the shore, on Third Street, in Manhattan Beach, but then moved a mile back from the water, to an eighty-acre ranch near what is now Sepulveda and Manhattan Beach boulevards. It was on these beaches that Jeffers first came to love the Pacific and to call it "the one ocean." Neither of his Manhattan Beach homes exist today.

Jeffers spent the summer with his family in Manhattan Beach and then decided to enter the University of Southern California for his master's degree in letters. He met Una in 1906, in a German class at USC. When he met her, however, Una was already married, to a prominent Los Angeles attorney named Ted Kuster.

Brophy's *Robinson Jeffers Newsletter* has published, from time to time, information on Una, the bored socialite wife. She appeared more than once on the society pages because she was, among other things, the Southland's premier woman automobile racer.

Brophy, who when I interviewed him had recently been reading newly found letters about Una's early days, said she was not altogether an appealing creature. She was very pretty, but very demanding. Her husband, who doted on her, supplied her with her own seamstress — for she insisted on having only the most exquisite clothes. "She was very manipulative," says Brophy, "and used her sexuality on everybody. She was very proud and very vain. Later, of course, as the wife of Robinson Jeffers of Carmel, she led a very austere life in Tor House. It's amazing how she changed later in life."

It was not necessarily love at first sight between Una and Robinson when they met at USC in 1906. In fact, it wasn't until 1909 — and quite likely later — that their romance became physical and passionate. Early on, when curiosity got the better of Una's friends and they asked about her constant companion, she is supposed to have replied, "He's a very gifted linguist and writes very immature poetry."

Row house at 1623 Shatto Street

In 1907, Jeffers's parents decided to move to Europe. Robinson followed for a short while, intending to enter the University of Zurich. But he felt hemmed in by constant parental supervision, and returned alone to Los Angeles. He re-enrolled at USC, this time in the medical school. He was living in a row house that still stands at 1623 Shatto Street, near downtown Los Angeles. He also began spending more and more time with the pretty Mrs. Kuster and the gossip began to sizzle.

In the summer, the Kusters lived in a house at Hermosa Beach. Jeffers rented a room with a Mrs. Melinda Nash, not very far away. While Kuster worked, Jeffers and Una, and sometimes other friends of hers, dallied on the beach. By now, things had gone quite far. They were exchanging daily love letters. During this period, Jeffers wrote his "At Playa Hermosa," in which he describes having neither "despair nor hope" as he watched the "gray waves rise and drop." It ends with these strangely prophetic words: "Strange and ominous peace abides. What will Fate exact of me/For this quiet by the Sea?"

Once, on a hike to Mount Lowe, in the San Gabriel Mountains, Mrs. Ted Kuster proposed marriage to Jeffers during a romantic interlude replete with a detective that the lady's unfortunate husband had hired. During this period, too, Lawrence Clark Powell wrote, "(Jeffers's) love of poetry and nature deepened. He had a passion for birds, winds, sunsets, long solitary walks, and would go alone on trips, afoot or on horseback, into the mountains." If he wasn't in the mountains, Powell said, he was at the beach, at Redondo or Hermosa. "On that blue Pacific bay he roamed the wharves and hobnobbed with longshoreman unloading fragrant Oregon pine from coasting schooners, or drank with them at night in waterfront saloons."

Of course, the romance with Una was still the most important thing that happened to him in Los Angeles.

Although he had returned alone to Southern California, his parents had soon followed. They again settled in Los Angeles but were soon off to Seattle. Jeffers took the opportunity to go away with them in 1910 and get away from Una. He thought he would study forestry in the Northwest. He didn't stay long, though. Una and Jeffers had said they must never see each other again. Within a half hour of Jeffers's return from the Northwest, he saw Una at a crosswalk, sitting in a large open roadster. They tried to avoid each other's eyes, but realized it was impossible. They were hopelessly in love.

In the meantime, the elder Jefferses had tired of the Northwest and moved back to Los Angeles, where they bought a house that still stands at 822 Garfield Avenue, in Pasadena. It was then, in 1912, that Jeffers published his first book of poetry, printed by a Los Angeles print shop at Jeffers's expense. Called *Flagons and Apples*, it was well received by at least one Los Angeles newspaper, whose reviewer asked Jeffers to write the review of the book. So Jeffers wrote the review, and it was run under the reviewer's byline.

One gets more insight into Jeffers's life during this time from his own description of the period just before the publication of *Flagons and Apples*. The reminiscence was one of the few pieces of prose that Jeffers ever published.

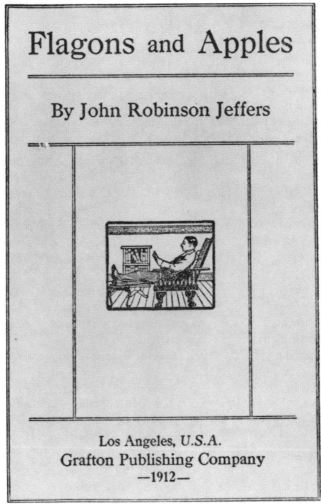

Flagons and Apples

By John Robinson Jeffers

Los Angeles, U.S.A.
Grafton Publishing Company
—1912—

First book of poetry

It appeared in 1932 in a fine-printing magazine called *The Colophonio*, which came from the presses of Ward Ritchie.

"This was in Los Angeles and I lived rather solitary at one of the beaches (Hermosa) twenty miles distant, and was too young for my age, and drank a good deal when I came to town. At Redondo, on my way home in the evening, I left the electric car to visit a barroom frequented by longshoremen friends of mine. I stayed there until the cars stopped running and had to walk the three miles home. For several hours I had thought of nothing about my verse, which only interested part of my mind, for I had no confidence in them. It was not until the next morning that I looked for the bundle of manuscripts which had been under my arm, but it must have been laid down somewhere...either at home or in Redondo."

Luckily, Jeffers goes on to explain, he knew his own verse by heart, and was able to retype another draft for the printers.

One of Brophy's friends and fellow researchers for the *Robinson Jeffers Newsletter* is Robert Kafka. He is a self-described Jeffers fanatic who has retraced much of Jeffers's life in Los Angeles, doing even such tedious jobs as researching county court records. Kafka knows, for instance, by first-hand research, the various bars Jeffers went drinking in, and has even uncovered the fact that Jeffers was involved in — though did not cause — a bloody barroom brawl in a place called the Ships' Cafe, which was built in the shape of a ship on the old Venice pier. Jeffers also used to haunt several bars, now all gone, on South Spring Street, in a downtown area that's now "all modern banks and parking lots."

Neither Brophy nor his friend Kafka have been able to uncover exactly where Mrs. Nash's house was in Hermosa Beach, where Jeffers stayed when he wanted to get away from the city, and also to see Una, which was often. A close relationship between the young Jeffers and Mrs. Nash quickly developed. Jeffers described her as his adopted mother. She kept his apartment always ready for him, and she looked after him when he was there. Young Jeffers was by no means a perfect tenant. One time he went away and, by oversight, left his dog locked in the bedroom. The dog tore up all the furniture.

Brophy's newsletter tracked down a John DeWitt of Costa Mesa who knew both Jeffers and Mrs. Nash. DeWitt said Mrs. Nash's place was "a big brown house on the crest of the hill in Hermosa, overlooking the Pacific to the west, and the Japanese vegetable gardens to the east." DeWitt told the newsletter that Jeffers used to take him walking, and "would read some of his poems to me, which at my tender age were not fully comprehended."

Mrs. Nash, said DeWitt, was an accomplished seamstress from Wisconsin, and had been an old and valued employee of the DeWitt family there. Mrs. Nash was apparently quite good at what she did and had made some money and retired to Hermosa Beach, and later invited the DeWitts to stay with her when they moved out to L.A. DeWitt said that Mrs. Nash had transferred her love from a dead grandson to Jeffers, who "was a temperamental, introspective and reclusive young man. He would be closeted in his room for hours, writing, completely oblivious to regular mealtimes. He would often go downstairs in the middle of the night and Mrs. Nash would get up and prepare a meal for him."

The tragedy of Mrs. Nash was that she was a strict Victorian. At one point late in the game, Jeffers and Una, not exactly a chaste bride, asked

Mrs. Nash along on a trip they wanted to take to Seattle. Mrs. Nash was to be the chaperone — a role that Mrs. Nash believed in very strongly. Such were the times. But she was so shocked at the impropriety of the thing that she refused Jeffers's request. Robinson and Una went to Seattle anyway. Mrs. Nash became quite depressed — DeWitt said he found out why when the headlines broke on Friday morning, February 28, 1913. The scandal-loving morning sheet, the Los Angeles *Times*, ran the story under the headline, "Love's Gentle Alchemy To Weld Broken Lives." It was the same newspaper that used to carry on and on about Mrs. Una Kuster's car-racing days on its society pages. But this time, a society matron had suddenly jumped onto the news pages. What the Friday morning edition told was the tale of prominent attorney Ed Kuster divorcing his wife Una; Kuster intended to take a plump lass from Bakersfield as his second wife.

Ah, delicious scandal! The Los Angeles *Times* story explained to the breathless denizens of L.A. that the divorce proceedings of the socially prominent couple had been "shrouded by a veil of mystery." But the newspaper had talked to people in the know, and it could authoritatively report that behind the Kuster divorce was the stalking, "unseen but potent figure of the inevitable triangle." The "potent figure" was a member of a mystic cult which "professes to believe that those things which conscience permits are right." Jeffers was named as the "potent figure."

The next day the same newspaper was still carrying on about the affair. "Two Points of the Eternal Triangle," the headline blared. There was a box with pictures of Una and Jeffers, and his poem, "On the Cliff," which was a love poem from *Flagons and Apples*, under the right side of the headline. On the left was a single-column deck head: "Parents Wash Hands of It." The point of this story was to report that Mrs. J.H. Jeffers, "mother of John Robinson Jeffers, the lyric expounder of melancholy poems of passion," wasn't going to comment on her son's affair, that his destiny was his own.

The newsletter went on to proclaim that Mrs. Kuster had, in reality, been "made the scapegoat of a coterie of faddists who egged her on. In the beginning," said the story, "Mrs. Kuster was used by these individualists," who are unnamed in the article, "to ascertain just how far society, or that portion of society they represent, would go in accepting the new thought wherein the 'I' becomes the absolute, and once conscience is muffled, all is right." Intriguing stuff? It seems also that poor Mrs. Kuster was "sincere in her actions, whatever they were," according to the newspaper. "When upon one occasion an attempt was made to induce her to experiment with another candidate for superman distinction, she turned from the proposition in abhorrence."

The story quite shocked Mrs. Nash and no doubt confirmed her worst fears.

Still, after Jeffers and Una had run off to Seattle and finally had gotten married in Tacoma, Jeffers wrote Mrs. Nash an affectionate letter. He said that they planned to return to "L.A. — and Hermosa" — but only for three weeks, before they departed for Europe. Jeffers signed the letter, "Goodnight, my dear Nash, Robin."

Una and Jeffers returned to the Southland, but didn't make it to Europe until some years later. Happy as lovebirds, the poet and his wife stayed with the senior Jefferses in Pasadena. Since she was pregnant, however, they decided to stay in the Southland and take advantage of American medicine. They rented a place in La Jolla, where they stayed a few months. They didn't return to Los Angeles until a month before Una gave birth to a girl, on May 5, 1914. They named the baby Maeve, but she lived only five days.

When the Jefferses first moved to La Jolla, Kuster and his new bride followed suit. The four of them used to go walking in the hills and along the beach in La Jolla, and no doubt that included nearby Torrey Pines. "Everything was so weird," commented Brophy, "but Jeffers always allowed things just to happen. His attitude seemed to be that that was the price of life, that's just how things were." Kuster later became a neighbor of the Jefferses in Carmel.

Soon after their first child's death, they realized they would have to find someplace other than Europe to settle, for the war was now very much on. Jeffers had been quite fond of La Jolla, however. During the months in La Jolla, he was becoming more and more attached to the sea, and less and less anxious to live in a city. Jeffers wrote an old Occidental classmate, Dan S. Hammack Jr., a Los Angeles lawyer, that he knew of no "Southern Californian beach more beautiful" than La Jolla. He mentioned that despite La Jolla's increasing amount of civilization, abalone, seals, porpoises, and pelicans still abounded. Still, they were not considering it for a permanent home.

The Jefferses first heard of Carmel, the oasis in the north, from one of Una's old friends. From the moment Jeffers and Una laid eyes on the Big Sur coast, they knew they had found what they were looking for. "For the first time in my life," Jeffers would later say, "I could see people living — amid magnificently unspoiled scenery — essentially as they did in the Idylls or the Sagas, or in Homers's Ithaca. Men were riding after cattle, or plowing the headland, hovered over by white sea gulls, as they had done for thousands of years, and will for thousands of years to come. Here was contemporary life that was also permanent life."

As is now clear from his poetry, Jeffers found his voice in the granite house he built himself on the Big Sur coast. His restlessness and need to move from place to place, obviously brought on by his father, disappeared. Yet in looking back on his life, Jeffers himself noted some of the formative elements in his mature work, and they were all things that occurred in turn-of-the-century Los Angeles.

For example, at nineteen years of age, he came across the quote from the German philosopher Friedrich Nietzsche: "The poets lie too much." Jeffers decided he agreed with that and worked on making himself the exception that proves the rule. He became a very uncompromising kind of poet, who wrote only about the things he thought would last, would be eternal.

And it was also in Los Angeles that Jeffers met Una. Intellect nourished their love. Jeffers credited her as the co-author of everything good that he went on to write, even though "she never saw the poem until I had finished it." Often it was Una who would go out and listen to the gossip, the legends, which Jeffers wove so powerfully into his narrative poems of Big Sur.

She was the sociable half of the couple; he liked only good friends, such as George Sterling, the unofficial California poet laureate. Once, Una actually got her husband to agree to go to a party of literati in Carmel. He faked a faint after a few minutes and they had to go home.

While Los Angeles was important in Jeffers's development, Carmel was his nirvana. For him and Una, Carmel became their entire identity. While Jeffers didn't write anything summing up his life in Los Angeles, he did mention how much Una hated the Southland. Jeffers himself encouraged people to think of the Jeffers before Carmel as a different person than the Jeffers of Carmel. To one fellow who later complained that he wished he had known Jeffers in his Los Angeles decade, Jeffers replied that "Luckily perhaps…we didn't meet in 1911. I remember humbly a rather queer young person by that name then."

Una and Jeffers seemed to profoundly change each other, just as Big Sur profoundly changed them both. He wrote his best poetry there, and in the 1920s, he had a large popular following. His books went through many printings, even though he didn't do the things that successful poets are supposed to do, such as go on the poetry-reading circuit. Jeffers was a hermit. He didn't like groups of people. He was an oddity, hard to categorize.

Although the Jeffers of Carmel was a staunch Republican, very conservative, the critic who did the most to put him on the map was the editor of the then-influential Communist magazine in New York, *New Masses*. James Rorty not only wrote about Jeffers but used all his influence to get others to do so. The irony of a Marxist literary czar promoting a poet with politics only slightly to the left of Attila the Hun was not lost on Rorty himself, who said, "I think Jeffers is one of the best poets alive. I don't share his philosophy. What of it? He writes with greater poetic intensity than any other living poet I have read." Jeffers's poetry had a sizable audience behind the Iron Curtain, even when Marxism was the official ideology.

I was finally able to get in touch with Lawrence Clark Powell, author of

Robinson Jeffers, The Man and His Work, published in Los Angeles in the mid-1930s, and chief librarian at UCLA for many years. Today Powell feels vindicated by his early championing of the cause of Jeffers. The last decade has seen a Jeffers renaissance, Powell proclaims. "There's been half a dozen books about him. There's a Robinson Jeffers newsletter now coming out of Occidental College. And his books are back in print."

Powell denied that Jeffers was just a misanthropic visionary. "He was a very hard-nosed, intellectual realist. He wasn't embittered. He was in his daily life a very happy man who said he'd like to go on living as he did for centuries."

Powell also does not believe that Los Angeles or the scandal involving Una embittered Jeffers. He said the great anti-city sentiment in Jeffers's later poetry was written "about no place whatsoever. It was a philosophical concept of cities. He was writing out of his mind, not his life."

Maybe so, but I've never been able to believe that the life of the mind can be separated from that of the surrounding environment, especially in Jeffers's case, where he constructed the stages for his poetic sagas out of recognizable parts of the landscape, both in Big Sur and in Los Angeles.

In Search Of
Upton Sinclair

Despite the fact that the centennial of Upton Sinclair's birthday was celebrated in 1978 at California State University at Los Angeles, the sad truth for Robert O. Hahn is that the greatest muck-raking author of them all has fallen on hard times in his own country — even here

Upton Sinclair, candidate for governor

in Southern California, where Sinclair lived and worked and was very much a part of local history for more than half a century. Hahn, now retired to the Santa Cruz area in Northern California, is the former education professor at the university who used to publish *Uppie Speaks*, also known, for the sake of proper academicians, as the *Upton Sinclair Quarterly*. Hahn is still further saddened to note that if people remember Upton Sinclair's name at all, they confuse him with his now more famous protege, Sinclair Lewis. Yet Sinclair Lewis himself admitted that his *Elmer Gantry* was inspired by Upton Sinclair's *Profits of Religion*. Back in 1906, Sinclair Lewis had been a member of Upton Sinclair's utopian commune, Helicon Hall, just outside New York City. At that time, Sinclair Lewis was a young, unknown writer and Upton Sinclair had just become a national celebrity because of *The Jungle*.

Hahn does not necessarily disagree with those who say Sinclair Lewis wrote consistently better literature than Upton Sinclair. But if you count the thousands of letters, pamphlets and magazine articles, in addition to some seventy-eight books that Sinclair wrote, Hahn says it would certainly be impossible to argue that no writer ever had a greater impact than Upton Sinclair. And some of Sinclair's books were acknowledged masterpieces — books such as *Jimmie Higgins* and *The Goose-Step*, an expose about higher education that focused on the University of Southern California.

Not only was Sinclair incredibly prolific; he was also a self-published author, operating out of post office boxes in Pasadena, Long Beach and Monrovia. He published hundreds of thousands of copies of his own books from the various Southland homes he lived in after 1915. Yet when Sinclair Lewis accepted the Nobel Prize for literature in 1930, he chastised the prizegivers for not having so honored Upton Sinclair, "of whom you must say, whether you admire or detest his aggressive socialism, that he is internationally better known than any other American artist whosoever, be he novelist, poet, painter, sculptor, musician, architect."

Lewis was not the only person who wanted Sinclair to have the Nobel Prize. Albert Einstein, Bertrand Russell and George Bernard Shaw, among others, signed petitions to the Nobel committee. Many people are shocked to learn that Sinclair never received the Pulitzer Prize for *The Jungle*, the book which forced the president and Congress to pas the nation's first Pure Food and Drug laws. In fairness to the Pulitzers, they were not even started until 1918. Ultimately Sinclair was finally given the Pulitzer for *Dragon's Teeth*, one of his immensely popular Lanny Budd series, written later in his life.

Hahn is of the opinion that Sinclair's name has not received a fair shake in the post-war world for much the same reason Lewis mentioned in his Nobel speech. It was simply, says Hahn, that his militant socialism branded him as someone to ignore. Hahn says that even at Cal State L.A., "the snobs, the literati in the English Department ignored him," and that is that way across the nation in all the country's colleges and universities now. The result, Hahn says, is that Sinclair, whom the Europeans regard as the American Balzac, isn't being presented to students in high schools any more, either.

Yet in Europe, Sinclair remains a popular American writer, whose work is always being reprinted. There's a new biography of Sinclair in German, Hahn says, and German television once did an in-depth documentary which was shot in Los Angeles and the San Gabriel Valley. "That tells you something. Television here has just ignored him."

Hahn points out that the only reasonably current biography of Sinclair was Leon Harris's *Upton Sinclair: American Rebel*, published in 1975. Hahn adds that Harris might as well have subtitled his book *The Forgotten American Rebel*, because it didn't do very well, "even though it was a pretty good book." When Hahn taught an unusual course on Upton Sinclair as part of Cal State L.A.'s American Studies program, he had trouble buying copies of Sinclair's last book, his autobiography.

But was Sinclair a great writer? I asked Hahn more than once. Hahn agreed that this is not an easy question to answer. For one thing, because his books were self-published he had to edit them himself. Most writers, including the best, need editors, Hahn pointed out. So Sinclair is inconsistent, but his problem is that he was different as well. His style was quite different from other styles at the turn of the century, Hahn believes. "It's almost a documentary style, closer to the current journalistic style; you know, something like Truman Capote's *In Cold Blood*. The thing about Sinclair is that he had an incredible lifespan. He was a link in our history. He began writing for a living at seventeen and wrote into his eighties. It's a curious thing," said Hahn; "it's as though the social put-down of his time has lived with him all these years."

Hahn was introduced to Sinclair's writings when he was growing up in the East before World War II, and once he had discovered Sinclair, he could not stop hunting for more to read. By the time he arrived in Los Angeles in 1948, he had thirty Sinclair volumes in his personal library.

Sinclair came to Coronado, on San Diego Bay, in 1915, and settled in Pasadena in 1916, a decade after *The Jungle* had made him a national celebrity. His expose of the meat-packing industry may have hit the public's stomach and not its heart, but it had propelled him into world-class fame. Sinclair and President Theodore Roosevelt developed a rather tense but personal relationship over the book; Roosevelt was sometimes a "trust-buster," but he most certainly was no socialist. And in fact, Sinclair's writing may have made more converts to vegetarianism than to socialism. Although he himself was both a vegetarian and a socialist, his graphic descriptions of the adulteration and contamination of meat products as well as the unsanitary conditions which were commonplace in packing houses revolted the public. Further investigations revealed that *The Jungle* was not only a gripping novel, it was devastatingly accurate reportage.

After *The Jungle*, Sinclair couldn't do anything without it showing up in the penny-dreadful New York "yellow press." By 1908 he was close to a nervous breakdown. His breakup with his first wife, Meta, had become lurid headlines everywhere he went. At the same time George Sterling, who seems to have been a friend of every important California writer of the day from Jack London to poet Robinson Jeffers, was coaxing Sinclair to come west. So was another socialist, millionaire H. Gaylord Wilshire, after whom Los Angeles's Wilshire Boulevard was named. Wilshire had a gold mine in the Sierras, whose two unusual main features were plenty of "high wages and socialist propaganda." Sinclair finally came west, and stayed both in the Sierras and in Carmel.

He was welcomed by no less a personage than his fellow muckraker, Lincoln Steffens, who wrote him in Carmel, "You are in my state, you know — California, the most beautiful lady in the union — and you are in a beautiful place in that beautiful state." At that time, Steffens wanted Sinclair to come to Sacramento, and visit the Steffens household there. Sinclair didn't go to Sacramento that time but, ironically, in 1934 when Sinclair ran for and almost won the governorship, he did visit the Steffens home — for the Steffens home in Sacramento had become the governor's mansion.

Those who grew up in the Golden State during the great Depression no doubt remember Sinclair and his "End Poverty in California" movement, the EPIC plan. It won him the Democratic nomination, and he lost to the Republicans with forty-five percent of the vote only after one of the most vicious political smear campaigns ever launched. Nonetheless, Sinclair's candidacy forced a realignment of the two major political parties, and out of the EPIC movement came such later Democratic officeholders as U.S. Senator Sheridan Downey, Governor Culbert Olson, Congressman Jerry Voorhis and Los Angeles County Supervisor John Anson Ford.

But that is jumping ahead of our tale a bit. After his first visit to California, primarily Northern California, during 1908, Sinclair was forced to return to the East. He did return to Southern California in 1915, and the reason was simple. Like everyone else, he loved the climate. "It's good for the body and it's good for the mind," he announced. By the end of his long stay here, he had decided he could not imagine ever having to live in any other part of the world.

Sinclair's first view of California had been George Sterling's writers' and artists' colony at Carmel in 1908. But when he finally found the ideal place for himself and his new wife, Mary Craig, in 1916, he chose that most unsocialist of places — Pasadena. He described Pasadena as "the city of millionaires" and he was certainly right. The nation's "plutocracy," to use Sinclair's word, had been spending their summers in Pasadena, for some while — in the days before air conditioning, they used to like to leave the muggy, hot East, and spend their time in the mansions and great hotels of Pasadena. One of their favorite activities was playing tennis. As a matter of fact, one of Sinclair's favorite activities was playing tennis. He once ranked as Pasadena's seventh best tennis player.

It was certainly not out of character for Sinclair to love what was then that most plutocratic of sports, tennis. For the nation's most notorious socialist was in fact very much a genteel aristocrat. His father had been a drunk, but, like Sinclair's mother, he was proud of his family's Confederate Navy aristocracy. Furthermore, through his mother's family Sinclair was related to the Blands, one of the wealthiest families in Baltimore.

The split between poor and rich was very real to Sinclair. A great part of his childhood was spent in wretched poverty in New York, but sometimes he lived in the mansions of his rich relatives in Baltimore. In *Upton Sinclair: American Rebel*, author Leon Harris suggests that it was this double exposure that had formed his character. Sinclair's life was an odd variation on the Horatio Alger theme: he had risen out of the slums to make himself a great success through his writing, but he had never aspired to riches, as did most other successful Americans who lifted themselves from poverty and slums by their own bootstraps. Instead, he wanted an explanation for the chasm he saw between the rich and the poor. Social justice, not wealth, was his obsession.

Significantly, Sinclair discovered socialism in *Wilshire's Magazine*, which was published by H. Gaylord Wilshire. He first saw the magazine in 1902 in a New York editor's office. He used to prowl editorial offices for work because he'd discovered early on that he had a knack for writing pulp magazine fiction, and while he was still a teenager he supported himself and his poor parents with his hack work.

One of the greatest moments in his life was when he finally got to meet Wilshire. Wilshire had made and lost several fortunes in L.A. real estate, but whenever he made money he always plowed it into his socialist ventures, be they magazines or mines. By 1895, Wilshire had been sure that the boulevard to which he had given his name would become the "fashionable concourse and driveway" of L.A. He was right, of course — Wilshire Boulevard was destined to become L.A.'s answer to the Champs Elysee of Paris, Fifth Avenue in New York and Michigan Avenue in Chicago.

Yet in a sense, Wilshire's great visionary powers may have affected the world more through their impact on the young mind of Upton Sinclair than through their impact on L.A. maps. After discovering Wilshire's magazine,

Sinclair spent the rest of his long career pouring his socialist vision into nearly everything he wrote. It has often been pointed out, however, that Sinclair's greatest accomplishments were social reforms, rather than a transformation of society from capitalism to socialism. Thus such varied people as John Kennedy, Bertolt Brecht, Aleksander Solzhenitsyn, Leon Trotsky, Sergei Eisenstein, Herbert Marcuse, Ramsey Clark, Robert McNamara, Eric Sevareid, Patrick Moynihan, Norman Mailer, Maxim Gorki and Mahatma Gandhi claimed to have been deeply affected by his writings.

Although Sinclair was often called a communist, Lenin contemptuously dismissed him as "an emotional socialist." Sinclair's socialism was not generally of the Marxist variety; it was more of utopian populism, with deep roots in the American experience. There was something almost religious, almost saintly, about Sinclair. In appearance, he was a frail, rather ascetic-looking man. He was often described as an American Zola or Balzac, but he was puritan in his private habits. He certainly was no hedonist. He didn't drink and probably spent most of his lifetime, after his disastrous first marriage, as a celibate — at least that is what Dr. Hahn believes.

He was also a health-food nut, always experimenting with yet another miracle diet. Both he and Wilshire fell prey to a San Francisco homeopathic physician named Abrams, whose "I-An-A-Co" machine was dismissed by most of the medical profession as a fraud.

In some ways, he fit right in with some of his millionaire neighbors in Pasadena, especially the contingent in Pasadena which was the American counterpart of the Fabian Socialists in England of the time. Two Fabian authors, H.G. Wells and George Bernard Shaw, regularly communicated by letter with Sinclair in Pasadena. And Wilshire, who was Sinclair's neighbor, traveled to England constantly.

Others in Pasadena society who were part of the Sinclair group included Charles Chaplin, the "plant wizard" Luther Burbank, Mrs. Kate Crane-Gartz of the Crane plumbing fortune, Bobby Scripps of the newspaper chain, and land and oil heiress Aline Barnsdall, whose name is perhaps best remembered today because of the park that carries it.

Sinclair owned several cottages in the 1500 block of Sunset Avenue (long since torn down for a freeway). He used to go walking with Henry Ford in the San Gabriel Mountains behind Pasadena; they would discuss politics and economics. Finally Sinclair realized that he wasn't getting anywhere with Ford. He reasoned that perhaps another millionaire, a socialist, could better convince Ford. So he asked King Gillette, the socialist razor king, to argue with the capitalist flivver king. Gillette was no more successful than Sinclair had been.

Of all his friends, aside from Charlie Chaplin, Wilshire was the closest.

When Wilshire's gold mine was going badly, Sinclair gave him most of what he had left from the fortune he had made with *The Jungle*. He also encouraged other socialists to do so — but the gold mine went under anyway.

Sinclair made thousands and spent thousands — usually on his crusades. He published his own books in California because the New York publishers had proven fickle and unreliable. A steady stream of books, magazines and pamphlets issued forth from Sinclair's Pasadena post office box. Sinclair had far less trouble with his publishers overseas; he kept the same publisher in England for half a century. The Russians published millions of copies of Sinclair's works. But Sinclair did not always run his publishing business like a business. He distributed thousands of copies of *Flivver King* at cost to auto workers organizing in Detroit.

The group of millionaire socialists around Sinclair often came up with money for their crusades — but the financial dealings between Sinclair and Wilshire had been especially close. At one desperate point, Sinclair had offered to sell himself into indentured servitude to Wilshire for several years, for a certain amount of money. Wilshire declined the author's offer, but he lent and gave plenty of money to Sinclair over the years of their friendship.

Sinclair's name was closely connected, in quite a different way, with yet another of L.A.'s illustrious pioneers, General Harrison Gray Otis, proprietor and editor of the Los Angeles *Times*. Sinclair and Otis had one of the city's legendary feuds.

Back in 1882, according to David Halberstam's *The Powers That Be*, General Otis was made an offer by the city's circulation czar that the general couldn't refuse. Harry Chandler, who controlled the circulation of most of the city's several dailies, struck a bargain with Otis, and the general's competitors simply ceased to have viable newspaper properties any more. The ambitious young Chandler then went to work as circulation manager for the *Times* and ascended the ladder of success even further by the simple device of becoming Otis's son-in-law. The following year, Southern Pacific gave L.A. its first rail link to the outside world, and the City of the Angels ceased to be a dusty little village of five thousand souls. Thus was the Chandler dynasty born.

Harry Chandler, who controlled the circulation of most of the city's several dailies, struck a bargain with Otis, and the general's competitors simply ceased to have viable newspaper properties any more. The ambitious young Chandler then went to work as circulation manager for the *Times* and ascended the ladder of success even further by the simple device of becoming Otis's son-in-law. The following year, Southern Pacific gave L.A. its first rail link to the outside world, and the City of the Angels ceased to be a dusty little village of five thousand souls. Thus was the Chandler dynasty born.

The general died in 1917, the year after Sinclair settled in Pasadena.

When in 1920 Sinclair published his book *The Brass Check*, much of his famed study of American journalism was about the general. In *The Brass Check* Sinclair repeated a story about Otis that Wilshire had told him. It seems that once, close to the turn of the century, Wilshire met the general on the street. Otis was being solicitous about a newspaper based on the utopian socialist ideas of Edward Bellamy, which Wilshire and others were publishing. In view of various editorials which had appeared in the *Times*, Wilshire was surprised that Otis was so concerned about the *Nationalist*.

"I see you people have got a weekly paper," the general said. Wilshire nodded in affirmation.

"Well now," said the general, "the *Times* has a new and modern printing plant. We would like very much to do that work for you. Suppose you give us a trial."

The *Nationalist* was being printed in the print shop of the old *Express*. Wilshire said he personally wouldn't object to its being printed at the *Times*, but he was sure that some of his associates would probably say the general didn't treat their ideas fairly in the *Times*.

To this the general is supposed to have replied, "Oh, now, now, you don't mind a thing like that. Surely, now, you ought to understand a joke." Whereupon for the next several days the *Times* carried cordial editorials upon the ideas of Edward Bellamy's socialism. This went on for two or three weeks, but when the *Nationalist* kept on being printed at the *Express*, the general "shifted back to his old method of sneering and abuse," Sinclair reported.

If you get the impression that Sinclair was trying to say that the general was a venal and corrupt character, you are quite right. Sinclair's dislike of the general, however, was not based solely on something that had happened years ago to his friend, Wilshire. Shortly after settling in Pasadena in 1916, Sinclair had been invited, as a celebrity author, to give a lecture to one of the ladies' cultural clubs, "which," he noted, "pay celebrities to come and entertain them, and next to marrying a millionairess, this is the easiest way to get your living in Southern California." Sinclair was no more averse to making a buck than the next socialist, and when he made his appearance before the Friday Morning Club, he was a success. He scandalized and shocked the audience, as they wanted, but he also entertained. Everyone seemed quite happy with the arrangement.

Sinclair was not so well received, however, the next morning in the august pages of the Los Angeles *Times*. The account of Sinclair's speech had been written by the general himself. The general's news account said the speech was "more-or-less brilliant quotations upholding anarchy, destruction, lawlessness, revolution, from the lips of an effeminate young man with a fatuous smile, a weak chin and a sloping forehead, talking in a false treble, and accusing them of leading selfish, self-indulgent lives." The *Times* story said that Sinclair had expressed his sympathy with dynamiters and murderers, and it added that "never before an audience of red-blooded men could Upton Sinclair have voiced his weak, pernicious, vicious doctrines. His naive, fatuous smile alone would have aroused their ire before he opened his vainglorious mouth. Let the fact remain that this slim, beflanneled example of perverted masculinity could and did get several hundred women to listen to him."

The general followed up this news account with editorials for the next several days demanding that Sinclair be incarcerated forthwith.

Not surprisingly, Sinclair wasn't very fond of the general either. "I have yet to meet a single person," he wrote in *The Brass Check*, "who does not despise and hate his *Times*. This paper, founded by Harrison Gray Otis, one of the most corrupt and most violent old men that ever appeared in American public life, has continued for thirty years to rave at every conceivable social reform, with complete disregard for truth, and with abusiveness which seems almost insane. It would seem better to turn loose a hundred thousand mad dogs in the streets of Los Angeles than to send out a hundred thousand copies of the *Times* every day."

The year the general died was a momentous one. The Russian Revolution had broken out toward the end of World War I, the czar and his family were in jail, and a socialist by the name of Kerensky was wondering what to do with them. (Kerensky, who was later overthrown by Lenin and his Bolsheviks, ended up living in Berkeley.) Sinclair sent him some advice. He suggested the czar and family be sent to Catalina Island, since this island off the coast of Los Angeles "is populated by sheep, the proper subject for autocracy." His idea was that Catalina should be made a "refuge for rulers abdicating or dethroned." Sinclair said his suggestion was made to boost the "wonderful outdoor climate and beautiful islands with wild goats running over them, and deep sea fishing to be found" in Southern California. This sounded like a satire of the general's obsessive boosterism of Southern California, which Sinclair once described as a "smug and self-satisfied" community that is "a parasite upon the great industrial centers of other parts of America."

Wilshire read *The Brass Check* and warned its author that he'd never get away with publishing it. He urged Sinclair to get copies of it into the hands of socialists all over the country as fast as he could, and then have them hide their copies in their homes.

Sinclair took Wilshire's advice seriously. "It was an easy way to get rid of books," he later commented, "but a hard way to make money." The fact is that *The Brass Check* would eventually go through many printings, although Sinclair often had to connive to get the paper to print it on. He was convinced that this was no accident.

Sinclair wasn't much enamored of Los Angeles's other major publisher, William Randolph Hearst, either. He talked about the "daily cat and dog fight" between Hearst's *Examiner* and Otis's *Times* with obvious contempt for both papers. On the other hand, not so many years before, Sinclair had regarded the young Hearst as something of a messiah who might have led the country into the promised land if only he had made good on his ambition to be president. Furthermore, Sinclair wrote for the Hearst press. As late as 1923, he was writing a series in Hearst's New York *American*, which ran his stories with such sensational headlines as "Plutocracy Rules American Colleges," "U.S. Colleges Under Control of Morgan Gold," "Secret Societies Rule Yale," "Democracy is Gone," and "The Desperate Struggle for the World's Oil." Sinclair wrote on a variety of other subjects for Hearst, ranging from psychology to women's liberation.

Also in 1923, Sinclair was jailed in San Pedro during a "Wobbly" strike. He was arrested while speaking to seven hundred strikers. He stood on private property, and he had written permission from the owner to be there. He was reading the Declaration of Independence and the First Amendment to the Constitution. He was held incommunicado overnight — and out of the incident came the Southern California branch of the American Civil Liberties Union. Of all the things Sinclair accomplished in his life, he listed the founding of the Southland branch of the ACLU as one of the most important.

The Brass Check was received with accolades all over the world. The notorious cynic and wit H.L. Mencken wrote of the book to Sinclair: "I find nothing that seems to me to be exaggerated. On the contrary, you have, in many ways, much understated your case." But Mencken could not go along with Sinclair's suggestion that socialism was the answer. "To hell with socialism," he said. "The longer I live, the more I am convinced that the common people are doomed to be diddled forever. You are fighting a vain fight. But you must be having lots of fun."

Mencken and Sinclair carried on an exchange of their views over the years, and Mencken even came and visited Sinclair in Pasadena. They argued about booze and Jack London. Mencken was, of course, firmly committed to booze. Sinclair was a prohibitionist — it's been suggested more than once that the sight of his drunken father made him that way.

Part of the reason *The Jungle* had been such a success was because London had trumpeted its cause. When they met, however, London told Sinclair about various alcoholic and hashish debauches he had witnessed. At the time, London was getting drunker and drunker as they talked. Sinclair was shocked and upset. To his way of thinking, London had ruined himself with drink. But Mencken argued that had it not been for booze, London probably wouldn't have been a great writer.

Certainly Sinclair's presence in Southern California added to the area's intellectual atmosphere. Not long after Sinclair had settled down in Pasadena, George Bernard Shaw wrote to him, saying, "I hear about all sorts of interesting people being at Pasadena, which I suppose is due to your having settled there (for six months as usual, eh?). If I ever get to the States I will try to find where Pasadena is."

Sinclair also carried on a lengthy correspondence during his early days in Pasadena with a young English writer named Winston Churchill. And there was always considerable correspondence between Sinclair and Sinclair Lewis. When Lewis came and visited Sinclair in Pasadena, the younger man went way out of his way to arrive sober — which was not necessarily his most natural state.

Both Eugene Debs and Clarence Darrow, the famed socialist and crusading lawyer, respectively, were visitors in Pasadena. Later, of course, Albert Einstein, when he was at the nearby California Institute of Technology, spent long hours with Sinclair. Both were amateur violinists, and they liked to get together in Sinclair's backyard and drag horsehair over cat gut.

Then there was correspondence from the great playwright Eugene O'Neill, who told Sinclair how much he had been affected by *The Jungle* and how he was thinking of moving out to California soon. Thomas Mann and Sinclair had corresponded even before Mann, forced to flee Germany, ended up in exile in Los Angeles.

When all the letters, manuscripts and papers Sinclair had accumulated over a lifetime were moved from his last home in the Southland, there were eight tons of material. Sinclair lived in his Monrovia home (which is now an unmarked national monument at 464 N. Myrtle) until the mid-'60s. He offered his papers to the Huntington in San Marino, but at the time the famed museum said it wasn't interested. Finally, the Sinclair collection went to the Lilly Library at Indiana University.

Sinclair replied to almost anybody's letters. He wrote hundreds of letters, giving advice on everything from sex to diet and politics. He was known as a soft touch for any young writer who wanted an opinion from a famous author. But toward the end of the '20s, the correspondence had grown overwhelming; he wasn't getting his own work done.

So in 1927, the Sinclairs moved to a modest house in Long Beach. It is still there, at 10 58th Place. According to John Ahouse, Sinclair's Long Beach period was especially productive. Ahouse points out that he produced such classics during his Long Beach period as *Oil!*, *Boston*, *Money Writes* and *Mental Radio*.

Sinclair's wife, Mary Craig, had a passion for real estate speculation, like the rest of Southern California in the '20s, and she owned a couple of parcels on Signal Hill in Long Beach. The discovery of oil there put her square in the middle of the Signal Hill oil boom, which was one of the biggest in the nation at the time. She made a few thousand dollars from her speculation. More important, Sinclair got the raw material for *Oil!* He watched with fascination as the drama of the oil boom unfolded; soon he was taking notes and interviewing everyone. He wrote his yarn against a backdrop of wheeling and dealing, bribery and corruption. "A picture of civilization in Southern California," he said. All of Sinclair's favorite subjects are to be found in *Oil!* — there are evangelists and college presidents and newspaper publishers. The book is also the most convincing of Sinclair's novels from a psychological as well as a political standpoint — and after *The Jungle*, critics usually rate it as his best work.

During the Long Beach period, Mary Craig also drew Sinclair's prodigious attention to psychic phenomena — he was so convinced that she had ESP that he wrote a book called *Mental Radio*. The book drew the attention of the famed pioneer psychic researcher J.B. Rhine of Duke University. But Sinclair's old friend Bertrand Russell refused to write an introduction to the book, flatly dismissing ESP. Albert Einstein, on the other hand, did do an introduction to the German edition.

Mental Radio produced correspondence from Sir Arthur Conan Doyle, creator of Sherlock Holmes, in 1929. Doyle, who had said he regarded Sinclair as "one of the greatest novelists in the world, the Zola of America," shared Sinclair's interest in ESP. In one of his letters to Sinclair, Doyle said that he was impressed with Sinclair's famous attack on organized religion, *Profits of Religion*. But Doyle added: "Don't run down Spiritualism. It is the one solid patch in the whole quagmire of religion. Of course there are frauds, quacks, though that has been exaggerated."

The Long Beach period came to an end in 1930 because Sinclair was getting involved in Hollywood studio work. It was the time of the Great Depression, and Sinclair purchased a genuine Beverly Hills mansion at 614 N. Arden Drive; it was cheap, he pointed out, because there was no market then for big houses. Sinclair was doing very well financially — so much so that his old friend Charlie Chaplin got him both financially and creatively involved with the great Russian film director Sergei Eisenstein. Eisenstein spent several months and a pile of Sinclair's money working on his *Thunder Over Mexico*.

The late Sol Lesser, who produced such films as *Stagedoor Canteen*, *Our Town*, *The Red House* and *Kon-Tiki*, was deeply involved with Sinclair on *Thunder Over Mexico*. Eventually, however, Sinclair sold the unedited reels of the film to Stalin, just to try and recoup a fraction of what he had lost, and started becoming even more anti-Communist than he had under Mary Craig's promptings.

Politics was ultimately to direct Sinclair's efforts away from the studios. The Depression was deepening. Sinclair had already taken out his typewriter and knocked off a book telling what he would do about the country's financial problems — *I, Candidate for Governor, and How I Ended Poverty: A True Story of the Future*. This was fiction, but among the people it impressed was the owner of one of the town's biggest hotels. The hotelier liked his ideas, and kept urging him to run for governor as a Democrat, not as a socialist.

So while living in the Beverly Hills mansion, Sinclair changed his voting registration from Socialist to Democratic. He pointed out that he had been raised a Democrat; in fact his great-grandfather, Commodore Arthur Sinclair, had been one of the original founders of the Democratic party. But Sinclair had become disillusioned with the Democratic party during his youth in New York City, as he watched how Tammany Hall was ruining Gotham.

Unlike the communists and his former socialist comrades, Sinclair had made a discovery about California. "There is little working-class mentality." Talking about the Golden State's inhabitants, he observed: "They were middle-class in their thoughts and feelings, and even the most hopeless among them were certain their children were going to get an education and rise in the world."

Thus it was out of a book, a book that was really only fiction, that Sinclair's EPIC movement — End Poverty in California — was born. The EPIC plan became a giant grassroots movement such as California had not seen since. There were EPIC clubs, EPIC theatres and an EPIC newspaper, which had a daily circulation of two million at one point in Sinclair's campaign.

EPIC forced a major realignment of both the Democratic and Republican parties in California. Despite the fact that the Republican Frank Merriam won against Sinclair in November, the Democratic party went on to become the majority party; before EPIC almost all the governors had been Republicans, as well as most of the voters.

The campaign against Sinclair was one of the most vicious smear jobs in political history. It also had the dubious distinction of being the first election where advertising men were hired to run a campaign. Republican Frank Merriam's campaign was managed by the firm of Lord & Thomas, financed by a cabal of powerful California interests, and led by Sinclair's old nemesis, the Los Angeles *Times*.

Sinclair told the story afterwards in his book, *I, Candidate for Governor: And How I Got Licked*. And David Halberstam's *The Powers That Be* describes a young New York *Times* reporter, Turner Catledge, who had come to California in 1934 with an assignment to find out about what had happened to the Sinclair candidacy. Catledge picked up the Los Angeles *Times* but could find no mention of where he might go and listen to Sinclair. The Los

Angeles *Times* didn't run that kind of information about Sinclair. Instead there was simply a story saying that Sinclair was attacking the Bible and was un-Christian.

Later Catledge went to dinner with Kyle Palmer, the political correspondent and king-maker of California politics for the Los Angeles *Times*. Palmer told Catledge to forget "that kind of crap that you have in New York of being obliged to print both sides. We're going to beat this son of a bitch Sinclair any way we can. We're going to kill him."

Halberstam's book goes on to describe some of the things Catledge was not aware of when he had dinner with Palmer. The Los Angeles *Times* had lent Palmer to Louis B. Mayer, the movie mogul, who had decided to use the studios in any way he could to stop Sinclair. Newsreels were faked, and the Depression-packed movie houses up and down the state were required by the studios to run them — not as political advertising but as legitimate news. In one of these newsreels, for instance, there was a wild-looking, bearded Russian anarchist telling the camera crew that he was going to vote for Sinclair because "His system vorked vell in Roosia, vy can't it vork here?" Other newsreels showed hordes of unemployed laborers sitting at the California border, waiting to come and get Sinclair's welfare when he won the governorship. The only problem is that the "unemployed" were movie extras!

Hahn claims that during the election the Los Angeles *Times* employed one gentleman full-time in a secret room in the *Times* building. His job was to go through all of Sinclair's books and find juicy quotes on subjects ranging from free love to religion. These quotes were then run, wildly out of context, in big black borders on the front page. The amazing thing, Hahn says, is that despite the smear job, Sinclair still got 45 percent of the vote in the general election.

Sinclair has been portrayed as some sort of hedonistic, devilish creature when in truth he was very much a Puritan. If anything, some of his radical friends found Sinclair just too much of a saint, a fanatic on "clean" living. It was also obvious to a lot of people that Sinclair directed his sexual energies into his work, for there had to be some explanation for the incredible amounts of work he accomplished.

There was something out of sorts in Sinclair's sexual makeup. His first marriage had foundered on his wife's infidelity. She actively pursued and believed in the free-love ideas popular at the time. It then seems as if there was almost no physical passion at all in his second marriage. Mary Craig married Sinclair only after long agonizing between Sinclair and his old Carmel poet friend George Sterling. In 1928 in Long Beach, Sinclair actually published some of Sterling's love sonnets to Mary Craig.

One can see his puritanical sensibilities in his shocked description, in *The*

Brass Check, of a certain "gorgeous and expensive leisure-class hotel" in Pasadena. Sinclair wrote with obvious horror about "the elderly ladies of fashion who were putting paint on their cheeks, and cutting their dresses halfway down their backs, and making open efforts to seduce" the young men on the premises. He complained that young matrons "disappeared for trips into the mountain canyons nearby" with members of the opposite sex. Then there was "the married lady of great wealth who had been in several scandals, who caroused all night with half a dozen soldiers and sailors, supplying them all with all the liquor they wanted in spite of the law, and who finally was asked to leave the hotel — not because of this carousing but because she failed to pay the liquor bill."

At the same time Sinclair was a leading exponent of women's rights — and a great friend and ally of pioneer feminist Margaret Sanger. But he carried on about the treachery of "fast women" with all the righteous indignation of an old-fashioned Episcopalian minister. At one point he proclaimed: "Take it from me, there is no possibility of happiness in sex life — under our present social system, at any rate — except to find a decent girl who will be true and to whom it's worth being true." The problem with these lofty sentiments, of course, is that one's strong impression is that Sinclair and his second wife eschewed sex.

And Sinclair's first wife, Meta, had offered this analysis of Sinclair: "He is conservative by instinct and a radical by choice. Mr. Sinclair is an essential monogamist, without having any of the qualities which an essential monogamist ought to possess."

During the Second World War, Sinclair began his immensely popular Lanny Budd series, and he spent a lot of time nursing his ailing wife as well. They had moved to the pleasant house on Myrtle in Monrovia. Finally, because of the smog, Sinclair and his wife moved away for a while to Arizona. But finally they returned to California, where Mary Craig died in 1961.

Sinclair subsequently married May Hard Willis and outlived her. He died in 1968 at ninety years of age in a New Jersey nursing home, one year after being honored by President Lyndon Baines Johnson during the signing of a new meat packing reform bill.

Was Sinclair a great writer? John Ahouse is willing to admit that Sinclair's prose did not always "offer the literary substance academic English departments are looking for." Ahouse says that Sinclair becomes really intriguing only when you're looking at his life as a whole, and not judging him by any single piece of writing. "You have to become aware of the issues he was fighting for," and then "his sense of personal integrity begins to communicate itself."

Ahouse says he does not find it surprising at all that Sinclair's popularity has slipped in his own country while it has maintained itself in some European countries. The idea of "fiction put to the service of an idea" is a less popular notion in our country than in other countries, he says. "When the smoke clears, his place will perhaps have been more in social history than purely literature." Hahn, on the other hand, derides the notion that one can study literature without connecting it with history, or that one can know history without knowing the literature of the period. Also, literature and history have to arise in a place — the place helps define both. Los Angeles helped give Sinclair to the world.

In Search Of
Literary L.A.

T he year 1980 began with some furious storms. My series of articles examining Los Angeles and her great writers was leading me to a conclusion with which I was not very comfortable. This realization came to me one night as all around me L.A. seemed to be disintegrating in mud slides, rain and yet more rain. I was one of the lucky ones. The roof of my Silverlake apartment had only sprung a minor leak. Usually the view from my second-story apartment shows me all of Hollywood, including the Griffith Park Observatory. But that night the rain was falling so hard that I wondered if I was back in London. Suddenly, an unholy amount of lightning, such as I had rarely seen in Los Angeles, flashed awesomely and the roof literally rocked from the thunder. I laughed at the realization that in Los Angeles one's thoughts turn to apocalypse when it rains a little harder than usual. Of course there was all the inevitable bad news on the international scene. Worse, the newspapers had been full for the last several months of articles talking about The Big Earthquake, and about how the San Andreas fault was moving this way and that, so that almost everyone agreed that the Big One — the Really Big One — was on the way. You couldn't see all of Hollywood that night and maybe the big earthquake or these rains or an atomic war was about to wipe out Los Angeles, but at the moment the sound of the rain was nice. It had turned the lights of Hollywood into a diffused, rain-smeared image of warm, shimmering colors. The outlines of the city were visible, and yes they could have been on the set of a futuristic city before the Apocalypse. Could such a place produce valid literature? Would it be around long enough to do so?

Then one of the lightning bolts hit only a few feet away, in the empty lot across the street. I saw at close range the cold, death-like glow from that lightning, and it sobered me even more than had the sight of suicides, car-crash fatalities and other such things I had seen during my years as a police beat reporter. Perhaps what was terrifying was that this wasn't a man-made killer, that lightning bolt. I felt as if I had seen death close-up.

All of the four great literary works of the twentieth century that Los Angeles had a hand in were works of apocalyptical vision. They had been written during the Depression and the Second World War, but the fact is that they had been produced at least in part because of Los Angeles. The four works were also quite dissimilar. *Doctor Faustus*, Mann's novel of gloom and doom, was inspired not only by what was going on in his homeland, but also by the proximity in L.A. of his neighbor and acquaintance, Arnold Schoenberg, granddaddy of avant-garde music.

Malcolm Lowry's *Under the Volcano* owed a lot to Los Angeles, even though he hated the place.

To go on with these four horsemen of the apocalypse, Nathanael West wrote his famed *The Day of the Locust* about actual people and places of Hollywood. Then, toward the end of the Second World War, a countryman of Lowry's, Aldous Huxley, wrote the ultimate apocalyptical vision of Los Angeles in his novel, *Ape & Essence*.

Why, I wondered, had L.A. produced so much gloom and doom? Is it because it truly is the City of the Future?

In the post-war years the Bohemians became part of history. They were replaced by the beatniks, who congregated in coffeehouses in Venice and in old L.A. neighborhoods like Echo Park. Yet interestingly enough, the thread that links the Bohemians and the Beats can be found in an area south of downtown called Watts.

One of the most important of the nation's black writers grew up here at the turn of the century. In his classic work called *Anyplace But Here*, Arna Bontemps went back to his childhood memories of the sweetness as well as the problems of Watts. What he was doing was tracing the evolution of black ghettos, and Watts became his archetypical "Mudtown" (his name for northern ghetto communities).

Bontemps originally was shipped to Watts by his father after his mother died in his native Louisiana. He grew up and went to school in Watts and worked at the post office at night. But after college he went to Harlem, where he teamed up with Langston Hughes to help create the Harlem Renaissance of the 1920s.

In *Anyplace But Here*, Bontemps wrote of Watts with great love. He wrote with special fondness of Jelly Roll Morton and his coterie of New Orleans jazz greats whose heyday was in Los Angeles during the '30s. Bontemps told of how, before the Second World War, "Los Angeles in legend became 'paradise west' to Negroes still languishing in Egyptland of the South."

In a book of letters between Bontemps and Hughes, editor Charles H. Nicholas makes the point that these two writers grew out of the American tradition of Whitman and Twain. He goes on to say, "The Beat writers owed even more than they acknowledge to writers like Hughes and Bontemps." Mentioning Jack Kerouac and Norman Mailer, he contends that these writers even owed the word "beat" to black. "Beat is a word derived from the language of lower-class Negroes, meaning 'poor, down-and-out, dead-beat, on the bum, sad, sleeping in the subways'", Nichols declares.

John Fante

While black literature was often overlooked, or dismissed as ethnic or folk culture at best, now it appears as if the future of writing will indeed come out of the city's multi-ethnic reality. Oddly enough, the lineage for this could well be traced to John Fante, who was Charles Bukowski's L. A. mentor, even though Bukowski does not write much about L.A.'s multicultural background. If anything, Bukowski revels in his European, Polish-German background. Still, at one point Bukowski moved into the old hotel on Bunker Hill where Fante had once lived, went to the hospital to visit Fante during his lingering bout with diabetes, and dutifully attended his funeral. Bukowski obtained a sense of legitimacy from Fante in his own efforts. Fante wrote a powerful novel somewhat overlooked in 1939 when it was first issued because it came out the same year as *The Day of the Locust, The Grapes of Wrath* and other great books. *Ask The Dust* was not republished until 1980 when Black Sparrow, Bukowski's publisher, reissued it with an introduction by Bukowski. *Ask the Dust* paints a vivid and powerful picture of Bunker Hill when it was still home and neighborhood to thousands of ordinary folks like Fante.

When *Ask the Dust* first appeared, critics suggested that Fante was to California's Italians what William Saroyan had been to California's Armenian community. But although Fante was pigeonholed as a strictly "ethnic" writer — an Italian writer, to be exact — he wrote about everyone in his short stories and novels, from Jews to Filipinos to Mexicans to blacks. Previous to Fante only one person really captured the multi-ethnic character of the city, and that was Louis Adamic in the '20s, and one of Fante's earliest and most loyal supporters, Carey McWilliams, who wrote nonfiction about the multi-ethnic character of the Golden State in the '30s. Adamic, a good friend of both McWilliams and Jake Zeitlin, worked in the pilot house in San Pedro, guiding the ships in and out of Los Angeles Harbor. Adamic went on to become an important, even if undervalued, writer who concentrated on the immigrant experience in America. He is remembered more as the most famous writer of his native Yugoslavia today than he is in his adopted town which he wrote so much about in the '20s and '30s. McWilliams wrote a biography of Adamic published in 1935 called *Louis Adamic and Shadow-America*. Adamic was obsessed with the notion that all Americans were "shadow-persons, with nothing substantial and permanent, nothing to hold on to." In *Grandsons* Adamic writes about Americans, instead of having roots, being possessed by shadow-selves, a kind of exile from a forgotten past.

Raymond Chandler also portrayed the city's mixed ethnic bag with a strong sense of style and sense, but Chandler was a misanthrope, and a bigot especially when it came to blacks and Jews. Fante, on the other hand, who also wrote in that "hard-boiled" style that was pioneered in Los Angeles writing in the '30s, was a "hyphenate" American and very conscious of the fact, and that is why he wrote fondly and pointedly of L.A.'s ethnic diversity. While Chandler's style was to evoke a powerful nightmare image of L.A. akin to his own alcoholic disillusionment, Fante took L.A.'s reality not only seriously but humorously. Dope, sex, love, drunkenness, work and rejection were all features of his works, especially the four books in which Los Angeles appears as a central character.

Certainly by the 1950s and '60s one of the obvious features of L.A.'s burgeoning coffeehouse scene was the mixing of black and white, often through the medium of music. *The Air-Conditioned Nightmare* by Henry

Louis Adamic, in a signed portrait to Jake Zeitlin

Miller was the bible of the disaffected, who played chess and listened to jazz. But after Kennedy's assassination in 1963, the civil rights and anti-war protests came hand in glove, and what had been a primarily spiritual and cultural protest became political.

Today in New York, you will find many of critics who have wrongly assumed that Los Angeles has no literary tradition to draw on, save those grafted onto it by Hollywood. This is because New York thinks it all has to happen in Gotham. But this is not true. When one understands the fullness of the literary tradition that has emerged and will continue to emerge in Los

Raymond Chandler, in a snapshot by his publisher, Alfred Knopf.

Angeles, one sees that the City of the Angels has had an intellectual and literary life of distinctive merit and great potential.

True, since the Second World War, the Beat scene has come and gone. And there seems to have been no more Mark Twains anywhere in the nation, on the West or the East Coasts. As to be expected, Los Angeles has also had its share of pretenders to the throne of great writer — Steve Erickson is one name that comes to mind. For a long time people were carrying on about Joan Didion too, who wrote about driving cars too fast on the freeways as if that were some sort of transcendental experience.

Has Bukowski any competition for the title of L.A.'s greatest living writer? Julia Stein, who comes from and writes out of a working class background, whose book of poetry called *Under the Ladder to Heaven* showed far more real comprehension of the human condition than a hundred Steve Ericksons, says that L.A. has produced many good if not great writers — Joseph Hansen, Ross McDonald and Mike Nava, all of whom wrote hard boiled detective fiction in the Chandler tradition. She regards James Ellroy as a real writer, a master of the noir detective story, whose stuff began being published in the early '80s. She says Ellroy (she is particularly fond of his *The Big Nowhere* and *The Black Dahlia*) creates detective heroes who are as mad, possessed and obsessed as Poe's great detective Dupin and that he captures the L.A. streets all too well.

She also insists that L.A. poetry did not end with Bukowski. Having been active in PEN, and as a writing teacher at both UCLA and in various jails and a frequent participant in various poetry readings around town, she knows the local scene well. She admits that all too many of L.A.'s poets are busy writing imitations of New York School poets or Sylvia Plath. But L.A. has also participated in the upsurge of Third World writing, with such superb voices as black poets Wanda Coleman, Kamau D'aaood and the Japanese-American Garrett Hongo, she insists. In the mid-'70s Stein edited a feminist populist newspaper and pioneered a multi-cultural/feminist/populist vision for L.A. poetry she calls post-modernist. She was appalled by the elitism of modernist literature, but felt vindicated when the 1990 Los Angeles Art Festival copied the multi-cultural programming she and others were pioneering in the late '70s; from this a new West Coast multi-cultural radicalism in literature, she argues, a major American writer or two may yet to emerge.

It would be nice to think she's not being overly optimistic.

Scenes From Home

I have thought long and hard about what in particular united all the disparate elements of California Bohemianism. It shows in California literature, and in Los Angeles literature as well as San Francisco literature — whatever it is. What shows is the pristine innocence of Bohemia, later jaded by the apocalyptical strain in writing which Huxley and Mann introduced to the Southland. The decay and the innocence — that is the true L.A.

Despite the superficial cosmopolitan atmosphere Los Angeles has been developing the last few years, don't think that authors — and even mere mortal residents — haven't perceived the rawness, the primitiveness of this place correctly. Time and place have been called disappearing characteristics of modern fiction about New York for decades now, but in Los Angeles time and place are still the stars of our dramas. Perhaps time and place are ephemeral phenomena, in life and to a lesser degree in literature — maybe both are but a writer's conceits, constructs, facile artifices. But the fact is that Los Angeles has put its garish mark on world literature with them. Desert sun and fire, the multivaried moods of nature and light, and artificial spotlights and glows have given the place its own luminescence. Were it not for the sun, there would be no fires, no doubt. But there are primeval fires in Los Angeles — fires that consume the way the flames must lick their victims in hell — that seem to come from the bowels of the earth.

If you really want to understand the way Los Angeles looks and feels, you have to understand the desert sun and the land, the heat and the fire and colors, over which a thin veneer of civilization has been laid in the last century or so. Go just the other side of the mountain pass out of the Los Angeles basin on Highway 5 to Newhall. This is on the other side of the San Gabriel Mountains that form the Los Angeles Basin. Being only 35 miles from downtown Los Angeles means that the old town of Newhall, now officially known as the City of Santa Clarita, is only half an hour away by freeway. With its California Institute of the Arts, an arts university initially patterned after the Bauhaus, and Magic Mountain amusement park, and suburbs and malls and mini-malls, its riverbed and streambeds as well as its hillsides covered with condos and homes, Newhall seems far away from the bright lights of Hollywood Boulevard.

But here is where you can see just how raw and primitive the Los Angeles basin really is. The area is still far from built-up, so those who have lived there a while can still find a bluff above it all, and watch the great red fires sweep out of its hilly canyons early in every summer, and contemplate the buzzards and condors that circle the almost lunar desert landscape where you

167

half expect dinosaurs to be roaming and pterodactyls to be roaring and wobbling through the air. Right there at the edge of the L.A. basin, you get to understand — to feel the rhythm of the fires in summer and the torrential rains, floods and even occasional snows in winter, and dread the inevitable punctuating earthquakes.

Straight ahead north are the Tehachapi Mountains, and northeast by hardly more than ten miles is the beginning of the Mojave Desert where giant rock structures have been dramatically uplifted by the earth's violent geology. It is tentative, primitive land in either direction — and it's the same land that formed the Los Angeles basin that's now been covered over with the appurtenances of the city.

Consider that one of the ritziest part of Los Angeles's Wilshire Boulevard goes over a patch of ancient surface oil. They pulled a museum full of beast skeletons and bones out of the still percolating tar pits. And remember that the San Gabriel mountains forming the northern part of the basin near Newhall are also the beginning of condor territory, ancestral home of a nearly extinct, primitive bird. Just how wild a land this is wasn't driven home for me until one day in the late '60s I got a call early one morning. It happened that a huge Abyssinian hornbill — a giant, primitive bird out of another eon — had escaped from the Los Angeles Zoo a few weeks before. "Abby's" misadventures around the Los Angeles basin were featured on the front pages and on every television news show for day after day. Everyone cheered on the bird, who was obviously looking for freedom, and was spotted in different precarious situations all around the basin.

A good news source called me as a reporter on the Newhall *Signal* to tell me that a local father had been woken up early that morning by the sound of his son shooting off his rifle. It seems that Abby had finally found her way through the pass in the basin walls into Newhall and was flying north, because the rocky high desert landscape reminded her of the North African land she had come from. She stopped for only a second on a fence in Newhall — and a kid looked out the window, saw Abby, and did what any good red-blooded American boy would do. He shot and killed her. The embarrassed father asked me not to reveal the identity of Abby's killer.

By six o'clock that morning, the bird, with its 14-foot wingspread, had been folded into my icebox. She stayed there while I wrote the story, and then we called the zoo officials to come and take her body and identify her. Abby, who was a noble but rather ugly creature that looked almost like a pterodactyl, stayed in my icebox for a couple of days. When the paper came out with our story, my exclusive in the *Signal* was widely noted on various television stations. But it was Abby's poor body, filling up the entire refrigerator, that really gave me an intimate sense of the attraction that land had had for her. Suddenly the primeval fires and light were revealing their secrets to me.

In 1902 John C. Van Dyke wrote in *The Desert* that sunlight "falls fierce and hot as a rain of meteors…it is the one supreme beauty to which all things pay allegiance" in Southern California. In 1906 the then-young poet Robinson Jeffers sat on top of a hill in Los Angeles and watched the night descend, describing at the perimeter of his view "furnace fire lights" whose "rolling fierce shafts" pierced the black sky. Even when there aren't fires and floods, there is always something about the light, natural and artificial, combined with the desert sun and spontaneous fires that impart a manic, primitive look to Los Angeles and environs.

Half a century ago in his classic *Southern California: An Island on the Land*, Carey McWilliams insisted that the strange interplay of light and air in the desert by the sea is unique, and different from those of the Mediterranean or even the tropics, which L.A.'s climate most closely parallels. Carey McWilliams noted that Los Angeles is bounded on one side by mountains and the other side by ocean, that it is a place where the sun and the air play odd little games with each other. This is no natural garden setting, gentle and woodsy, such as Tennyson and Wordsworth wrote about. Most European and eastern American cities are carved out of gentle, old worn hills and woods. But L.A. is a different kind of American city — this was never the Garden of Eden — there's hardly a plant in the Los Angeles basin that wasn't imported and isn't kept alive by water imported from elsewhere. The land itself is almost an inert ingredient — it's mostly the Mojave Desert sun and air suddenly full of ocean moisture that's unique, McWilliams insisted.

Both inside the basin walls and outside, the land is hilly, with, as we said, jutting and often dramatic rocky geology, covered naturally with chaparral, sagebrush and some scrubby oaks. Sometimes seen in plain light, L.A. landscape becomes commonplace. But if you live in L.A. — within the basin or just beyond it — the memory of the fires and floods and the sunlight begins to work its magic. The longer you stay in L.A. the more the magic works because you always know how quickly the commonplace disappears.

Nathanel West's vision that inspired *Day of the Locust* came from a terrible summer he spent in a Hollywood boarding house at the height of the depression when he was both ill and broke. The heat of the summer sun combining with the deadly red from the brush fires in the nearby Hollywood Hills colored his L.A. perceptions forever. The great fires that every summer burst out of the canyons — in Newhall or in the Hollywood Hills — are the same. They certainly inspired West to his best work and it had an incredibly apocalyptical feeling. Throughout West's "Day of the Locust," his protagonist, a movie studio artist, is working at home on his masterpiece, "The Burning of Los Angeles." Explained West, "He was going to show the city burning at high noon, so that the flames would have to compete with the desert sun...He wanted the city to have quite a gala air as it burned."

It's been suggested that like desert air, which produces great, strange mirages, L.A.'s air is like a giant movie lens that makes the place always seem bigger than life. Others have noted how fast the sun slips out of the hilly desert canyons as it sinks into the Pacific, in imitation of a Klieg light being turned off. In *After Many a Summer Dies the Swan*, Aldous Huxley creates a nearly hallucinogenic quality to the light of Los Angeles by combining both of these effects. And this was before the landscape had driven him to LSD. Note this passage: "It was a winter day and early in the morning; but the sun shone brilliantly, the sky was without a cloud. The car was traveling westwards and the sunshine, slanting from behind them as they advanced, lit up each building, each sky sign and billboard as though with a spotlight, as though on purpose to show the new arrival all the sights."

Authors personalize the light. In *What Makes Sammy Run?*, Budd Schulberg wrote that "the sun was taking its evening dipping, slipping down into the ocean inch by inch, like a fat woman, afraid of the water."

In the '20s Upton Sinclair wrote an incredibly Balzacian novel of some 500 pages called *Oil*, which painted a sparse landscape that was, literally floating on oil, oil that would propel the development of a city even more than its famed dream factories. In 1912 he has an oilman and his son racing across the Southern California landscape, "no hat on Dad's head, because he believed that wind and sunshine kept your hair from falling out..." Sinclair describes the scene as the car roars across it: "A barrier of mountains lay across the road. Far off, they had been blue, with a canopy of fog on top; they lay in tumbled masses, one summit behind another, and more summits peeking over, fainter in color, and mysterious. You knew you had to go up there, and it was interesting to guess where a road might break in. As you came nearer, the great masses changed color — bushes of a hundred shades. They were spotted with rocks, black, white, brown, or red; also with the pale flames of the yucca, a plant which reared a thick stem ten feet or more in the air, and covered it with small flowers in a huge mass, exactly the shape of a candle flame, but one that never flickered in the wind." A few miles further, dad remarks, "If that sun doesn't get over the hill in three minutes, she's late." Sinclair also notes that in the West they tried to light up even the small towns with far more artificial light than back east. Sinclair insisted Western towns were different: "The width of the street, the newness of the stores, the shininess of their white paint, and the network of electric lights hung over the center of the street..." In the 'teens the basin probably had a pristine, gentle quality as the orange orchards and bean fields got planted and roads and Red Car tracks were laid out. But that period lasted only a short time. Raymond Chandler describes how when he first got to L.A. in 1912, he found a pristine world with year-round sun, hot and dry in the summer, with great tropical rains in the winter. By the time his hard-boiled prose in the Philip Marlowe books is maturing, he is writing about the Depression, and the pristine past is as lost as the Garden of Eden. By the '50s, he sadly announced, the climate remained hot but became sticky and humid and befouled with smog. The sunshine had turned "as empty as a headwaiter's smile." But maybe what is the most memorable line from Chandler came when he immortalized our Santa Ana conditions, those terrible hot desert winds blowing through the valleys into the basins. These are the times, said Chandler, when meek wives look longingly at the backs of their husbands' necks and sharpen their kitchen knives.

By World War II, Huxley had descended into apocalypse for a literature that reflected the Southern California desert he was living in. The sun has set the stage for the apocalypse ever since. The great flashes of light from the nuclear bombs, Hiroshima and Nagasaki, were on his mind as he wrote this book, especially because Huxley was practically blind. Light became his obsession. He discovered the source of Los Angeles's unique light by living in the desert at Llano. The desert light enabled him to see more, he believed. He even drove his car across the desert floor, able to make things out because of the direct desert light and distinct shadows.

Sun, light and ultimately fire — this old high desert island by the ocean has also left big imprints on international literature. Take Thomas Mann's *Doctor Faustus*, which many people think is the greatest novel of the 20th century. It never mentions L.A., but it was conceived and written in L.A. The book is about the decline of Germany into total barbarism during World War II. The germ of the novel was said to first have come to Mann when he was on vacation in Palestrina, Italy, as a young man. For it was during Mann's Palestrina period that he developed his sense of his own German identity; he hated the palm trees and blue skies in Italy because they were so un-German. No doubt Mann's subconscious was awakened during the Holocaust as he sat in the pleasant green hills by the blue Pacific, the blue, desert-sun lit bright air of the Pacific Palisades making him think of that early time in Palestrina. One thing no doubt led to the next. The palm trees and sun of L.A. commingled with Mann's Palestrina memories. Along with his own forebodings about the land from which he was exiled, *Doctor Faustus* must have been provoked.

In Malcolm Lowry's *Under the Volcano*, which takes place in Mexico on the verge of World War II, the Consul ultimately disappears into the volcano. He is consumed by the fire of the volcano. Everything was ultimately consumed around Lowry — even the dead dog goes into the cabalistic furnace. Lowry wrote much of the manuscript while cooped up in a dingy Los Angeles hotel room.

Compare Sherlock Holmes, the greatest detective of London, to Philip Marlowe, Raymond Chandler's most Los Angeles of all detective heroes.

What lives and breathes about Holmes is the same quality that lives and breathes about London even to this day — it is a cosmopolitan international city, older and wiser than Los Angeles, it would seem, and very rational and sophisticated with its Victorian soul.

Holmes deducts. Marlowe reacts. What lives and breathes in Philip Marlowe is not his intellect but a sharpened sense of L.A.'s place and time, invariably cast in a continuum of fire and sun and garish artificial light.

Bohemianism was the pristine beginnings; but apocalypse was the later message. L.A. literature was born in a baptism of fire.

BIBLIOGRAPHY

BIBLIOGRAPHY

BIOGRAPHIES, STUDIES AND MEMOIRS OF SPECIAL NOTE

Bennett, Melba Berry. *The Stone Mason of Tor House: Life and Work of Robinson Jeffers*. Ward Ritchie, 1966

Brophy, Robert. *Jeffers: Myth, Ritual and Symbol in his Poems*. The Press of Case Western Reserve University, 1973.

Cross, Richard. *Malcolm Lowry: A Preface to His Fiction*. University of Chicago Press, 1980.

Day, Douglas. *Malcolm Lowry*. Oxford University Press, 1973.

Epstein, Perle. *The Private Labyrinth of Malcolm Lowry*. Holt, Rinehart, and Winston, 1969.

Hamilton, Nigel. *The Brothers Mann: The Lives of Heinrich and Thomas Mann*. Martin Secker & Warburg, 1978.

Harris, Leon. *Upton Sinclair: An American Rebel*. T.Y. Crowell, 1975.

Heller, Erich. *The Ironic German: A Study of Thomas Mann*. Little Brown & Company, 1958.

Keats, John. *You Might As Well Live: The Life and Times of Dorothy Parker*. Simon and Schuster, 1970.

Light, James F. *Nathanael West: An Interpretative Study*. Northwestern University Press, 1971.

Mann, Katia. *Unwritten Memories*. Alfred A. Knopf, 1975.

Mann, Thomas. *The Story of a Novel: The Genesis of Doctor Faustus*. Alfred A. Knopf, 1961.

Martin, Jay. *Nathanel West: The Art of His Life*. Farrar, Straus & Giroux, 1970.

Martin, Jay. *Always Merry and Bright: The Life of Henry Miller*. Capra Press, 1978.

Powell, Lawrence Clark. *Robinson Jeffers: The Man and His Work*. Primavera Press, 1934.

Sinclair, Upton. *Autobiography of Upton Sinclair*. Harcourt Brace & World, 1962.

Stone, Irving. *Jack London: Sailor on Horseback*. Doubleday & Company, 1977.

CORRESPONDENCE

Steinbeck: A Life in Letters. Viking Press, 1975.

The Selected Letters of Malcolm Lowry. J.B. Lippincott, 1965.

Arnold Schoenberg Letters. Faber and Faber, 1964.

Letters of Thomas Mann. Alfred A. Knopf, 1970.

The Selected Letters of Robinson Jeffers. John Hopkins Press, 1968.

BIBLIOGRAPHY

BOOKS OF GENERAL INTEREST

Dardis, Tom. *Some Time in the Sun*. Charles Scribner's Sons, 1976.

Walker, Franklin. *A Literary History of Southern California*. University of California Press, 1950.

Walker, Franklin. *The Seacoast of Bohemia*. Peregrine Smith, 1973.

ADDITIONAL NOTES

Much of the material in *In Search of Literary L.A.* was drawn from limited-edition books and from newspapers and magazine articles in special collections not easily available to the general public, as well as from the better-known biographies and collected letters of the different writers. In addition, the author conducted interviews with authors, or with people who knew those authors, or who had become experts on their lives and works. Special mention should also be made of a series of articles by Lawrence Clark Powell which appeared in *Westways* magazine, called "California Classics Reread." Two on-going publications deserve special mention. *The Robinson Jeffers Newsletter* is published by the library at Occidental College, but, sad to tell, *The Upton Sinclair Quarterly* no longer is being published.

INDEX

You can order additional copies directly from the publisher.

California Classic Books
Post Office Box 29756
Los Angeles, California 90029

For $11.95, we will pay shipping and sales tax if you are a
California resident. Discounts available on quantities.
Ask for literature about our other books.

Los Angeles typographer Ken Boor set the text of this book in 11/12.5 Goudy Old Style,
which was output on a Mergenthaler/Linotype digital phototypesetter. The color cover
was the creation of art director Bill Winters. Three thousand copies were printed on 60
pound acid-free Vellum by Delta Lithograph Co. in Valencia, California.